JESUS

GOD, MAN *OR* MYTH?

An Examination of the Evidence

by

HERBERT CUTNER

Published 2000
The Book Tree
Escondido, CA

Published by
The Book Tree
Post Office Box 724
Escondido, CA 92033

We provide controversial and educational products to help awaken the public to new ideas and information that would not be available otherwise. We carry over 1100 Books, Booklets, Audio, Video, and other products on Alchemy, Alternative Medicine, Ancient America, Ancient Astronauts, Ancient Civilizations, Ancient Mysteries, Ancient Religion and Worship, Angels, Anthropology, Anti-Gravity, Archaeology, Area 51, Assyria, Astrology, Atlantis, Babylonia, Townsend Brown, Christianity, Cold Fusion, Colloidal Silver, Comparative Religions, Crop Circles, The Dead Sea Scrolls, Early History, Electromagnetics, Electro-Gravity, Egypt, Electromagnetic Smog, Michael Faraday, Fatima, Fluoride, Free Energy, Freemasonry, Global Manipulation, The Gnostics, God, Gravity, The Great Pyramid, Gyroscopic Anti-Gravity, Healing Electromagnetics, Health Issues, Hinduism, Human Origins, Jehovah, Jesus, Jordan Maxwell, John Keely, Lemuria, Lost Cities, Lost Continents, Magick, Masonry, Mercury Poisoning, Metaphysics, Mythology, Occultism, Paganism, Pesticide Pollution, Personal Growth, The Philadelphia Experiment, Philosophy, Powerlines, Prophecy, Psychic Research, Pyramids, Rare Books, Religion, Religious Controversy, Roswell, Walter Russell, Scalar Waves, SDI, John Searle, Secret Societies, Sex Worship, Sitchin Studies, Smart Cards, Joseph Smith, Solar Power, Sovereignty, Space Travel, Spirituality, Stonehenge, Sumeria, Sun Myths, Symbolism, Tachyon Fields, Templars, Tesla, Theology, Time Travel, The Treasury, UFOs, Underground Bases, World Control, The World Grid, Zero Point Energy, and much more. Call **(800) 700-TREE** for our *FREE BOOK TREE CATALOG* or visit our website at www.thebooktree.com for more information.

FOREWORD

I make no apology for the fact that this work is controversial. It was unavoidably so, as many of the defenders of the "man" Jesus, as well as those who insist that he was a "God", have bitterly assailed, not only on critical but on personal grounds, those of us who have insisted that the story of Jesus is just a myth. I hope, however, that readers will see something beyond the controversial part—will find a real criticism of the so-called evidences brought forward to prove that Jesus Christ lived on earth.

I have tried to leave no relevant argument untouched and have refrained from dealing with many disputed and speculative points, such as the actual origins of Christianity or who was the author of the original Gospel.

The works listed in the Bibliography will give any student fuller details on any problem I have not adequately dealt with.

H. C.

ACKNOWLEDGMENT

My grateful thanks are due to Mr. C. M. Hollingham of Brighton for many valuable suggestions and corrections and for so carefully revising the proofs of this work.

H. C.

CONTENTS

INTRODUCTION

This is an interesting piece of investigative work by an author, Herbert Cutner, who sets out to prove that Jesus, as an actual man, never existed. It is an extremely well researched book and, although all may not agree with what the author says, it is highly informative and well worth reading.

Cutner makes a continuous effort to support his arguments, using many references that provide ample backing—especially for the argument that the "miracles" performed by Christ did not happen. According to Cutner, these miracles were instead certain mythologies that were used to enhance Jesus as a "God" and to inject pagan themes into a new faith that was trying to enlist new members. Because of the strong evidence that myths were created or borrowed to portray these miracles, Cutner also asserts that no such man as Jesus ever existed, either. He claims that beyond the miracles, there is not enough evidence to prove there was such a man. Although I disagree with this particular premise, I still respect Cutner for having written the book as he brings out many interesting facts that are not found elsewhere. If Christian, one is likely to rethink one's entire religious belief structure after reading this book.

The author asserts that those who believe that Jesus had lived are holding on to "primitive and childish fantasies." He claims that in following the life of Christ, we find a mythological story throughout that effectively destroys the idea that Jesus ever lived. An interesting point he makes is that the evidence continually found always refers to Jesus as the Christ—a divine savior figure, and thus a myth. Not a man, but elements from a story (or stories) that came before the time of Christ. Cutner is seeking references to a man and man alone, not a mythological, godly figurehead. And in this respect, he finds the evidence sorely lacking.

A fascinating area of the book and the key to it may be found in the areas of Gnosticism and the Apostle Paul. Cutner does not rule out the Gnostic views of Christ. The Gnostic Christ is often found within oneself, as opposed to being an historical personage. Paul, according to Cutner, never portrayed Jesus as a man, but as a spiritual being—exactly as the Gnostics had portrayed him. Paul was almost rejected by the Church for his Gnostic views and was approached very carefully by them before finally being accepted. With the Church's acceptance of Paul, Cutner asserts that this inner Gnostic reflection was outwardly projected by the Church into an actual man—a savior. This was probably why Paul was almost rejected—his views posed a great "danger" to those who might rely on their own spiritual knowledge, or *gnosis*, rather than the authority of the Church. One thing is clear from this highly interesting and informative book. Whether Jesus really lived or not, we still have a great deal to learn about ourselves and our true place in the universe.

Paul Tice

CHAPTER I

Some Preliminary
Considerations

EVER SINCE DUPUIS (1742-1809), IN HIS FAMOUS
Origin of All Worships, showed that Christianity was but another form of the Solar Myth, and that therefore no such person
as Jesus Christ ever lived, his theory has been increasingly discussed. Actually, Dupuis refused to examine "into the question
of a philosopher, or impostor, named Christ, the founder of a
religion known by the name of Christianity. For even if we were
to concede this point," he says, in the ninth chapter of the
abridged edition of his work, "Christians would not be satisfied
unless we were to acknowledge Christ to be an inspired man, a
son of God, nay, himself a God, crucified for our sins. They require a God who once took food on earth and is now the food of
his people. Now, we are far from granting so much as this . . ."
He invites his readers to study the proofs he gives to show "the
nature of Christian worship", and claims he can prove that "the
hero of the legends known by the name of gospels is the same
hero who has been celebrated with far more genius in the poems
written in honor of Bacchus, Osiris, Hercules, Adonis, and
others."

I

Dupuis has never, I think, been translated in full into English, and his work as a whole is almost unknown to English readers and, for that matter, also to French readers. But the problem he posed was taken up by a few writers, notably in England by Robert Taylor (1784-1844) and John M. Robertson (1856-1933).

There are three views on the question of Jesus Christ. The first is, that he was the Son of God, the Second Person of the Trinity, God himself, the Messiah, the Redeemer, the Savior—and so on. He came down to earth either as a fully grown man or as one born of the Virgin Mary, performed many miracles, was crucified under Pontius Pilate and rose from the dead after three days, ascended to Heaven, and will return to earth when he thinks it is time for the Second Advent. This view, held by almost the whole of Christendom, is propagated by the British Broadcasting Corporation and from nearly every Christian pulpit.

The second view is that Jesus Christ is not really the Christ; that is, the Anointed, the Messiah, but just plain Jesus; that he was merely a man who went about "doing good" and preaching a simple faith; that he never performed any miracles; that we know very little about him; but that after he was crucified under Pontius Pilate, his followers began to weave many romances into his life which accounts for the legends and myths surrounding the story in the Gospels. If these are put aside, we get the picture of a—more or less—fine character, who died, in a way, for all humanity. This view is held by many Theists, Unitarians, Jews, and other religionists, as well as by numerous Freethinkers and Rationalists.

The third view is that the whole story of Jesus as related in *all* the Gospels, Canonical and Apocryphal, is just myth and legend; that there never was a Jesus Christ, or a man about whom these legends grew. Nor was any being crucified, as related in the New Testament, under Pontius Pilate. In short, we have in the picture drawn for us by the Gospel writers a literary creation, grown and expanded from some inward religious experiences, perhaps of a man like Paul. This is the view of a comparatively small number of students and writers, some of whom do not disbelieve in God.

In the present work we shall deal with some, at least, of the evidence produced by the three classes in support of their views. It is necessary at the outset to be quite clear as to the nature of the problem.

The question we are to discuss is *not* whether, at the back of the Gospels, there was an obscure individual about whom we know literally nothing, but who *must* have been there to give rise to Christianity. If we know nothing whatever about him, it is useless to discuss him. A. D. Howell Smith, in his *Jesus Not A Myth* (page 199), says:

"The Gospel story then is truly a legend. . . . But beneath the mystical and mythical crust there lie hidden historical facts, though it is exceedingly hard—nay impossible—to bring them all to light."

If it is impossible to bring them *all* to light, it would be interesting to know *which* have been brought to light. Of course, if there was a real man behind the Gospel story, obviously he had to eat, drink, and sleep.

In his last work on the problem, *Jesus and Judas*, J. M. Robertson admits, as an hypothesis, a "wonder-working Jesus" who was "not a teacher, not an utterer of *logia*, not the head of a band of Twelve Disciples, not crucified under Pontius Pilate, etc." It seems to me that it is an utter waste of time to discuss the existence of such a being who has left no trace in history and who seemingly did nothing to account for such a religion as Christianity. There were, as a matter of fact, quite a large number of these "wonder-working" religious fanatics all over the East, and we have many traces of them. Our special concern, however, is not with such as these, but with the recognized founder of Christianity. What is the evidence for *his* real existence?

The curious thing is that while many of the historicists are ready to give up a miracle-mongering Jesus, they show increased reluctance to put someone, clearly defined, in his place. Many years ago George Solomon wrote a provocative and controversial work on *The Jesus of History and the Jesus of Tradition Identified*. His thesis was that Judas of Galilee and the Jesus mentioned by Josephus during the Roman siege of Jerusalem as crying "Woe to Jerusalem" on its walls, both gave rise to the Jesus cult and

legend. But the historicists never took kindly to such a prototype as the latter. Although Christians have perhaps used the
"Woe . . ." phrase more than any other religious body, they
steadfastly refuse to believe in Mr. Solomon's explanation, and
even those who do not believe in a Divine Jesus are not prepared to accept this particular madman. They prefer to argue
about some vague or shadowy Jesus of whom we know nothing
whatever, but who was the real founder of Christianity; only he
must not be the kind described by Josephus.

There is also another point which must be made clear. The
historicity of Jesus does not depend on proving that the upholders
of the myth theory have made mistakes, or do not agree with
each other. The problem is a very big one and requires an ex-
ceptional acquaintance with the literature of myths, legends, folk
lore, anthropology, history, as well as theology in general and
Christianity in particular. There is no one "key" to the riddle.
Thus one writer might well speculate on the facts before him one
way, while another deduces something quite different.

For C. F. Dupuis, the explanation of the Christ Myth was in
its connection with solar worship. In his day there had been
hardly any scientific study of anthropology, sociology, and psychology; and there is no single solution to such a complex problem.

Robert Taylor followed, in the main, the theories of Dupuis.
In his two books, the *Syntagma* and the *Diegesis*, he went very
carefully into the literary documents which are the chief "evidences" of Christianity, and on this study formulated his thesis
that his readers had "all the sufficient evidence that can be adduced for any piece of history a thousand years old, or to prove
an error of a thousand years standing, that such a *person* as Jesus
Christ never existed; but that the earliest Christians meant the
words to be nothing more than a personification of the principle
of reason, be it what it may, which may most benefit mankind in
the passage through life." As Taylor was a fully ordained Church
of England clergyman (he was, it might be added also, a qualified surgeon) with a remarkable knowledge of languages, his
analysis of Christian documents stands almost as true today, after
a century of critical Biblical scholarship, as it did in his own

day. Later, in a series of lectures published as *The Devil's Pulpit*, delivered at the Rotunda in Blackfriars Road in 1830-1 and for passages in which he was eventually condemned to two years imprisonment, his second term, he developed his theories on the solar myth and the Zodiac. References to some of his conclusions will be made in later chapters.

In 1841 appeared *The Existence of Christ as a Human Being Disproved!* by a "German Jew"—probably J. C. Blumenfeld. It is a work full of suggestion and well worth reading, though rather more "dated" than either Dupuis or Taylor.

Unfortunately, the theory was never very enthusiastically received by Rationalists; and though many writers in the Freethought press probably agreed that such a person as Jesus Christ never existed, it was not until John M. Robertson towards the end of the last century was writing a sociological view of the rise of Christianity and fully believing in the existence of both Jesus as a man and of his apostles, became convinced that the Christian deity and his twelve apostles were myths and that there was a pre-Jesus cult. In his five subsequent works (see Bibliography) he held tenaciously to his theory, and started a controversy which has shaken the Christian churches more than has any other attack. It was one thing to ignore and boycott Dupuis and Taylor—who, in any case, had long been dead. It was quite another thing to pretend that the arguments of one of the keenest literary critics in England, with a first class brain, were just not worth the proverbial two hoots. We shall have occasion to consider later some of the replies made by the clergy.

Robertson's thesis was that there was a pre-Jesus cult, and in this he was followed by Professor Arthur Drews in Germany. On the other hand the American Professor W. B. Smith saw in the Gospel stories almost pure symbolism written to propagate Monotheism. He insists in *Ecce Deus* (1912) that "there are no texts in the Gospels that indicate that the Jesus was a man." Jesus was in fact God Almighty—which is the view of Christianity.

Thomas Whittaker and L. Gordon Rylands follow Robertson in his view of a pre-Jesus cult, with certain variations—for example, Rylands is concerned greatly with the conceptions of God or the Christ held by Jewish and Greek Gnostics; while Whittaker wishes to place the pre-Jesus cult at a much later date than Robertson.

The two Frenchmen who have ranged themselves on the side of the Mythicists are Dr. P. L. Couchoud and Edouard Dujardin. First, in his "destructive" work, *The Enigma of Jesus,* and later, in his *Creation of Christ,* Couchoud gives reasons why there is no evidence for the existence of Jesus as a man, and then shows how he was "created" by literary means. Dujardin, claims his translator A. Brodie Sanders, in *Ancient History of the God Jesus* (1938) "clearly demonstrates that Jesus was the god of a prehistoric mystery religion of Palestine which emerged on the fringe of the Jewish national cult that had attempted to suppress it, in the same fashion that other local mystery religions of antiquity reappeared, after long periods of obscurity, alongside the national religions of Egypt, Greece, Persia, and other countries."

All these writers are careful scholars who made tremendous research over many fields of literature in the hope of arriving at the truth and elucidating the Jesus problem. Their books could never be "best-sellers", so that the possible material gains were very small. And in addition, their attempts to show that Jesus was a God in the same sense as Osiris or Mithra or Krishna, not merely incurred the hatred and scorn of Christians, but brought down on the unlucky heads of the writers even the scathing criticism of certain Rationalists.

All, or nearly all, of the most eminent Biblical critics of the nineteenth century, even the most advanced theologians in Germany and Holland, however much they were ready to admit myth, symbolism, and allegory in the four Gospels and Acts, refused to give up Jesus as an historical character. The greatest theologian of his day, the late ex-Abbé Loisy, "disintegrated" the Gospels and other New Testament writings as much as nearly any militant Freethinker, but refused, almost with cold fury, to give up Jesus.

Thousands of "lives" or "biographies" of Jesus have been written. From the Freethought point of view those of Strauss and Renan are perhaps the most famous. Strauss, though he riddled the Gospel stories with trenchant criticism, held steadfastly to Jesus; Renan looked upon Jesus as the greatest of the sons of men. In England we have similar testimony from Thomas Paine, John Stuart Mill, and the historian W. E. H. Lecky. Even Robert Ingersoll in America said that "for the man Christ [sic] I have infinite respect." Ingersoll radically changed his opinion later in life, but he obviously believed that there was a real Jesus behind the Bible story.

On the other hand, the semi-Rationalist Dr. F. C. Conybeare, though ready to admit that myths and miracles permeate the Jesus story, came in with a bitter attack on Robertson and the Mythicists in general in his *Historical Christ*. He was heartily supported by most Freethinkers, including the redoubtable Joseph McCabe, the author of a hundred trenchant Freethought works, and later, by A. D. Howell Smith in *Jesus Not a Myth*, and well known atheists like Archibald Robertson, the author of *The Bible and Its Background*. It is curious to note, however, that Strauss studied theology and was ordained at the age of 22, Renan was meant for the priesthood and almost became a priest, McCabe was a Roman Catholic priest for many years, Howell Smith is the son of a Church of England clergyman and once hoped to follow his father in the same path, and Archibald Robertson also comes from a clerical family. It is not easy to throw off childhood impressions.

Even the world-famous author of *The Golden Bough*, perhaps the greatest of all studies of folk lore and religious customs all over the world, took his stand in that work with the historicists—his method exposing the primitive beliefs and legends underlying almost all beliefs with, in his opinion, the exception of Christianity. As, however, he later wrote a very sympathetic Preface to Couchoud's *Engima of Christ*, his views may have considerably changed by then—or at least they were perhaps very much shaken.

To enumerate all the replies to the Mythicists made by the Christian and Unitarian Churches is impossible in these pages. Some of these works will be dealt with as well as, if possible, their most telling and persuasive arguments.

It must be admitted that, once granting the existence of God, anything whatever can follow. As was pointed out long ago by d'Holbach in that masterpiece of atheism, *The System of Nature*

—in the original French, not in the garbled English translation—
once you admit the greatest absurdity, that is, God, you can admit
what you like. Jesus Christ and his miracles, Osiris, Krishna, and
even Aladdin and his wonderful Lamp—all can logically follow.
Admit the "Creator" of the Universe, and there is no story on
earth which can be proved impossible.

Needless to say, I do not admit the existence of God, but for
the purpose of the next chapter that will have to be put aside.
What—apart from God—are the arguments Christians use to
prove the reality of Jesus Christ? They have been given countless times, and that they have been proven effective is shown by
the number of believing Christians. Let us examine some of the
principal arguments.

CHAPTER II

Christian Evidences

THE EVIDENCE FOR THE EXISTENCE OF JESUS Christ as a God is contained in the New Testament. It is true that thousands of Christian writers have contributed other works dealing with this evidence more in detail, like those of Archdeacon Paley, which were long considered the best text books on the question; and it is true that secular writers and historians like Josephus and Tacitus have had to be called in for additional confirmation. But it is the books in the New Testament which form the principal authority behind the Christian Church.

Who guarantees the authenticity and credibility of these documents? The answer is—the Church of Christ. And obviously the next question must be—who or what guarantees the Church of Christ as having the sole authority to guarantee the New Testament? And the answer is—the New Testament.

It is claimed that when Jesus said, as reported in Matt. xvi; 18, "And I say also unto thee, That thou art Peter, and upon this rock I will build my church; and the gates of hell shall not prevail against it," the Roman Catholic Church is the "Church" here spoken of. Thus, the Gospels guarantee the Church, and the Church guarantees the Gospels, which in logic is known as argu-

9

ing in a circle. It is because so many apologists and defenders of
Christianity have been more or less conscious of this that they
have come to the rescue and tried to prove that the Gospels are
true history, and that the Church of Christ really has authority
from God to expound and propagate them. The Gospels and the
New Testament abound with what are known as "miracles" and
it has been one of the duties of the Church to prove to the world
that these miracles actually occurred as described. This has not
been easy. It is interesting to note that the demand for proof of
the Gospel miracles has been far more insistent these days than
in the past.

W. J. Bolton points out in his Hulsean Prize Essay for 1852,
The Evidences of Christianity from the Early Fathers:

> The reader must not expect to find the early Apologists offering
> any regular proof of the reality of the Christian miracles, or of
> the authenticity of the writings that narrate them. This strange
> task has fallen to the lot of the modern apologists; and has been
> called for by our doubting critics, who under every disadvantage,
> have thought fit to question facts which a Tiberius, a Celsus, a
> Porphyry, a Julian, a Hierocles, a Symmachus did not deny . . .
> it had evidently not yet entered into the minds of either Christian
> or Pagan, Jew or Gentile, at the only proper time, seriously to
> doubt the reality of such a body of facts as Christianity presented.
> The historical testimony to the miracles was considered on all
> hands sufficient and conclusive. Any set attempt therefore to
> confirm it would have been worse than superfluous; it would
> have introduced suspicion into the very grounds of the con-
> troversy.

Bolton, who was a thorough Victorian Fundamentalist, was
constrained to add that, anyhow, "it was the prevalent opinion of
early times that a miracle, though ever a proof of power, is not
necessarily a proof of *Divine* power"; but "the tendency of the
present age has decidedly set in against any theory of the sort, and
all parties agree in allowing that a miracle, if it can be proved
authentic, is one of the strongest evidences any cause can possess".

The miracles described in the New Testament are nearly
all about Jesus, or those which he performs; and however

much the Church may object to their being criticized, the fact remains that it is no longer a question of demanding "evidence" for them these days, but of the utter *rejection* of all miracles, evidence or no evidence.

Hundreds of books have been written dealing with miracles, grave discourses taking to task the unbeliever in general, and special works like Hume's famous *Essay on Miracles,* in particular; solemn enquiries and disquisitions ranged under many heads like, *A Dissertation on Miracles* by Dr. George Campbell, once considered the ablest of all answers to Hume, but now quite forgotten; or a closely reasoned argument like the first part of Cassels' iconoclastic *Supernatural Religion.* There is no necessity in these pages to take up the problem again. All I need say is, in Cassels' words, "Every consideration, historical and philosophical, has hitherto discredited the whole theory of miracles". No evidence can be produced or has ever been produced in favor of a miracle. Believers insist that one has no right to make such a dogmatic statement, and instance the undoubted fact that if anyone had claimed a hundred years ago that a vulcanite disc could reproduce the music of a full orchestra, or that a voice from a box could be heard clearly giving a speech delivered 10,000 miles away, or that a man could "fly" to America in a day or so, he would have been called a liar, or such feats be classed as miracles. And they certainly would be miracles, if anyone could have produced them *on the spot.* But the gramophone did not come into being in one minute, so to speak; the radio was the result of many years of close and continuous research, as was the aeroplane. They are all "miracles" of science, if you like, but every step taken to produce them had years of work behind it, with scientific theory tested by scientific practice.

The miracles of Jesus on the other hand are—to believers—unique. He is the only God, we are told, ever born of a Virgin; he is the only God carried about by a real Devil and put on the pinnacle of a Jewish temple. No other God has ever really quelled a storm by word of mouth, or come to life after being put to death. A curse from his mouth destroyed a fig tree, and he fed thousands of people with a few fishes and a few loaves of bread. Finally, his ascension to Heaven, in full view of many people, to sit at the right hand of God Almighty, is surely without a parallel in the history of gods. To compare such scientific facts as the radio, the gramophone, and the aeroplane with the Gospel miracles seems to be a waste of time.

It may be said, however, that people do not believe in Christianity because of the miracles, but, as Cassels says, "miracles are accepted because they are related in the Gospels which are supposed to contain the doctrines of Christianity". This is probably quite true; and it may be worth while to examine some of these statements, whether of doctrines or miracles, in the light of modern thought.

First as to the Virgin Birth.

The exact date of the birth of Jesus is quite unknown, though 4 B.C. is now usually accepted by orthodox believers. To prove to the Jews that he was descended from David—as he would have to be if he were their long expected Messiah—two genealogies are given in Luke and Matthew, each differing from the other, and from the Old Testament. In addition, both genealogies are of Joseph, the husband of Mary, and as Christians claim that Jesus was the Son of God, and Joseph had no part whatever in his birth, they are obviously irrelevant.

Jesus was born of a virgin according to Matthew in fulfillment of a passage in Isaiah vii; 14, "Behold a virgin shall conceive and bear a son, and shall call his name Immanuel". Gallons of ink have been used to explain—or explain away—this passage, but as the very orthodox *Catholic Encyclopedia*, written for Christians who believe in the Virgin Birth more ardently than any other sect, now admits the prophecy is invalid, it can safely be given up. The exact quotation is from the fifteenth volume, page 451:

> Modern theology does not grant that Isaiah vii: 14, contains a real prophecy fulfilled in the virgin birth of Christ; it must maintain, therefore, that St. Matthew misunderstood the passage.

Christians have also found it difficult to explain how "an angel of the Lord appeared to him [Joseph] in a dream" and talked. How does an angel (a real "angel", not a dream angel, of course) talk to anyone in a *dream*?

There is no need to go into the other "prophecies" given by the Gospel writers to prove that Jesus was the Jewish Messiah. In writing up the account of the Son of God, they had the Old Testament in Greek before them, and they freely made use of it. It was not Jesus who "fulfilled" any prophecy; it was the Gospel writer, searching the Scriptures for a text he could work into the story to look like a prophecy, who made his Jesus fulfill the prophecy.

Although Matthew and Luke, who deal with the Virgin Birth story, are considered "inspired" writers (which means, if it means anything at all, that they wrote under the guidance of God himself), they yet disagree on minor details. It was to Joseph that the angel appeared according to Matthew; it was to Mary according to Luke. And the Annunciation took place *before* Mary's conception, if Luke is the authority; and *after,* if Matthew is the authority. Also Matthew says Joseph was a resident of Judea; Luke, of Galilee.

Was Jesus born in Nazareth or in Bethlehem? Here again Matthew and Luke say it was in Bethlehem; but, as far as possible, every other statement in the New Testament *implies,* at least, his birthplace was in Nazareth. If it were not, how comes he to be called Jesus of Nazareth? Why did he say in Acts xxii, 8, in answer to Paul, "I am Jesus of Nazareth"?

In the *Encyclopedia Biblica,* Dr. Cheyne, a (more or less) devout Churchman, argues that there was not at the time—the beginning of our era—any town called Nazareth.

In a little work entitled *The Career of Jesus Christ,* Dr. Milton Wooley, insists that Nazareth is the Zodiac. Here are his words:—

That I am correct here let me refer the learned to Job xxxviii, 32, where he will find *Mazaroth* translated (see in the margin) *"the twelve signs."* [In the Variorum Teachers' Bible, it gives, *"according to tradition* the signs of the Zodiac."] Both Gesinius and Fuerst have *"the twelve constellations of the Zodiac."* Both agree upon the root. It is *nazar,* the m being changed to n, which is allowable in Hebrew. *Nazar,* as a verb, means "to surround, to enclose, to encircle." (Fuerst's Heb. Lex. p. 919.) Nazareth then is the same as Mazaroth (Parkhurst has but one z). The idea of their identity I claim as original with me.

In his *Jesus Not a Myth* (p. 192), A. D. Howell Smith contends that "surely an imaginary village could not have been invested with reality by all the Evangelists." That may be so, but surely that seems like begging the question. It is for Mr. Howell Smith to prove that "Nazareth" was meant to be "invested with reality" by the first writers of the Christ Myth. If Dupuis is right when he claims that Jesus is a "God" like Osiris, Hercules, and the others, that these are mere representations of the Sun, we can well see the connection between "Mazaroth," the twelve signs of the Zodiac, and Jesus, who is also a representation of the Sun.

Matthew claims that a "prophet" also said—in the Old Testament—"He shall be called a Nazarene". There is no such prophecy there, but in Judges xiii, 5, there is the passage in which an angel of the Lord appeared unto a barren wife and told her she would have a son "for the child shall be a Nazarite unto God". There is no connection between "Nazareth" and a "Nazarite" but commentators have done their best to explain or explain away two words with such a similar sound in the hope that whatever else may happen, the "inspired" Matthew must be proved right.

There is a curious sidelight on the place Joseph is made to take in the Gospel story. Joseph is merely the husband of Mary, and he very quickly disappears altogether without it being quite clear why he was dragged in at all. But in Luke, the text of our Authorized Version says (ii, 33), "And Joseph and his mother marvelled at those things which were spoken of him". This gives one clearly to understand that Joseph was—merely Joseph. But in nearly all the best codices the Greek is not "Joseph" but "his *father*". That is, "And his father and his mother marvelled, etc." In other words, the A. V. deliberately mistranslated the verse— as indeed it had to if God and not Joseph was the father. But how can this be reconciled with the doctrine of the Virgin Birth?

In the same chapter, however, is a verse which has not been mistranslated—verse 48. It is, "His mother said unto him, Son, why hast thou thus dealt with us? behold thy father and I have sought thee sorrowing". Here Mary, who ought to know, distinctly declares *Joseph* to be the father of Jesus. Again what becomes of the Virgin Birth?

So little is known of Jesus in detail that there are dozens of opinions as to his age when he began his ministry. It ranges from 22, according to one calculation from Luke, to 37 if Wiesler is right; but as Dr. Geikie admits in his *Life of Christ*, "Amid such differences, exactness is impossible." However, when Jesus did begin, he found John the Baptist as "the messenger" sent to announce him. A plausible case has been made out by H. J. Schonfield in his *Lost Book of the Nativity of John* to prove that John was actually looked upon as the veritable Messiah, and that his Messianic attributes were quietly transferred to Jesus by the early Church when gathering materials for their own Christ. It is curious to find that according to Matthew xi, 14, Jesus (who ought, as God, to have known) said that John the Baptist was Elias, that is, Elijah; while according to John i, 21, John himself said he was *not* Elias. This is one only of many inconsistencies in the accounts of Jesus and John.

But in the fourth chapter of Matthew we get the celebrated journeys through the air which Jesus made in the arms of the Devil. The existence of a real Devil is assumed as well as his ability to fly through the air, and he not only placed Jesus on a pinnacle of the temple (as the temple had only one pinnacle the Revised Version reads "the" instead of "a") but showed him from the top of a high mountain *all* the kingdoms of the world—a miracle if ever there was one.

Upon the ministry of Jesus it is quite impossible to get a coherent account from the Gospels. Either the Synoptics disagree with John in details or with themselves. Even the most orthodox Bible dictionaries admit that difficulties abound. As an example, who were the parents of James the Less and Joses? Matthew xiii, 55, and Mark vi, 3, claim they are the sons of the Virgin Mary, and therefore the brothers of Jesus. The difficulty of reconciling a Virgin with the mother of a family made both Matthew and Mark change their minds about James and Joses; for later Matt. xxvii, 56 and Mark xv, 40 calmly tell us that they are the sons of another Mary, presumably the *sister* of the Virgin. If the earlier Matthew and Mark are right, then Joseph must have been their father; unfortunately, Matt. x, 3, and Mark iii, 18, tell us that James the Less was the son of Alpheus. John, on the other hand, (xix, 25) make it look as if Cleophas was their father. Smith's *Bible Dictionary* says, "This is one of the most difficult questions in Gospel history". But perhaps the real reason for the mix-up is that we are dealing not with history but with fiction.

The chronology of the Gospels has given more than one theologian a headache, and it has never been solved. Over and over again the "timing" of John is quite different from that of the other writers, even when dealing with the same story. For instance, Luke v, 6, puts the miraculous draught of fishes at the beginning of the ministry of Jesus; John xxi, 11, actually *after* his death and resurrection. The Lord's Prayer was delivered during the Sermon on the Mount before the *people* according to Matthew. Luke shows it was before the *disciples* alone (xi, 1). And the list of these differences in time could be extended in dozens of cases.

As for specific miracles performed by Jesus it is astonishing how the four Gospel writers either contradict one another, or are ignorant of what happened according to each other. For example, Jesus stilled the tempest *before* Matthew was called from the receipt of custom (Matthew ix, 9); but according to Mark, it was *after* Matthew (Levi) was called (Mark ii, 14; iv, 35-41). The miracle of expelling a devil, or a number of them, from men and forcing them into two thousand swine occurred, according to Matthew, in the country of the Gergesenes; according to Mark and Luke it was in the country of the Gadarenes; while a number of manuscripts declare it was in the country of the Geresenes. Voltaire wanted to know how swine could, in any case, have been kept in a Jewish country? It is interesting to note also that while the Synoptics are full of miracles of the expelling of—presumably—real devils, John never mentions them.

Even such a world-famous miracle as the feeding of the multitude is given contradictory accounts. Matthew, Mark, and Luke say the food was brought by the disciples (Matt. xiv, 15-17; Mk. vi, 35-38; Lk. ix, 13). John says it was brought by a lad (Jn. vi, 9).

According to John, we find Jesus walking across the sea; according to Matthew and Mark, he only walked half way. Only Matthew relates the incident of Peter also trying to walk on the sea and failing. Mark and John, each of whom gives a detailed account of the voyage, do not mention it.

Just as the raising of the widow's son from death to life at Nain is only related in Luke, so the raising of Lazarus, a similar miracle, is related only in John; both omissions in the other Gospel writers are quite unaccountable, especially as far inferior miracles are related by all of them.

Matthew, Mark, and Luke declare that the purging of the temple was made a few *days* before the death of Jesus; John says it was at the beginning of his ministry—three *years* before his death. He cursed the fig tree, according to Matthew, *after* he purged the temple; *before*, according to Mark. And so one could go on exposing the most blatant contradictions in the Sacred Narrative, contradictions which could not occur had the writers, as is claimed by the Church, been divinely inspired.

There is no doubt also that the Last Supper is meant by the Synoptics to have taken place on the Passover—it was for them the Paschal meal. But John makes it an ordinary meal a day *before* the Passover, and this discrepancy has never been reconciled. Yet, if the story were true, if the Last Supper had really taken place, it is difficult to see how the inspired writers could have made any mistake. Not that the description of the meal is even accurate. Jewish scholars claim that none of the Evangelists had ever seen a Paschal Feast, so gross are their errors of detail.

And there is still something worse. The Eucharist was instituted at the Last Supper according to Matthew, Mark, and Luke. John says the ceremony instituted was the washing of feet. John actually does not mention the Eucharist, while the other writers do not mention the washing of feet. Considering the tremendous importance of the whole ceremony of the Mass these are astonishing discrepancies, and the orthodox commentators have been at their wits' end to account for them. They have never been able to do so.

Again, for John the ministry of Jesus was mostly confined to Judea; for the Synoptics, to Galilee. John says it lasted three years, while the Synoptics say, one year. Irenaeus, one of the most famous of the early Church Fathers, claims that the ministry lasted over twenty years. And Christians are still wrangling over the question to this day.

The accounts of both the Crucifixion and the Resurrection bristle with so many difficulties that the only way to accept the events is by an act of supreme Faith. Reason must be ruled out. That this is so can be shown by dozens of quotations from earnest Christian writers themselves. Their works are full of the most candid admissions which, fortunately for the Faithful, are hardly ever read except by students and the few persons who are specially interested in Biblical problems.

In *Exploratio Evangelica*, Dr. Percy Gardner says, "The tale of the physical resurrection of Jesus belongs evidently to the same circle of thought as that of the miraculous birth. This tale likewise rests on a historical substruction which falls to pieces on a careful examination". Similarly, many Christian scholars would have said the same of the Crucifixion if that had been a miraculous event; but of course they throw overboard the miraculous surrounding it, and prefer to stick to the bare "fact".

Matthew and Mark make Jesus announce his betrayal *at* the Last Supper, John *after* the meal. Matthew and John make Jesus say who should betray him, while Mark and Luke say he did not. Matthew makes Jesus say to Judas when he was betrayed "Friend, wherefore art thou come?" Luke says Jesus said, "Judas betrayest thou the Son of man with a kiss?" And another point: Matthew and Mark say that the Jewish council, who planned to arrest Jesus, decided *not* to do so on the feast day, the very day on which the same writers say he *was* arrested! John says the preliminary examination of the prisoner was before Annas; the other three writers say it was before Caiaphas. As is clearly shown by the author of *Supernatural Religion* "The narrative is a mistake, and such an error could not have been committed by a native of Palestine".

Jesus was charged, according to all the Gospel writers, with blasphemy, but there was no Jewish law against anyone calling himself a "son" of God; and in any case, the Jews could not have asked for the death sentence for blasphemy for that had long been abolished. Moreover, the Jews were forbidden to hold any criminal trial during the Passover, or any feast for that matter. And certainly not on Friday, the day preceding a Passover held on a Sabbath day. Again, the Jews *never* employed crucifixion as a punishment—apart altogether from the fact that, as John expressly makes them declare in xviii, 31, "It is not lawful for us to put any man to death". This was true, as the Sanhedrin's authority ceased in or before 30 A.D.

Although Pilate declared that Jesus was innocent, and although he hated the Jews, yet he handed Jesus over to them to be crucified. It is difficult to trace any *history* in such a proceeding. In any case, here again we get discrepancies between the Gospel writers. It is John who says that Jesus was handed over to the Jews; but it is clear that Matthew and Mark say it was to the Roman soldiers—they at least are shown to have crucified him and not the Jews. In Acts (v, 30) Peter says it *was* the Jews, but they did not *crucify* him: ". . . Jesus whom ye slew and *hanged* on a tree." Most Christian commentators claim that in the Bible and where Jesus is concerned, hanging on a tree is exactly the same as crucifixion on a cross.

On the way to the place of execution, the Synoptics show that "a man of Cyrene, Simon by name," was compelled to carry the cross. John, on the other hand, makes Jesus carry the cross himself. Mark says Jesus was crucified at "the third hour", that is, our nine o'clock in the morning. Luke says it was "the sixth hour", our noon. But John says, at the sixth hour Jesus had not been sentenced; so that, according to him, the crucifixion took place much later still. Theologians have tried hard to harmonize the Gospel writers, but with such little success that Professor Sanday, one of the most eminent orthodox authorities, has been forced to admit that the "attempt to reconcile the two statements" by supposing that Mark and John reckoned the time of the day differently, "breaks down."

According to Matthew, on the day of the Crucifixion, "Many bodies of the saints which slept arose, and came out of their graves after his resurrection". This wholesale coming into life of old and perhaps even young Jewish saints seems to have been quite unknown to the other Gospel writers, to the Jews, and even to the Romans, who might have added such a piece of stupendous history to the other recitals which filled their official archives. And it is not altogether surprising to find that Christians on the whole rarely mention this event; it is astonishingly unpopular. The picture of Jewish saints waiting for Jesus to get out of his grave first (out of politeness, as Ingersoll said) before they could go into the holy city and appear "unto many", is one that somehow has never appealed even to the out-and-out Fundamentalist ready to swallow anything coming from the Bible.

The mother of Jesus, according to John, who expressly names her, was present at the Crucifixion; she is not, however, named as being present by the other Evangelists though they do name Mary Magdalene several times. As for poor Joseph, he had long since disappeared. Mary, it is true, is mentioned once again in Acts and that is all "authentic" history has of her. All the rest is silence except dozens of most dubious legends which not even the Roman Catholic Church requires its members to believe.

When was Jesus crucified? This has been a most difficult question to answer, for the event must have taken place under Pontius Pilate and when Caiaphas was High Priest of the Jews; that is, any time between 26 to 36 A.D. As Remsburg in his *The Christ* sums up, "Of 100 Christian authorities who attempt to name the year in which Christ was crucified, twenty-three say 29, eighteen 30, nine 31, seven 32, thirty-seven 33, and six 35 A.D."

If the Synoptics and John disagree on the date of the Last Supper, they must also disagree on the Crucifixion date. The Synoptics say it was on Friday the 15th of Nisan; John says it was on Thursday the 14th of Nisan. There are many Christians who have argued that the New Testament writers (or its interpreters) are altogether wrong, that Jesus was crucified on a Wednesday so as to give him three clear days before his resurrection. In any case, the early Christians were bitterly divided over the issue, most of their quarrels dealing with the question as to whether Jesus himself was or was not the Paschal Lamb which Jews ate at the Paschal feast. That question is not yet settled.

Though it is generally agreed that Jesus was about thirty-three years old at the time of his death the matter is complicated by the testimony of Irenaeus who disagreed with the Gospel story and roundly declared in his work *Against Heresies* (c. 180 A.D.)

that Jesus was over fifty years of age when he died. Irenaeus also knew nothing about any Crucifixion under Pontius Pilate for he says that "Jesus came on to death itself, that he might be the first born among the dead, that in all things he might have the pre-eminence; the Prince of Life, existing before all, and going before all." And he claims he got this "testimony" from Polycarp who actually got it from John, "the disciple of the Lord". In his *Anacalypsis*—a scarce but valuable work dealing with the origins of religions—Godfrey Higgins says, "The Church has been guilty of the oversight of letting this passage escape". But the real point is, is Irenaeus right? What becomes of the Christian scheme of salvation if Jesus did not die on the cross? And have the Historicists produced any arguments worth reading against Irenaeus?

Hundreds, probably thousands, of books have been written defending the story of the Resurrection as related in the Gospels, but the fact remains that, stupid as are the contradictions in the accounts of the Crucifixion, they are far worse and infinitely more stupid in the story of the Resurrection given by the "inspired" writers. Unless one has them clearly set out in order the average reader is almost bound to pass them by. The narrative in each Gospel is a hurried one, and the details, though well known to theologians and those students who deliberately study them, are almost unknown to the greater body of Christians. The chapters in *Supernatural Religion,* and in such works as *The Gospels as Historical Records,* and Thomas Scott's *English Life of Jesus,* dealing with the Resurrection in detail, give an almost unbelievable number of gross contradictions and absurdities. Here I can deal only with a very limited number.

According to John, Mary Magdalene alone first visited the tomb on the morning of the Resurrection; but the number is increased gradually—for instance, Matthew gives Mary Magdalene and the other Mary; Mark, Mary Magdalene, and Mary the mother of James, and Salome; Luke, Mary Magdalene, and Joanna, and Mary the mother of James, and other women. Perhaps if another canonical Gospel could have been added, both the numbers of women and of Marys would have been increased.

Mark says they came "At the rising of the sun". John says,

"When it was yet dark". Luke says the stone covering the tomb
had been rolled away; Matthew says the tomb was closed. Matthew says the women met "an angel"; Mark says it was "a young
man"; Luke says it was "two men"; and John, not to be outdone,
says "two angels". Matthew says he or they were outside; Mark,
Luke and John say they were inside the tomb. Luke says they
were standing; Matthew, Mark, and John say they were sitting.

According to Matthew, the women actually saw Jesus. According to Luke, they did not. Luke says that only one disciple,
Peter, visited the tomb; John says there were two, Peter and
John. John says that Peter went into the sepulchre; Luke says he
did not—he merely *looked* into it, and departed.

And if we compare the accounts of the appearances of Jesus related by the Evangelists with that told by Paul, we find again the
most hopeless contradictions.

Matthew says Jesus appeared to the two Marys, and to the
eleven in Galilee; Mark says it was to Mary Magdalene, to two
of his disciples, and to the eleven at meat; (it should be made
plain that these appearances are related in the last 12 verses of
this Gospel admitted by most authorities to be "apocryphal",
that is, a late addition, and not found in some of the best MSS).
Luke says the appearances were to Cleophas and his companion;
to Peter; and to the eleven and others. The order is quite different in John, who has, first to Mary Magdalene, then to ten
disciples, then to the eleven, and finally to Peter, John, and
others. (Again it should be made clear that this last appearance
occurs in the last chapter in John also considered a late addition.
See Couchoud's *Creation of Christ*, pp. 258-259.)

Paul in 1 Cor. xv, 5-8 gives quite another list and, of course, in
another order. According to him Jesus after his resurrection was
seen by Cephas, then by the twelve, then by "five hundred
brethren at once", then by James and all the apostles; and
finally by Paul himself "as of one born out of due time".

This is a complete mix-up and contradicts all the Evangelists.
In particular, who are the "twelve"? There were only at the
time eleven apostles as the twelfth had not been elected to take
the place of the late much-lamented Judas. No wonder Strauss
plays havoc with the accounts; and even two thoroughly ortho-

dox Churchmen like Dr. Westcott and Dr. Farrar are forced to admit the recitals "contain difficulties which it is impossible to explain with certainty" (*Introduction to the Study of the Gospels*); and the ". . . scattered notices, which in strict exactness, render it impossible, without many arbitrary suppositions, to produce from them a certain narrative of the order of events". (*Life of Christ*).

According to the "sacred" narratives it is impossible to say to whom Jesus *first* appeared. Mark and John say it was to Mary Magdalene alone, Matthew says it was to Mary Magdalene and the other Mary, while Luke says it was to Cleopas and his companion. Matthew says Mary knew it was Jesus when he first appeared to her, while John says quite clearly she "knew not it was Jesus". And again, it is fairly evident that according to Matthew, Jesus appeared to his disciples in Galilee, while according to Luke, it was in Jerusalem. This is such a grave discrepancy that in his notes on the passages, Dean Alford, in his Greek New Testament, says "We must be content to walk by faith, and not by sight".

When they saw Jesus, Luke says, the disciples "were terrified and affrighted". John, on the other hand, says "The disciples therefore were *glad* when they saw the Lord". (R.V.) Here faith must again come to the rescue.

According to Paul, Jesus was not seen by any *woman* after his resurrection; and it is the same with Luke. The name of Mary Magdalene does not appear in their accounts. Women, although most fervent and uncritical believers in Christianity, have rarely been theologians, otherwise it would have proved very instructive to read their comments on this fact.

In his elaborate work, *Supernatural Religion*, the author gives a very close analysis of the narratives of the Resurrection, and he points out that there were no witnesses whatever of the stupendous event. The details given in one Gospel are contradicted in one or all of the others, the whole story bristles with the supernatural, miracles abound everywhere, and yet upon them the complete structure of Christianity rests as an organized religion. Five hundred millions of people believe the story of the Resurrection led by hordes of priests, who hold up the terrors of Hell as the penalty of unbelief. In an age of science and discovery, in an age which has given us *The Origin of Species* of Darwin, *The Golden Bough* of Sir James Frazer, the *Anthropology* of E. B. Tylor, to say nothing of the works of Herbert Spencer on Evolution or those of Arnold Toynbee on History, it is amazing that so many persons more or less intelligent in the every day things of life, should accept one of the most childish stories ancient religion has handed down to us. We know nothing whatever of the men who first wrote the story, but even if we did, the story itself would not be one whit more credible. As Cassels says, "It comes to us as bare belief from the Age of Miracles, unsupported by facts, uncorroborated by evidence, unaccompanied by proof of investigation, and unprovided with material for examination. What is such belief worth? We have no hesitation in saying that it is absolutely worth nothing".

As if the Resurrection were not enough to prove to the world the Divine source of the Gospels, the writers have added the story of the Ascension. It is worth noting here that only two of the Evangelists actually mention it, Mark and Luke. That is, the two authors who are admitted *not* to have been actual disciples of Jesus (like Matthew and John) and who never saw it. Now, of those writers who detail the story of Jesus it is not unfair to expect that Matthew and John, who must have seen it should have described the Ascension. Yet they say *absolutely nothing* about it. The verses in Mark, on the other hand, which give one account of the Ascension, are not in the earliest MSS. Many books have been written for and against their authenticity without any positive result. So that the words of Luke who never saw it—"he parted from them and was carried up into heaven"—are the only "proof" which Christians have from the four Gospels that Jesus Christ was wafted to the abode of his Heavenly Father.

I have very briefly dealt with the Virgin Birth, the Crucifixion, the Resurrection, and the Ascension, three miraculous events in the life of Jesus, and one certainly bordering on the miraculous, because they are brought forward to show that, at a specified time, they prove that God Almighty was born "in the flesh" on this earth and that this God was the Jesus Christ of the New Testament.

Nobody knows anything for certain about the New Testament except that it exists. Who wrote any of it, when were the different parts written or where, is absolutely unknown. Thousands of books have been laboriously compiled analyzing every problem connected with the Greek text, mostly with the view of proving its absolute integrity, authenticity, and credibility. The New Testament has produced an enormous literature of speculation; for, by and large, that is all it amounts to. We still know next to nothing about the real origin of the Gospels and the Epistles.

The figure of Jesus Christ depicted in them is impossible. There can never be a "God" coming from Heaven to earth whether born of a Virgin or ready made. There have never been "miracles" coming either from God or man. The blind never gained their sight, the halt and the lame never walked about, the lepers were never cured, the deaf were never made to hear, the dead were never raised to life, by the methods attributed to Jesus in the Gospels. If the stories relating these events are taken literally, they never happened; if they are only meant to be symbolic or allegorical, then again, they never happened.

The dates given by the orthodox Churches to the composition of the Gospels have been proved to be utterly erroneous. The four Gospels as we have them were certainly unknown to the early Church Fathers (before about 180 A.D.). A typical instance is the case of Justin Martyr whose date is somewhere about 150 A.D. His works in defence of Christianity contain hundreds of quotations from the Old Testament and many from some kind of Gospels, Apocryphal or otherwise, but he never mentions the names of Matthew, Mark, Luke, or John. Some of his quotations come near to similar passages in these four writers, so that there can be no doubt some Gospels were known in his day, though he himself calls those he quotes the "Memoirs of the Apostles". He even quotes things which are not in the canonical Gospels as "gospel" truth; and also, according to some authorities, quotes from a "Gospel of Peter". Here is one of the earliest and greatest of Christian apologists, writing in defence of Christianity, and he appears to know nothing at all about our four Gospels, all of which, we are given to understand, were in com-

mon circulation in his day, having been composed between 60
A.D. and 90 A.D. or thereabouts. (Christian authorities vary.)
W. R. Cassels, after an exhaustive analysis of Justin, says:

> We have shown that there is no evidence that he (Justin) made
> use of any of our Gospels, and he cannot therefore be cited even
> to prove their existence, and much less to attest the authenticity
> and character of records whose authors he does not once name.
> . . . We have seen that Justin's *Memoirs of the Apostles* contains
> facts of Gospel history unknown to our Gospels, which were
> contained in apocryphal works, and notably in the Gospel ac-
> cording to the Hebrews; that they further contained matter con-
> tradictory to our Gospels, and sayings of Jesus not contained in
> them; and that his quotations, although so numerous, systemati-
> cally vary from similar passages in our Gospels. (*Supernatural
> Religion,* one vol. edition, p. 267.)

On the other hand, it may be well to quote here *The Critical
Handbook* by E. C. Mitchell, D.D., published by the Religious
Tract Society (1880) and described as "A Guide to the Study of
the Authenticity, Canon, and Text of the Greek New Testament".
Dr. Mitchell claims to have consulted the best recent authorities,
so it should prove interesting to see what he says about Justin:

> His works contain about 200 citations from the New Testament
> Scriptures. A tolerably complete life of Jesus might be compiled
> from them. Says Rawlinson (*Hist. Ev.,* p. 215): "No one can pre-
> tend to doubt that in Justin's time the facts of New Testament
> history were received as simple truth, not only by himself, but
> by Christians generally, in whose name his apologies were ad-
> dressed to the emperors."

The lay reader coming across this passage would certainly believe that Justin quoted the New Testament, yet the statement
is quite untrue. Even Dr. Mitchell's authority, Rawlinson, does
not say this, though his name is quite artfully put in to give
weight to the "200 citations from the New Testament Scriptures".

Justin, it must be added, among other Christian documents
quoted from the "Acta Pilati"—the "Acts of Pilate". In his first
Apology he says, to support his contention that Is. xxxv: 6,
prophesied the miracles of Christ, "And that He did these things
you may know from the Acts of Pontius Pilate". Needless to say

the copies of these Acts which have come down to us "are unauthentic" as Dr. Mitchell admits. They are, in fact, unblushing frauds.

If Justin never mentions our Gospels by name in either of his two *Apologies* or in his *Dialogue with Trypho,* written about the year 150 A.D., and yet chatters *ad nauseam* about Jesus, it is fairly good proof that in his day they were unknown, or not in the form we have them; and it is useless going more fully into the question here for it has been thoroughly discussed in great detail by Cassels in his *Supernatural Religion* to which I refer the reader. His conclusion is, "After having exhausted the literature and the testimony bearing on the point, we have not found a single trace of any of those (the four canonical) Gospels during the first century and a half after the death of Jesus". In other words, the Gospels, as F. C. Baur claimed, are "spurious".

And here it may be well to say a few words about *Supernatural Religion.* In *Jesus Not a Myth,* Mr. A. D. Howell Smith names the work in his Appendix, "Some useful books for students", at the same time taking care to refer to Dr. Lightfoot's "very able reply" which should also be read, and Cassels' "rejoinder".

Dr. Lightfoot was considered at the time the most able of all British theologians, and he had a unique opportunity in defence of his Church to make mincemeat of *Supernatural Religion.* Cassels' inquiry was into "the reality of Divine Revelation", which, according to Christianity, was proven by the miracles of Jesus as well as by the greatest of all miracles, Jesus himself, and his first care was to discuss the whole question of miracles. After that, he went on to study the evidence produced by Christians in defence of miracles, and then to analyze the one upon which the whole fabric of Christianity rests—the Resurrection.

Now, many centuries of controversy with unbelievers had made even the most courageous Christian controversialist very wary and chary of entering the field of battle. Long ago the celebrated Dr. Bentley, in trying to dispose of Anthony Collins, had found one very fine method: convict your Freethinking opponent of fraud, ignorance, and bad scholarship, and his thesis falls to the ground. I should say rather, *try* to convict your opponent by this method, for some of the mud thrown is sure to stick. A good

example is the way in which even an Agnostic like Sir Leslie
Stephen was quite convinced that Dr. Bentley "slashed and tore
poor Collins's scholarship" and of course other Freethinkers followed suit. By thus concentrating on mistakes of grammar or
Greek, the reader is unwarily led away from the main issue which
is exactly what the critic wants. Over and over again Christian
controversialists have pursued this method, as if it always mat-
tered greatly that a present tense in Greek should be the imper-
fect, or that a date should be *conjectured* as, let us say, 1702 when
it ought to be 1712 in the opinion of somebody else.

A large part of the Christian attack on Voltaire emphasized his
"ignorance"; and needless to say, in the vulgar abuse heaped
upon Thomas Paine for writing the *Age of Reason,* it was his
"ignorance" which received the heaviest attack. As for Robert
Taylor, who was not only an ordained clergyman and a fully
qualified surgeon, but also a B.A. of Cambridge, it was the
trump card of his opponents. It is not surprising therefore that
Dr. Lightfoot's first care was to examine his adversary's "learning" and he had little difficulty in finding a few errors of grammar
and pagination of authorities.

But Cassels' book was entitled *Supernatural Religion,* and one
would have thought that Lightfoot's principal task would be to
annihilate the objections to miracles which take up 120 pages of
close reasoning in that work. Will it be believed that his "very
able reply" refuses to touch miracles at any price? Not only
that, it also refused to touch the whole question of the Resurrection, a word, by the way, which does not even occur in the
Index to his *Essays on Supernatural Religion.* I know of few
books called "very able" which have made such a point of evad-
ing almost every relevant difficulty found in an opponent as
this one; and am not surprised that John M. Robertson in his
Courses of Study points out that in the *Development of Theology
in Germany and Great Britain,* Prof. Pfleiderer forcibly vindicates
"the critical value of *Supernatural Religion*" and gives "a severe
criticism of Lightfoot".

I have purposely devoted a little space to this discussion, for
if the most learned theologian of his time could make such a
poor showing against such an exposé of Christian pretensions in

the matter of the dating of the Gospels as is found in *Supernatural Religion,* the reader will be able to assess more accurately the value of Christian evidences and their defence. If the four Gospels (and they are four out of a large number) are late productions of the second century they can even at best be little but hearsay; that is, their witness to a God called Jesus is worth nothing at all.

This does not mean that portions of the Gospels, or parts which look a little like the Gospels, were not in existence even as early as 100 A.D. If we can trust anything at all of the "history" of the early Church which has come down to us, it is that Gospels of all kinds were being regularly composed. And even if everything in such a work as Couchoud's *Creation of Christ* cannot be sustained, he does give us a glimpse of the way in which Gospels may have been originally written. The writing of Gospels continued for centuries and even in our own generation many new ones have been produced.

Howell Smith in *Jesus Not a Myth* has a chapter on the "Dating of the Gospels", but it is impossible to say definitely how *he* would date them. It is so, it isn't so, and it may be so, are not a very clear way of invalidating a work like that of Cassels. For example, he quotes Ignatius and his Epistles, though "grave doubts about their authenticity do not seem to have been dispelled by Lightfoot's learned defence. . . . Apparently, the writer cites Matthew and Mark but not Luke, and doubtfully John." So what? I confess I do not know. But even Dr. Lightfoot does not go so far as this in his defence of the Ignatian Epistles. He says, "Quotations from the New Testament, strictly speaking, there are none." (*Apos. Fathers,* pt. ii., vol. i., 1885, p. 580). It would have been more to the point had we been given the appropriate citations from Matthew and Ignatius and Mark.

Sufficient has been said about the Gospels produced by Christians as unimpeachable evidence for the existence of Jesus Christ as a God. It is time we turned to Paul, who is nearly always put forward as a witness quite impossible to overthrow.

CHAPTER III

The Witness of Paul

STRICTLY SPEAKING, WE SHOULD GO FIRST TO
Paul to prove that God Almighty came to earth "in the flesh" in
the person of Jesus Christ, as his Epistles were, according to
Christian critics, written some years before the Gospels. They
appeared from about the year 50 A.D., to about the year 66 A.D.
It is all of course quite uncertain, so much so indeed, that the
modern orthodox theologian is quite content if only four out of
the thirteen formerly believed to be all by Paul are now accepted.
Actually, the number used to be fourteen because Hebrews was
ascribed to Paul. However, the "genuine" Epistles are now almost everywhere accepted: Romans, First and Second Corinthians, and Galatians, and these at least prove beyond the shadow
of a doubt, it is contended, the truth of Christianity, and the
existence of Jesus Christ as a Man as well as a God. Such certainly is the opinion of Christendom, and if we omit the Deity
part of Jesus, Paul is the principal witness for Jesus also for
all other Historicists.

There is no evidence that Paul ever claimed to have seen
Jesus, except in a vision; and he says himself—if the Epistle is
genuine—"The Gospel which was preached of me is not after

30

man. For I neither received it of man, neither was I taught it but by the revelation of Jesus Christ". The vision is described in Acts, but somebody in writing that work appears to have made some sad errors. There are two versions of Paul's vision. In the first it says, "And the men which journeyed with him *stood speechless*" (Acts ix, 7). In the second, "We were all *fallen* to earth" (xxvi, 14). In the first of these texts, the men, we are told, *heard* "a voice". But in Acts xxii, 9, Paul says, "and they that were with me saw indeed the light and were afraid; but they *heard not* the voice of him that spake to me".

Again in Acts, Paul clearly says that after his conversion he went straight to the synagogues to preach Christ, first in Damascus, and then in Jerusalem (Acts ix, 20-28). But in Galatians, there is nothing about preaching Christ in the synagogues immediately after his conversion. Instead, we are told he "conferred not with flesh and blood" but went into Arabia, back to Damascus where he stayed three years before he went to Jerusalem, "and abode with Peter" for fifteen days; while the only apostle he saw was James "the Lord's brother". And this account Paul, before God, swears is the true one. (Gal. i, 16-20). We laymen can of course take our choice of either account, but they both can't be true.

We also find Paul in Romans (xi, 13) and (xv, 16) clearly stating that he was the Apostle to the *Gentiles*. Yet in Acts, throughout his ministry, he never ceases to preach to the *Jews* in their own synagogues. Moreover, he claims that it was Peter's mission to convert the *Jews* (Gal. ii, 7); while Peter himself claimed that that was *not* true, "that the *Gentiles* by my mouth should hear the word of the gospel and believe" (Acts xv, 7).

Both Paul and Peter claim that Jesus was a "man" (1 Tim. ii, 5, and Acts ii, 22), while Paul, contradicting the "physical" resurrection described by the Gospel writers, taught only a "spiritual" one (1 Cor. xv, 44-50). Paul preached *deliverance* from the "law", that is, Judaism; Jesus, in Matthew v, 17-18 insisted that "one jot or one tittle shall in *no wise* pass from the law". Did Paul know this? He certainly had some sayings of Jesus at hand not recorded in the Gospels, as when he says that Jesus said, "It is more blessed to give than to receive" (Acts xx, 35).

It would be possible here to deal more fully with the "theology" of Paul, but nothing could be more wearisome. As the Duke of Somerset says in his *Christian Theology and Modern Skepticism*, "There is scarcely a single passage in the Pauline Epistles, or a single doctrine in the Pauline theology, which is not darkened or embroiled by the ambiguity of the expression". Yet it is to Paul more than to any other writer that the Mythicists are directed for proof that a Man-God or a God-Man really existed.

But if the Dutch theologian Prof. Van Manen is right, none of the Epistles ascribed to Paul was written by him, "neither fourteen, nor thirteen, nor nine, nor eight, nor yet even the four so long universally regarded as unassailable. They are all, without distinction, pseudographia". The reader should turn to the article on Paul in the *Encyclopedia Biblica* for a full discussion of the matter, or to Thomas Whittaker's *The Origins of Christianity*. If the Epistles of Paul are therefore forgeries of the second century, if the Christian Church is responsible for these forgeries, exactly how much can we rely on Paul as a witness?

We are distinctly told by Paul that Jesus was seen after his Resurrection by Cephas, by the twelve, by 500 of the brethren, by James, by all the Apostles, and finally by Paul himself. Now, if we accept Paul's Epistles as genuine, then we have here a real live witness who testifies to appearances of Jesus *after he died* on the cross and was buried. Do the Rationalist Historicists —like Howell Smith or Joseph McCabe—believe this? If not, what is the witness of Paul worth? Certainly it cannot be used by those who believe there was only a mere man in Jesus Christ; and if these particular texts are fraudulent—and can anyone doubt that they are?—what about the other texts which show us a "real" Jesus like 1 Cor. xi, 23-27? Here we have the distinct statement that "the Lord Jesus the same night in which he was betrayed took bread, etc." Was this written by a man who knew the facts, or is it a deliberate forgery?

The problem of Paul has produced a literature perhaps second only to that of Jesus, and to deal with all the theories and explanations as to what he meant or what he did not mean is quite beyond the scope of this work. But there are some things which must be dealt with if only to show how lying and forgery have crept in to Christianity to bolster up a dishonest creed and to give life to a literary creation.

That the Epistles of Paul have been tampered with is admitted even by orthodox theologians. Indeed, it cannot be denied that we have in them often two discordant voices speaking, and also that Paul, if he really were a disciple of a living Jesus, was often in complete disagreement with his fellow apostles. The quarrels between Peter and Paul, and Paul and Barnabas, are clearly shown in Holy Writ.

In his pamphlet *Paul the Gnostic Opponent of Peter* Gerald Massey proves quite clearly to any unbiased reader that "Paul was not a supporter of the system known as Historical Christianity, which was founded on a belief in the Christ carnalized; an assumption that the Christ had been made flesh, but that he was its unceasing and deadly opponent during his lifetime; and that after his death his writings were tampered with, interpolated, and re-indoctrinated by his old enemies, the forgers and falsifiers, who first began to weave the web of the Papacy in Rome. . . . The supreme feat, performed in secret by the managers of the Mysteries in Rome, was this conversion of the Epistles of Paul into the main support of Historic Christianity!"

Massey by the way, is often sneered at by persons who imagine that they are Biblical critics, as not himself being a Biblical critic. Without dealing with this typical piece of nonsense in detail, I should like to point out that Thomas Whittaker, who probably had never read anything by Massey, came to the same conclusion about Paul. Here are some extracts from his *Origins of Christianity*:

> According to the view taken in Van Manen's work the Pauline Epistles in our present text are slightly "catholicized." . . . The Pauline Epistles did not originally express the ideas of that which afterwards became the "Catholic Church." Paul—the ideal author of the series—was not, as Comte took him to be, "the founder of Catholicism." . . . He may be best described as the Father of Christian Gnosticism. (Pages 54-55).

And Whittaker further points out that when the Protestant Churches looked for a "basis" in Paul's writings there took "place a curious transition, which has scarcely been enough dwelt on, though Gibbon clearly perceived it. For the anti-judaic Paul of the Gnostics is substituted the essentially Judaising Paul of the Protestant Churches. That there are Judaising passages in the Epistles must, of course, be admitted; but it seems likely that the almost contemporary Gnostics had a truer feeling for the general drift of their ideal Apostle than late comers like the fourteenth-century precursors of Luther and Calvin." (p. 61)

It is surely very strange that though Paul talks incessantly of Christ Jesus, he never mentions "Jesus of Nazareth." He never mentions the wonderful teaching of Jesus, nor his still more wonderful miracles. Now, if the Gospel stories are true, and if Paul was converted so soon after the death of Jesus, and if he were also continually wrangling with the Apostles, how is it that in the Epistles we do not get more of Jesus of Nazareth, and a little less of Christ Jesus?

It is impossible to understand Paul unless one understands Gnosticism and what the Gnostics taught. Gnosticism, says Harmsworth's *Universal Encyclopedia,* "embodied attempts to formulate a cosmic philosophy or theory of the universe and a quest for a world religion. An example of syncretism, an effort to blend opposite and conflicting ideas into a harmonious whole, its sources were Zoroastrianism, Buddhism, and accretions from Judaism, Mithraism, the mythologies of Babylon and Egypt, and Platonism." This is a very brief description of an enormous subject, and cleverly manages to hide the one fact germane to the problem of Jesus Christ. But a hint is given when the article adds, "An example of a Gnostic view of Jesus Christ is in the apocryphal epistle of Barnabas". But how comes such a view of Jesus in an epistle produced by the Church if Jesus had been a living personage?

It was contended for centuries that Gnosticism was the name given to a sect, or some sects formed *after* the rise of Christianity, the truth being that the system was in existence long before the idea was evolved by the early Church to make the Gnostic Christ —a Being within one's own self—into a historical character. The Gnostics' principal task was to lead man to salvation through religious "mysteries". A good deal of the terminology used in

Christian theology, and for that matter in Theosophy, is nothing but Gnosticism, which means "knowledge". (Hence the word "Agnosticism", which has come to mean "no knowledge" or "I do not know".)

The Gnostics did not believe in the literal interpretation of the various stories they borrowed from other religions. For them, there was a "hidden wisdom", a "secret doctrine", *not* for the vulgar, that is, the ordinary people, in their teachings. Hence so many obscure sayings put into the mouth of Jesus as, for example, when the Gospels repeatedly admit that his hearers did not understand what he was talking about. Possibly, long before Gnosticism became something of a system, talking to the people in enigmatical terms, allegorizing and symbolizing, was a favorite method of public teachers, and accounts for so many ridiculous stories being accepted by the multitude as literally true, the priest claiming that he and his Church alone—Pagan, Jewish, or Christian—were able to interpret the "oracles".

Thus, in the Epistles of Paul, are large numbers of sayings which invariably give Christian commentators trouble, and which certainly mean different things to different theologians. I am sure that if I quoted something from one of these Epistles with my comment, I would be assailed on the one hand by the Christian as having misquoted or misinterpreted the text, and perhaps even more violently on the other hand by the non-believing Historicist, for whom Paul, as a valuable witness for his case, should be almost sacrosanct.

As an example, the reader should study the chapter on the Epistles of Paul given in *The Historical Christ* by Dr. F. C. Conybeare, in which the whole race of Mythicists is violently attacked. In this chapter, nearly all the texts which anybody familiar with even a little Gnosticism can see are typical of Gnostic ideas, that is, they contain the "hidden wisdom" of the typical Gnostic, are almost hysterically acclaimed as history. "Such a verse as Col. ii, 14", says Dr. Conybeare (p. 152), "where in highly metaphorical language Jesus is said to have nailed the bond of all our trespasses to the cross is an unmistakable allusion to the historical crucifixion; as also is the phrase 'blood of his cross' in the same epistle i, 20." Here we find something written in highly metaphorical lan-

guage easily turned into history by Conybeare just as no doubt he
would say that the story of Abraham and his bondwoman and
freewoman which Paul himself in Galatians (iv, 24) clearly calls
an "allegory" is not an allegory but actual history. We get another
example of this kind of reasoning in Mr. Howell Smith's *Jesus
Not a Myth*. On page 128 of that work he clearly recognizes that
"Paul's language is full of terms current in the pagan religions
and theosophies", and "again and again his thought seems to echo
one or other of the Gnostic systems". But does this make Paul
a Gnostic? No, we must not "infer from his occasional use of the
nomenclature of the pagan mystery religions that Paul had any
first class acquaintance with them". Paul, we are definitely told
"was a Jew and his modes of thought were primarily Jewish".
Well, it is true that Paul *said* he was a Jew *to the Jews*, but as
many Jewish rabbis have pointed out, there is otherwise very
little proof that Paul was a Jew, for his modes of thought are
definitely *not* Jewish. He certainly shows very little knowledge
of the Judaism of his time, quite positively not as much as Luke,
and Luke (or whoever wrote Luke) was not a Jew.

How does Howell Smith describe the Jesus of Paul? "The
Jesus of Paul", he says, "is a heavenly being, conceived almost
entirely along the lines of Jewish speculation". We must not,
however, jump to the conclusion that Paul had read all the Jewish
works such as the Wisdom of Solomon, the Old Testament, and
the Rabbinical commentary thereon, Howell Smith hastily adds.
Personally, I would like to know something more about the Rabbinical commentary he mentions which must have been current
about the year 50 A.D., and who were the rabbis responsible for
it. Be that as it may, if, as Howell Smith contends, the Jesus of
Paul is a "heavenly being", if he is (p. 129) a "Man from heaven",
if he is "a life-giving spirit", as well as the "Holy Spirit", or the
"Holy Breath", which terms we are definitely told are not "interpolations", how did this Jesus come down to earth and become,
according to his thesis, "historical"? How did Paul manage, as
we are informed on page 158, to proclaim "the belief in an historic Jesus"? Did Paul believe that his "heavenly being" did after
all come down to earth either as a complete Man and soon after
was crucified under Pontius Pilate; or that he came thirty odd

years before, and was born of a Virgin, and went about "doing good"? And I am completely puzzled as to what is meant by the term "heavenly being". Does it mean that Paul believed there was a being actually alive in "Heaven", or that Paul believed in "the Christ within you"—whatever is meant by this Gnostic term?

If Howell Smith wants us to believe in the historicity of Jesus as a Man, are we to understand that he himself believes that there is a "Heaven" in which resides a "Being"? And that (to confound the Mythicists, I suppose) this "Being" came down and became "History"? If he does not mean this, what does he mean?

Dr. Conybeare faces the fact that, even among orthodox Christian theologians, Colossians may not be a genuine work of Paul, but it is dragged in all the same to prove that Paul is a marvelous witness to the living "Christ", for it, together with "Thessalonians and the so-called Pastorals" form "so many fresh witnesses against the hypothesis of J. M. Robertson and his friends". Howell Smith also has doubts about Colossians being genuine, but does that matter? Not at all; the Epistle still acts as an unimpeachable witness for Jesus. Any bit of old writing, no matter who wrote it, or even when it was written, so long as it appears in the New Testament (and therefore in the "canon" and sacrosanct) and mentions Jesus Christ, is an unimpeachable proof of the existence of Jesus or—as Dr. Conybeare would say—of Christ. And it is obvious that if Paul had written that Jesus was seen after his Resurrection by 50,000 people instead of by 500, or if somebody else, forging Paul's name, had so written 100 years later, we should still have Paul brought to us as the great witness for—what? For Howell Smith's "heavenly being" Jesus, or Dr. Conybeare's "Christ"? Such a witness would not do for a mere man who could never have been seen alive, after he had been put to death, either by 500 or by 50,000 people.

Dr. Conybeare devotes many pages to the Epistles of Paul, pooh-poohing in his most angry fashion, any attempt on the part of the Mythicists to invalidate them by appealing, for example, to writers like Van Manen and Whittaker for proof either that they are full of "interpolations", or are unquestionably products of the second century. Now if there is one thing certain on this question of dates, it is that the whole of the New Testament, as we have it, is of a much later date than the Christian Churches will allow. It is unfortunately impossible in these pages to take up this problem in detail, but what I have already said as to the express findings of the author of *Supernatural Religion,* and the fact that he has never been adequately answered, is proof enough for any reader not hypnotized by Christian "authority". Whether the apostle who was called Saul and later became Paul, who is described in Acts as the opponent of Peter and Barnabas, really wrote any of the Epistles which go under his name, is impossible to say. But this is quite certain. Just as the Gospels have been interpolated so have these Epistles. Let the reader turn to the Variorum Teacher's Bible and see how much space is given to various "readings" and amendments, some taking up half the page in very small print. Over and over again this or that verse is pointed out as being corrupted, or suspected of being corrupted, or our translation as being "conjecture", with the opinion of many of the Fathers as well as of modern theologians as to what Paul meant or did not mean. Yet for Dr. Conybeare, so long as "Holy Writ" says something about a "cross" or about "crucifixion" that means "Christ". That means that Christ really lived, though I for one have never been quite clear as to whether Dr. Conybeare actually believed in "Christ" or in "Jesus".

To the argument that "in Acts there is no hint of Paul ever having written Epistles to the Churches he created or visited", he calmly asks "Why should there be?" And he proceeds in answer to tell us that "to Luke the letter-writing must have seemed the least important part of Paul's activity, although for us the accident of their survival makes the Epistles of prime importance". Here it can be seen that the worthy Doctor knows exactly what was important to Luke, or was not, while he also is certain that the survival of the Epistles is "accidental". Not that Conybeare is very comfortable (even to the Historicists) when he has to make admissions. "I admit", he says candidly, or at least trying to be candid, "that Paul's account in Galatians of his personal history is difficult to reconcile with Acts, and has provided a regular crux for critics of every school". I shudder to think what he would have said in defense of Paul, if John M. Robertson had made much more of such a plea.

Conybeare also admits that the "interest of Paul in the historical Jesus was slender and I have explained (in *Myth, Magic and
Morals*) why it was so". Of course, that should settle the matter,
and there ought not to be any more inconvenient questioning.
In this, however, some of us are incorrigible, and I for one still
fail to see how it was that the Epistles as a whole should never
mention the various wonderful happenings performed by Christ
(Conybeare) or Jesus (Howell Smith), or his still more marvelous sayings. It seems incredible that the number of emphatic
announcements regarding the Day of Judgment coming from
Christ Jesus, and the way in which Jesus himself was coming
back with, I believe, the Trump of the Lord, and other Heavenly
Happenings, should be so thoroughly ignored. We do not get
even his dealings with women like Mary Magdalene and Martha
referred to in the Epistles, nothing about the miracles, or the
Jewish dead rising after the Crucifixion, nothing about the Devil
who carried him in the air to the pinnacle of the Temple.

One of the standing proofs that there was a Jesus used by
Archibald Robertson is that Jesus distinctly declared in Matthew
xxiv, 34, and similar texts that the generation to whom he was
speaking would not pass away before his return—a prophecy quite
unfulfilled. This being the case, this prophecy could not have
been put into the mouth of a mythical person as the fact that the
prophecy utterly failed would have made it absurd. Therefore
somebody must have said it, and it was faithfully reported by his
hearers. There must have been therefore a Jesus. I hope that I
have put this argument clearly, as it has appealed to many Rationalists and particularly to Howell Smith who gives, in addition,
Matt. xvi, 28, "Verily I say unto you, There be some standing
here, which shall not taste of death, till they see the Son of man
coming in his kingdom". Mark, in ix, 1, makes the last clause,
"till they see the kingdom of God come with power", while Luke,
in ix, 27, has "till they see the kingdom of God". Here then we
have three texts put before us, all purporting to come from the
same Jesus, written by three "inspired" writers, who we are told
very dogmatically, could never have written such prophecies as
they were never fulfilled, unless they were genuine, that is, unless the speaker really lived. No forgers could possibly have put

them into the mouth of a myth, simply because there could have been no object in perpetuating an unfulfilled prophecy. "The strong witness of these texts", says Howell Smith (p. 160) "has to be explained away by the Mythicists."

What I do not understand, in the first place, is why the texts should be different? Matthew says quite clearly that it was "the Son of man" who would be "coming in his kingdom". That means that Jesus was coming into some kind of kingdom—or does it? What is meant by the word "kingdom"? Howell Smith says, as if there was no doubt about it, that by the "Kingdom of God" primitive Christians "envisaged the physical sovereignty of Jesus over an earth ruled from Jerusalem". This may be so, but it would have helped a lot if, say, a dozen authorities were given as proof, for I personally have been no more able to find out what primitive Christians meant by the term than I have been able to learn what they meant by the "Kingdom of God is within you". Possibly these terms are Gnostic, and if they are, then any explanation can be assumed for no one really knows everything the Gnostics meant.

In any case, why have we three different texts, and why is the one from Matthew generally singled out by some of the Historicists? Is it because they are not altogether certain what is meant by the "Kingdom of Heaven"? And it is much easier to confound the Mythicist by saying that a real Jesus must have said that *he* would be coming "in his kingdom" than to say that his hearers would merely "see the kingdom of God" while they were alive? For my part, I do not understand what Jesus meant—if a real Jesus said anything at all—by his "kingdom" (or to make the word more impressive, as Howell Smith puts it, "Kingdom"). Stupid as we know the primitive Christians must have been, I doubt very much if at least some of them really believed that Jesus would come again after his death and "rule from Jerusalem".

How do some Christian commentators understand Matt. xvi, 28? I have here before me the New Testament, translated afresh, published in America some years ago. The Greek text, which is given complete, is a facsimile of the famous Codex Sinaiticus, with corrections from the Codex Vaticanus, and the correctors of the original manuscripts. These are perhaps the oldest copies we have of the New Testament, and this version, called the "Concordant Version", claims to be as accurate a translation as possible. In addition, the translator and editor give a commentary, and on this text say:

> This prediction was fulfilled a week later when He took His most intimate disciples with Him and they saw His Power and presence and were spectators of His magnificence (2 Peter i, 16). It is fitting that at this juncture, there should be some plain intimation of the postponement of the kingdom. In the record the promise is immediately followed by its fulfillment, but there is a week's delay. Another cycle must run its course before the proper conditions reappear which precede the kingdom.

Whether A. Robertson or Howell Smith agrees with the Fundamentalist responsible for the above does not really matter. To the Christian or to some Christians, the famous passage in Matthew which almost completely confounds the Mythicist and which he "has to explain away" is answered very simply—Jesus Christ *did* come again a week later. Therefore the prophecy is not an "unfulfilled" one, and therefore it is rightly put into the mouth of the "Son of man", whatever is meant by this term, for I do not know myself.

It should be noted also that the prediction that Jesus would come again before his hearers tasted death was preceded by "the Son of man shall come in the glory of his Father with his angels; and then he shall reward every man according to his works". Here again was a prophecy unfulfilled, and yet it was allowed to stand in the text. So were quite a number of other prophecies as, for example, that some of the hearers of Jesus would not taste death till they see the Kingdom of God; till they see the sign of the Son of man in heaven; till *all* the tribes of the earth mourn; till the Son of man sends his angels with a great sound of a trumpet; and many more. All these prophecies completely failed, but they were allowed to stand. If the Gospels are products of the second century, it seems to me that their writers or editors kept these things in because it appeared to them to add that touch of verisimilitude necessary to give to a being claimed to be historical. It was the stock in trade of prophets to prophesy, it was impossible to write about a prophet without making him responsible for dozens of fulfilled and unfulfilled predictions.

This method of proving that there must have been a Jesus because he falsely prophesied can be extended a little further, with what seems to me rather unfortunate results to the Historicists. They are asked, for example, to explain away, if they can, the well known text in Acts where the Lord clearly promises that nothing whatever would happen to Paul if he carries on with his preaching: "Be not afraid, but speak, and hold not thy peace: For I am with thee, and no man shall set on thee to hurt thee: for I have much people in this city". (Acts xviii, 9-10.) No prophecy could be more explicit or better guaranteed, as God himself told Paul he would be perfectly safe to go on preaching. And was God right? In verse 12 we are told that so far from no one "setting" on to Paul, "when Gallio was the deputy of Achaia, the Jews made insurrection with one accord against Paul, and brought him to the judgment seat . . ." That was only a beginning, as he was later beaten by a mob, nearly torn to pieces, struck in the mouth, put in prison, sent in chains on a sea voyage, shipwrecked, starved for 14 days, and bitten by a viper. Thus the prophecy was completely unfulfilled, and thus, according to Howell Smith and A. Robertson, the Lord must have undoubtedly existed; otherwise one would have to explain how a forger could put in the mouth of God a prophecy which the sequel shows was nonsense.

And after all, some of the "prophecies" put into the mouth of Jesus were "fulfilled". In Matt. xxiii, 34, we get "Wherefore, behold, I send unto you prophets and wise men and scribes; and some of them ye shall kill and crucify; and some of them shall ye scourge in your synagogues, and persecute them from city to city; . . . Verily I say unto you, All these things shall come upon this generation". Mark and Luke say much the same, and everybody knows that their long, and more or less ghastly accounts of what was going to happen were always considered Jesus's marvelous predictions of the destruction of Jerusalem which took place about 40 years afterwards.

And here we can go back to Paul again for he also predicted many things which were quite unfulfilled. He gave out "by the word of the Lord" that "the Lord himself shall descend from heaven with a shout, with the voice of the archangel, and the trump of God: and the dead in Christ shall rise first . . ." Now it is undeniable that Paul, according to this passage from I Thes. iv, 16, and many others, was absolutely certain that the end of the world was coming in the lifetime of his contemporaries; that is, if Paul really wrote Thessalonians. And if the above prophecies of Jesus are cited as proving beyond the shadow of a doubt that Jesus must have uttered them, and that therefore he was a real personage because they are unfulfilled, in the same way Thessalonians must have been written by a real Paul because his prophesying the end of the world has turned out a complete failure.

But is Thessalonians the work of Paul? In *Apostolic Records* the Rev. Dr. Giles is most *uncertain* that the author was Paul, and in any case he wants to reject the second coming of "our Lord" passages "as being of little value for those who have but a slight tincture of modern scientific knowledge", the very passages which, as I have shown above, could be used to prove that Paul must be the author. ". . . . it looks more", adds Dr. Giles, "as if some later author or editor had issued these epistles, on the belief no doubt, that his doctrine and facts were on a Pauline basis."

Dr. Edwin Hatch, in the *Encyclopedia Biblica*, thinks I Thessalonians "is almost certainly" genuine, while the genuineness of the second epistle "has been much disputed". As a matter of fact, these two Epistles do not belong to "the big four" and their authenticity has long been a matter of dispute. But whether they are or not, does the fact that Paul's prophecy miserably failed prove that he unquestionably existed?

The most interesting phase, however, about the Epistles to the Thessalonians is the way in which they contradict each other on this vital point, the second coming of "Christ". In the first Epistle, Paul makes it perfectly clear that the second coming of Christ is quite near (I Thes. iv, 15-18), for it is "we that are alive" who are going to meet "the Lord in the air". But in II Thes. ii, 1-5, we are just as clearly told that we must not be deceived "for that day shall not come" unless "there come a falling away first" and (to make matters clearer, I suppose) "that man of sin be revealed the son of perdition". It is not for me to explain the contradiction which Dr. Giles declares "has not yet been satisfactorily cleared up", but I cannot help asking, which of these two statements is it which proves that Paul must be the author of both, the one in which he distinctly lays down the second coming of Christ will be in his lifetime, or the one in which he says it will not?

Dr. Conybeare, who pooh-poohs everything in the Myth theory with which he does not agree—though in *Myth, Magic, and Morals* he insists that whatever he himself says is a myth must be a myth—points out the text II Cor. v, 16, as one which J. M. Robertson passes over in silence. The text is, "Wherefore we henceforth know no man after the flesh: even though we have known Christ after the flesh, yet now we know him no more". Here we have it declared from Paul himself (though the meaning is not clear) that he had actually seen "Christ" in the flesh, though anyone familiar with the Pauline literature and its commentaries will know that it has always been urged that Paul never saw Jesus alive, but that after "persecuting" him as Saul, a vision direct from heaven converted him into Paul, the Great Apostle to the Gentiles. Even Howell Smith admits that Paul's Jesus was a "heavenly being". For Dr. Conybeare, this is one of the texts "most inconvenient to the zodiacal theory of the apostles", and so it would be, if we were sure that Paul wrote it, and that he actually saw Jesus alive *before* the Resurrection.

But the most searching examination of all the Pauline literature has resulted only, in the opinion of most theologians, that Paul's Jesus was "subjective", a "heavenly being", a "Christ" due perhaps to his intense religiosity and his conviction that the Messiah had come; or that it was the Gnostic "Logos" which had come to him, as the result of his eyes being "opened" in the same way that a similar religious teacher, Emanuel Swedenborg, had his eyes opened. In *Plato, Philo, and Paul* the Rev. J. W. Lake says, "Paul never saw Jesus, and never learned his doctrine, either from his disciples or his apostles. . . . So he preached Christ; for he recognized Jesus as the Messiah, not in the popular but in the spiritual sense, i.e., as the power and the wisdom of God.

But the power and the wisdom of God were the attributes of the Gentile Logos; the 'Divine Word' by whom the worlds were made. . . ." And this is the opinion of most writers on the subject, and it may have been Dr. Conybeare's but for the fact that he realized that the witness of Paul would be useless for the Historicists unless it can be shown that Paul had actually seen Jesus. Even the most dogmatic of them saw that Paul's witness for the reality of Jesus *after* the Resurrection only made them admit that he *did* rise from the dead, and in that case, it was not Jesus the man for whom they were contending, but Jesus the God.

Dr. Conybeare vigorously defends the authenticity of the Epistles of Paul against any idea that they are late productions; and in particular he refuses to recognize that those texts which allude to Jesus as the seed of David, or describe him as in I Cor. xi, 23-27, for example, at the Last Supper, are interpolations. Everything in the Epistles referring to Jesus is absolutely authentic. In fact, even if it could be proved that any of the Epistles "may not be from Paul's hand", insists Conybeare, "they are unmistakably early; and their forgers, if they forged, undoubtedly held that Jesus had really lived". Thus Paul is a witness absolutely unimpeachable; but even if he did not write what is attributed to him—well, the "forgers" are unimpeachable witnesses. And the point to note is that as Paul writes that, among many others, 500 people saw Jesus alive *after* he had been put to death, this proves there must have been a Jesus, otherwise how could he have arisen?

So impressed with Paul is Conybeare that one feels that if Paul had "testified", or a forger in his name had "testified", that Jesus had been carried about by the Devil through the air much as Aladdin was carried about by the Genie of his Lamp, he would have angrily asked how could John M. Robertson or W. B. Smith get over such testimony? How could a Devil carry anyone unless he had really lived?

In I Cor. xi, 23 foll., we get the text "For I have received of the Lord that which I also delivered unto you, That the Lord Jesus the same night in which he was betrayed took bread, etc." And Dr. Conybeare adds, "All this ill agrees with the view that Paul believed the Jesus of the Gospels to be an ancient Pales-

tinian Sun-God-Savior Joshua". I have rarely read a sillier comment, and can understand why Mr. Robertson felt it was hardly
worth while to discuss the problem of Jesus with anybody writing
thus.

In the first place, any critical reader will have noted that if
Paul really wrote this passage about the betrayal he could have
known nothing whatever about a "Gospel" Jesus: there were no
Gospels at the date given for the composition of the Epistles.
Moreover, the "Jesus of the Gospels", put in this way, supposes
that Paul only knew of a Jesus of the canonical Gospels—though
at the time those other written Gospels were making their appearance and the whole question, which were the "authentic"
Gospels and which were not, was not settled till centuries afterwards. Then again, the picture of Jesus given by the different
Gospels varies with their authors, and if there is one thing which
emerges pretty clearly it is that the Jesus of John is quite a different being from the Jesus of Mark, and both differ very considerably from the Jesus portrayed in the Apocryphal Gospels, and
probably also from the Jesus of the "Lost and Hostile" Gospels,
as the Rev. S. Baring-Gould calls them. And even in the name
"Palestinian Sun-God-Savior Joshua" we get an example of Conybeare's spite getting the better of his critical judgment, for the
word "Savior" is the actual meaning of the Hebrew word "Joshua".

There is another point which is not cleared up either in the
Gospels or in Conybeare. When Paul talks about the Last Supper,
does he mean Matthew's or John's? As I have already pointed
out, the Last Supper, according to the Synoptics, took place on
the Passover; according to John, it was not the Paschal meal at
all, and it took place the evening *before* the Passover. Did Paul
—or Dr. Conybeare—know which was the day? If Paul knew and
he had clearly said so, what a lot of argument he would have
saved theologians!

In any case, in accepting the authenticity of the text, Dr.
Conybeare accepts the whole betrayal story of Judas. There was
a Judas and there was a betrayal! It seems incredible that anyone writing for the Rationalist press could so implicitly believe
in the existence of "Judas", a real Judas, and a "betrayal", the
utter impossibility of which is one of the most patent facts that

has emerged from the contradictory and incoherent story of the arrest of Jesus.

"Was Jesus betrayed?" asks Prof. Drews in his *Witnesses to the Historicity of Jesus,* and the question can be answered only in one way. "The thing is historically so improbable, the whole story of the betrayal is so absurd, historically and psychologically, that only a few thoughtless Bible readers can accept it with complacency", adds Drews. Yet it is completely swallowed by Dr. Conybeare.

It is, says Drews, "a late invention founded on that passage in the prophet Isaiah liii, 12, (where it is said that the servant of God 'gave himself unto death') and Judas is not an historical personality, but, as Robertson believes, a representative of the Jewish people, hated by the Christians, who were believed to have caused the death of the Savior. Further, the 'night' in which the betrayal is supposed to have taken place, has no material background. It serves merely to set in contrast the luminous figure of Jesus and the dark work of his betrayer. Hence Paul cannot have known anything of a nocturnal betrayal on the part of Judas, and one more 'proof' of the historicity of Jesus breaks down. . . . This much is certain: If I Cor. xi, 23, etc., is not an interpolation in the text, there are no interpolations at all in the New Testament."

It may be urged of course that we have here only the opinions of two opponents, and Dr. Conybeare's opinion is worth at least as much as, or even more than, Dr. Drews'; and the answer to this is very plain. What evidence can be brought forward for the existence of Judas?

The reader will find the facts on this problem marshalled with great care in John M. Robertson's *Jesus and Judas.* It seems to me incredible that any investigator into the problem of Christian origins could possibly visualize a genuine Judas. Nothing more like deliberate fiction can be found in the Bible, nothing so utterly unlike real life than this melodramatic villain of the piece—a shoddy, theatrical figure designed to cast discredit on the Jewish race, even in his name "Jew"-das.

Apart from any other consideration, the story as given in Matthew, for instance, reeks with improbabilities. Jesus in Geth-

semane says to his disciples, "Rise let us be going: behold he is
at hand that doth betray me. And while he yet spake, lo, Judas,
one of the twelve came, and with him a great multitude
with swords and staves, from the chief priests and elders of the
people. Now he that betrayed him gave them a sign, saying,
Whomsoever I shall kiss, that same is he: hold him fast. And
forthwith he came to Jesus, and said, Hail, master; and kissed
him. And Jesus said unto him, Friend, wherefore art thou come
. . ."(Matt. xxvi, 46-50).

This is the sort of stuff put forward by Dr. Conybeare as proof
that there was a real Jesus. It is incredible.

Look at the story as it stands. We are asked to believe that a
"traitor" was necessary to point out which was Jesus, Jesus, who
had been going about "doing good" for one year at least (or
three years), whose sayings, and parables, and teachings, had
been listened to eagerly by the common people who were hungry
for "righteousness", the Jesus who had caused such turmoil among
the Sadducees and Pharisees, to say nothing of the Romans and
yet was so little known that Judas had to point him out as the
criminal! And on top of this, Jesus knew he was going to be
betrayed and knew it was Judas who would betray him, and
says so to his disciples. In spite of that, Jesus actually says to
Judas, "Friend, wherefore art thou come?"

Judas the traitor, the false disciple, whom Jesus knew to be
both, was called "Friend", and Jesus, the Son of God, knowing
perfectly well that the kiss was meant to be a traitorous act, actually asks "Wherefore art thou come?" Jesus, in short, pretends to
Judas he didn't know; and yet the narrative points out over and
over again that the betrayal was predestined, and that Jesus
knew perfectly well the betrayer would be Judas. As E. P. Meredith says in his *Prophet of Nazareth*:

> If it was pre-ordained that Judas should betray him, why de-
> nounce woe upon him? Why hold him responsible for an act, in
> the performance of which he was carrying out the decrees of
> Heaven? If the betrayal of Jesus was inevitable—was done as it
> *had been written,* in order *that the Scriptures might be fulfilled,*
> and was determined by an unalterable fiat, on what principle of

justice was Judas responsible for this act, in which he was but a mere instrument to fulfill the purposes of a superior Being?

But it was not enough to betray Jesus. We get an embellishment in John xiii, 21-30 which is the climax of sheer nonsense. Jesus tells his disciples who the betrayer would be: "He it is to whom I shall give a sop". And after it was given to Judas we are told "Satan entered him". If Satan is not meant to be a literal Satan, then the whole of John had better be recognized as equally symbolic. Satan in fact, seems also to have been predestined to play his part in the boyhood of Judas. In the first Gospel of Infancy, Judas and Jesus are there shown to be little boys playing together. Naturally, Satan was even then in Judas, and urged him to bite Jesus. This was too much for the Son of God, who thereupon turned his anti-Devil powers upon Satan making that infernal being come out in the form of a dog and run away. I see nothing more absurd in this farrago of balderdash than in the story in John. But if Paul had quoted it, Dr. Conybeare would have given it his heartiest support.

Of course, the story of Judas was such an asset that, apart from his appearance in the Gospel of Infancy, there was even a Gospel of Judas known to Irenaeus who pronounced it to be fictitious; as if anything could be more fictitious than the story as given in the "genuine" Gospels. Indeed quite a number of eminent Christians like Dr. Cheyne have been obliged to give it up or at least to indicate that grave doubts must always accompany its claim to be historical.

Why was Judas called Iscariot? This question has produced reams of discussion. Robertson's summing up is worth repeating. "If", he writes in *Jesus and Judas* (page 51) "the very interesting thesis that *Skariot* was but an epithet signifying "surrender" should be established, the problem is substantially solved in terms of the myth theory. Judas is once for all not merely not a historical person but a traditional *functionary*, the person who in the mystery drama played the part of "deliverer-up" of the divine victim, with Judas as equivalent to *Judaeus*, for praenomen . . . the rational explanation of the whole mystery is just that it never happened. . . ."

This should, I think, dispose of the famous text in I Corinthians (xi, 23) which Dr. Conybeare is certain is genuine, and which is so obviously an interpolation—and therefore is no witness to the existence of Jesus as a man.

Prof. Drews quotes with approval in *Witnesses* (p. 98) the opinions of the German theologians Wrede and Bruckner "that Paul was not concerned with the earthly life of Jesus, and his idea of Christ was formed independently of an historical Jesus". Wrede adds, "Of the life of Jesus one single event was of importance to him: the end of life, the death. For him, however, even this is not the moral action of a man; indeed, it is not an historical fact at all for him, but a superhistorical fact, an event of the supersensual world."

The truth is that the more the Epistles of Paul are studied the more one realizes how little they contain anything that shows any real knowledge of an *historical* Jesus. Apart altogether from their authenticity in the main, even conservative theologians often show an uneasy feeling that some of the passages which connect Paul with a "real" Jesus are "suspect". In any case, they are generally hard put to prove these passages are unassailable.

There is still one point about the Pauline Epistles which will have to be discussed before finally deciding as to the value of Paul as a witness to a real Jesus. This is the question, are they *genuine?* That is, were they written by the Paul of the Acts somewhere between the years 50-60 A.D. or thereabouts, and in the form we have them are they quite or almost free from interpolations?

First of all, it is rather difficult to account for the fact that Josephus never mentions Paul considering that in Acts xxiv, 5, we are told that "We have found this man [Paul] a pestilent fellow, and a mover of sedition among all the Jews throughout the world, and a ringleader of the sects of the Nazarenes". A man who led sedition against *all* the Jews then living, wherever they were, must have left a fairly hefty reputation behind him; yet there is not a line in the Jewish historian which indicates that he had ever heard of Paul. This is an astonishing fact even when one is not at all inclined to accept an argument from silence.

Then, again, how are we to reconcile Paul's own statements in his Epistles with the accounts given in Acts where they can be compared? Take up Acts, let us say from chapter ix, and read onwards, and it will be found that Paul's own detailed account in Galatians gives the lie to Acts in dozens of particulars. As is pointed out in the *English Life of Jesus* by Thomas Scott, (1869),

> The lie is given (for what other expression can we honestly use?) to almost every statement in the narrative of the Acts. . . . Paul, at this time did *not* go to Jerusalem; he did *not* make any attempts to introduce himself to the Apostles there; these Apostles did *not* express any fear or suspicion of him, and Barnabas did *not* vouch for the reality of his conversion. Paul did *not* at Jerusalem address himself to the Jews, and the Jews did *not* seek to kill him; he was *not* taken to Caesarea, he did *not* preach throughout the coasts of Judaea, he did *not* go from Palestine to Tarsus; he did *not* stay at Tarsus six or seven years; and he was *not* brought back from Tarsus by Barnabas to Antioch; he was *not* sent with alms to Jerusalem during the famine foretold by Argabus (i.e., according to the chronology of the Acts, about nine years after his conversion;) and he was *not* set apart in the following year by "certain prophets and teachers" for a joint mission with Barnabas to the Gentiles.

Thomas Scott deals with dozens of other statements thoroughly contradictory in the life of Paul, and therefore he claims that "in these two accounts of the life and labors of St. Paul we have a crucial test of any theories which regard the Bible as containing a history infallibly correct; rather, it is unnecessary to seek for further evidence that in the Acts of the Apostles we have a history which, for its utterly untrustworthy character, cannot be surpassed, if it can be matched, by any narratives of the Koran".

The "crucial test" has utterly failed; yet we are still told that the witness of Paul is unimpeachable. But the Epistles, it may be contended, are "authentic" even if not written by the Paul of the Acts; and that may be so, if we are agreed as to what is meant here by the word "authentic". From considerations of the style of the "Big Four", they are probably from one writer—at least in their first form; but who is the writer, and was he dealing with a real Jesus? These questions have not been answered.

I have shown that, though Paul claims he was a Jew, there is practically nothing in the Epistles which bears out his claim. The writer never quotes or makes any allusion to the Hebrew Old Testament; his quotations are invariably from the Greek Septuagint. Moreover the Gnostic Marcion, who was bitterly anti-Jewish, was the great champion of Paul; and if Gerald Massey is right—and he is, in my opinion—then Paul was the great Gnostic himself who violently opposed the "humanizing" of "Christ" into Jesus, and whose Epistles were later altered by the Church as it rose in power. How did Paul, a Jew, come to master Gnosticism so soon after his conversion from Judaism?

"It is simply inconceivable" says Van Manen, (quoted by Drews) "that Paul the Jew, who persecuted the community on conviction, brought about so extraordinary a revolution in the faith of this community almost immediately after he accepted it. It is not conceivable that this conscientious zealot for Israel's God, Israel's laws, morals, and customs, should perceive so suddenly, when he has overcome his repugnance to the cross, that this God was not the most high, but must make way for the father whom neither Jews nor Gentiles had known before the coming of Christ; that this Christ was not the one promised to their fathers, the Messiah, but a supernatural being, God's own son, who merely assumed for a time the appearance of a man like ourselves; and that the law, with all its prescriptions and promises, could and should be thrust aside as without value or significance. We must not forget that all this is new to the Pauline gospel, and has no relation to the 'faith' of the first disciples, who were full-blooded Jews in their Messianic expectations . . ."

What Van Manen is trying to express is his surprise that, if Paul had really been a Jew, he could possibly have changed overnight, so to speak, from a thorough believing Jew into the very opposite, a Christian with a complete theology the antithesis of Judaism. This is manifestly so impossible that the gravest doubts have been expressed that Paul (by Paul here I mean, of course, the writer of the Epistles, for the Paul of the Acts was in all probability quite a different person) ever was a Jew or that his letters were written as early as the orthodox date.

Howell Smith, who tells us that Paul was "a learned Jew" (p. 149) and a pupil of a famous Rabbi is, of course, at variance with Jewish scholars, who long ago saw no trace of Judaism in his writings. "Jewish scholars . . . by no means recognize", says Drews in *Witnesses* (pp. 117-8) "the contents of the Epistles as of their own spirit; they emphatically deny that their author could have been a pupil of the rabbis. There is serious ground for reflection in the fact that, as Kautzsch pointed out in 1869 and Steck has confirmed, the writer of the Epistles does not quote the Hebrew text of the Scriptures . . . the Epistles give no trace of an acquaintance of Hebrew . . . (Paul) thinks as a Greek, speaks as a Greek, uses Greek books. . . . Further, this supposed pupil of the rabbis interprets the law in a way that, as we are told is anything but rabbinical . . ." In a word, as Dr. Claude Montefiore puts it—and he was particularly sympathetic to Jesus and Christianity—"This man (Paul) was never a rabbinic Jew at all or he had quite forgotten what rabbinic Judaism was or is." (Jewish Quat. Rev., vol. xiii, pp. 205-6). So much for Howell Smith's "learned Jew", though in fairness it must be said that he makes no distinction between the Paul of the Acts and the Paul of the Epistles. If the Paul of the Acts did not write the Epistles he might well have been a Jew converted to the Christianity of his day like other Jews, and his name appropriated by the writer, whoever he was, of the famous Letters. But what proof have we that he is the author of Epistles which show such a profound knowledge of Gnosticism?

In his *Origins of Christianity* Thomas Whittaker, following the Dutch scholar Van Manen, minutely examines the four "genuine" Epistles of Paul. Some of his conclusions appear to me never to have been seriously confuted. It is impossible to say, for example, exactly what Howell Smith thinks about Paul except that, at one moment, Paul's Christ was a "heavenly being", and at another moment, an historical one. He does not agree with Dr. Conybeare that when Paul said (II Cor. v, 16) that he once "knew Christ after the flesh", he really had seen Jesus. All it means is that he may have held "the traditional Jewish idea of the Messiah", an opinion which may be so or not. But if the

Epistles are carefully studied, say, with the help of Mr. Whittaker, there seems no basis whatever to believe that Paul knew very much about any Jewish Messiah. His Christ was purely a Gnostic conception. As Massey says, "The Christ of the Gnosis was not connected with *place* any more than personality, or line of human descent. His only birthplace was in the mind of man. Consequently, in his gospel, Marcion, who was a Gnostic Christian, does not connect his Christ with Nazareth. His Christ is not Jesus of Nazareth. And this note of the Gnosis is apparent in the writings of Paul. His Christ is nowhere called Jesus of Nazareth, nor is he born at Bethlehem, either of the Virgin Mary, or of Mary the wife of Cleopas, who was not the Virgin".

Whittaker points out that, while the Epistles may have had as a basis some kind of letter, "on the whole these compositions should not properly be called epistles. The contents generally are those of a book rather than a letter". And if we take Romans as an example to be studied, it must be obvious at once that the writer was addressing people who were already Christians. Why he should do so, especially as these Christians were unknown to him and at Rome, it is impossible to say. And what impression did this letter make upon its readers? No one knows. We do not even know if there were in Rome, at the time Paul is supposed to have written Romans, any Christians—that is, followers of Jesus of Nazareth—at all. But there quite conceivably may have been Gnostics.

Moreover, "the uncertainty in which we are often left as to the writer's meaning," says Whittaker, (p. 128) "is due to the presence of contradictory utterances . . . according to the ordinary view, it (Romans) was sent about 59. After that there is no trace of it until, more than half a century later, we find it held in honor by—the Gnostics! Where was it preserved before it came, we know not how, into the hands of men like Basilides and Marcion?"

Those who, like Dr. Conybeare, claim that the witness of Paul is irrefutable, never of course worry about questions like these. They never trouble to show how or why, when the Epistle to the Romans was written, "there already existed a whole vocabulary of technical terms belonging to Paulinism", as Whittaker says. "With these the reader is assumed to be familiar. 'Faith' and 'grace', 'righteousness' and 'love', 'justification by faith' and 'by works of the law,' and so forth are used without any feeling of difficulty in altogether peculiar senses." And most laymen skip over these things because it is easier to suppose the existence of a real Jesus who went about "doing good" than to bother trying to elucidate the mysteries of Gnosticism.

The Epistles are full of "mysteries" of which Paul claimed to be the true interpreter, as "We speak the wisdom of God in a mystery, even the hidden wisdom which God ordained before the world unto our glory"; "How that by revelation he made known unto me the mystery"; "Whereby, when ye read, ye may understand my knowledge in the mystery of Christ"; "This is a great mystery, but I speak of Christ"; and so on. Conybeare, Howell Smith, and all the other Historicists say this refers to Jesus of Nazareth. I claim to have shown as clearly as one can on such a subject to any unbiased reader that Massey is right when he said that Paul was a Gnostic Christian, with a "Christ in you" complex and that if any references in the Epistles are considered to refer to a "real" Jesus of Nazareth, these are obviously *forgeries*.

Paul's Christ is, as Massey shows, strictly masculine. He refused to consider that woman had anything to do with his Logos or Messiah who had replaced the feminine Wisdom called "Sophia". "None but the initiated", continues Massey, "in these matters could possibly know what was meant", when Paul insisted on the substitution of Christ for Wisdom or the second Adam for the first.

As I have pointed out, the average layman simply will not be bothered in trying to hammer out for himself what Paul meant by "mystery", just as he has no time for an intelligent study, say, of the Jewish Kabbalah, which is nothing but the ancient "mystery" of Gnosticism after it had passed through the minds of the mystics of old Jewry responsible for such strange works as the "Zohar".

There is no doubt whatever that there were two factions at

work at the beginnings of Christianity, and that it was the side
which proclaimed a Jesus "in the flesh" which eventually became the historic Church. It is far easier to understand the birth
of a son of God than a "Christ in you", and, strangely enough,
this has often been one of the principal planks of those Rationalists who are fighting to save Jesus almost at any price. The Myth
theory raises far more problems, they tell us, than the simple—
and beautiful—story of Jesus of Nazareth. But until the Gnosticism which is the core of Paulinism can be satisfactorily explained how can anyone accept the witness of Paul to a real live
Jesus?

Is it not remarkable that Justin Martyr who wrote two "Apologies" for Christianity and whose *Dialogue with Trypho* proves
how certain he was that Jesus was "prophesied" in the Old
Testament, and that therefore all Jews should accept him as the
promised Messiah, never mentions Paul? And is it not strange
that, if Paul of the Acts is Paul of the Epistles, we are not so
told in Acts, nor that in Acts, which deals more with Paul than
any other Apostle, nothing is said about his martyrdom or death
in Rome?

When John wrote (i, 14) "and the Word was made flesh and
dwelt among us" he was literally saying what had happened.
The Word, which was merely an idea of Gnosticism, and which
had no material life whatever, was "made" into "flesh" by the
simple expedient of writing a piece of fiction embodying various
stories culled from Paganism, but giving them a new life in their
Greek phrasing, and cribbing quite a number of ideas from Josephus so as to get the background right—just as an historical
novelist has to read up his period to get the correct atmosphere.
I shall later refer to some of the ways Josephus has been made
use of.

I hope that I have sufficiently dealt with the "witness" of Paul
to a real Jesus. It would have been possible to extend this chapter
and to have dealt in detail, as Drews does, with the many
separate texts which are the joy of people like Conybeare. I
prefer to quote Drews finally on the problem of Pauline Epistles;
they "give no support whatever to the belief in an historical Jesus.

This also, as we said, puts an end to religious interest in the historicity of Paul, and profane historians and philologists may be left in peace to reconstruct, out of Acts and the so-called Epistles of Paul, a picture of the real sequence of events which accompanied the rise of Christianity."

CHAPTER IV

The Cross

THAT JESUS OF NAZARETH WAS CRUCIFIED ON A Cross is the convinced belief of all Christendom, and certainly of all but a very few Jews, and of most Rationalists and Free-thinkers. The Gospels say so, the Churches say so, the ordinary lay reader, content to follow his leaders, has no doubt whatever about it, thousands of pictures showing Jesus dying on the Cross have been painted and seen by hundreds of millions of people, while the sale of crucifixes, fashioned in metal, wood, and ivory, has been enormous. The witness of all this, backed by the most impassioned preaching every Easter, is too much for the average man. He gives in without a struggle; and nowadays the only story which can beat the Crucifixion in popularity is the Resurrection.

Yet there is not a scrap of evidence worth hanging a dog for to attest the truth of the Crucifixion. It is sheer fiction and, in all probability, was never meant to be anything else.

I have already dealt with the problem in Chapter II as far as the Gospels go. Here I want to deal a little further with the Cross of Christ, which has been such a perfect Godsend to Christianity. The picture of the dying Christ on the Cross has aroused so much sympathy and pity, the agony of such a horrible death has been painted in such frightful colors, every child almost from infancy has had it dinned constantly in its ears, that it would be surprising if the story had not caught the imagination of the world. Nothing in the way the Nazis poisoned the mind of German youth can equal the propaganda the Church has put forward on behalf of the "crime" of putting "our Lord" to death. There were two objects in this, making the most of the myth for the benefit of the Church, and inculcating the most violent hatred of the Jews for being guilty of the "crime". And that they have succeeded is proved by the fact that even Rationalists, who are supposed to submit to reason in the final test, not only believe in the Crucifixion, but also defend it to the utmost. That is triumph indeed.

First of all, does the word in Greek in the Gospels which we have translated "Cross", and does the word in Greek translated "Crucifixion" actually mean Cross and Crucifixion? The simple and sufficient answer is that they do *not*.

The Greek word is *stauros* and it does not mean "cross". It means a stake or pole. Any Greek lexicon will show the reader that with the Greek element "staur", which means "impale", we get *stauroō, anastauroō* and *sustauroō*; and there is also the word *prospegnumi*, all of which are in the Gospels. Not one of these words means "crucify", though that is the way it is translated in our Authorized and Revised versions. *Prospegnumi* definitely means "to fix to" or "upon".

I have called attention to an American work entitled the *Concordant Version of the New Testament*, which is a new translation of the Codex Sinaiticus, the text of which is also given. The translator boasts that every word is correctly translated as far as humanly possible, and he has published as a guide to the Greek a very clever and full concordance of every Greek word. It is instructive to see what he has to say when he came to use the word Cross:

> When I first discovered that the word *stauros* stood for a plain stake without a cross piece or any other fancy addition, I used stake in the (Concordant) version and submitted it to a friend who was somewhat in sympathy with my work. But this change

so incensed him that I withdrew the rendering. He seemed to think that I was cutting out the great truth of the cross though I was only clarifying and emphasizing it. The "cross" with its ornamental shapes, its artistic forms, especially when made with precious metal and adorned with gems, suggests the exact reverse of the shameful, ignominious stake. To me the word is spoilt by association with false religion. It is a symbol of apostacy, of pride, in place of a degrading and dreadful death which puts an end to the flesh and prepares us for the utmost grace of Paul's epistles. But I bear with it, and point out the better rendering to those who have been initiated into the deep lesson of their own shameful end and their glorious place in Christ. (*Unsearchable Riches*, Jan., 1943)

The writer of this, A. E. Knoch, is a Fundamentalist, and believes that every word in the Sinaiticus is inspired by God, for which reason he has used it as the basis of his version. He claims that our Authorized Version is badly translated, and he wants to replace it with the true rendering of "God's Word". But he was obliged to follow the crowd with regard to *stauros*. It is a Cross in the A.V. and in the R.V. as well, as in all modern versions, and a Cross it must be in his. But the fact remains that the word is not "Cross" but "stake" and that ought to make even the most fanatical Historicist think again.

A *stauros* was a mere stake, and horrible to contemplate; it was used in the cruelest fashion to execute criminals and other persons obnoxious to the governing classes. It was sometimes pointed and thrust through the victim's body to pin him to earth; or he was placed on top of the stake with its point upwards so that it gradually pierced his body; or he was tied upon it and left exposed till death intervened; and there were other methods, too. There is not a scrap of evidence to show that a *stauros* was ever in the form of a cross or even of a T shape.

With regard to the other words used in our translations, I have shown that they do not mean either crucify or crucifixion. Indeed, it is said more than once in the New Testament that Jesus was "*hanged* upon a tree".

What was the earliest representation of Jesus made, as far as it was possible in those days, in pictorial art? It may be said at once that there is no clue whatever to his appearance in anything left by the early Christians. The well known portraits of him by Italian and other early artists appear to show a more or less bearded European of a Saxon type, whereas if there had ever been a real Jesus he must have looked like the Jews of his day, and that means that he would have been undoubtedly dark-skinned like an Arab. Most of his contemporaries and their children were, in all probability, wiped out in the war against Vespasian and Titus about 70 A.D. and later in the rebellion of Bar Cocheba. The real Jews were, it is almost certain, nearly exterminated; a few might have escaped and made converts from the various white races living around the Mediterranean; hence the peoples who call themselves Jews these days in Europe are for the most part white, and not like the Arabs, dark skinned. The Jews are very mixed and cannot really be called a race. Be that as it may, Jesus certainly could not have been of a Saxon type, if his story as related in the Gospels is true.

Some of the earliest representations show Jesus as a Fish, called Icthus; and Christian authorities have had a hard time trying to explain why the Cross was not early associated with Jesus. By the Cross I mean, of course, the kind which Christians always associate with Jesus. As Mrs. Jameson is obliged to admit in her classic work *The History of Our Lord*:

> It must be owned, that ancient objects of art, as far as hitherto known, afford no corroboration of the use of the cross in the simple transverse form familiar to us, at any period preceding or even closely succeeding the words of St. Chrysostom (4th Century). But if the simple form be not found in any relics of art, there is no doubt, on the other hand, that another form of it exists on objects coeval with Chrysostom, and that in such abundance . . . this is, namely, the so-called monogram of Christ, in the more or less complex tracery of which the cross, if not actually seen, is at least indicated. This monogram is composed of two Greek letters, the X or Ch and P or R, which by a usual Greek abbreviation formed one composite letter out of the first consonants of the name of Christ. . . . It is found on innumerable monumental stones . . . in every collection of Christian relics . . . but it would be difficult to find as early a speci-

men of the cross in its simplicity as now familiar to us. (Vol 2.,
pp. 315-6)

The form of the Cross we know appears to have been quite
unknown to the early Christians; yet if Jesus had been crucified
on such a Cross surely that would have formed some of the
earliest Christian representations of the Christian Deity.

The explanation generally given of this is the plea that death
by crucifixion was regarded with such horror that the early
Christians would never show it or even refer to it. But Roman
crucifixion was admittedly not on a cross at all but on a stake.
What we wish to know then is why was crucifixion on a trans-
verse cross substituted for the real thing and when? It is extremely difficult to get a clear answer from Christians, though
there are some who are brave enough to admit that the Cross
is a pagan symbol, and ought never to have been introduced into
Christianity at all.

Let me quote from a work which at one time was well known
among Protestants during the 19th Century. Its title is *The Two
Babylons* by the Rev. Alexander Hislop. Its thesis is the similarity
between Roman Catholicism and the worship of Nimrod and his
wife Semiramis in ancient Babylon. Mr. Hislop collected hundreds of similarities between the two religions, and no one can
read his book without coming to the conclusion that there is very
little to choose between Popery and Paganism. Freethinkers had
long before Hislop shown the same resemblances—indeed many
things given by Hislop and believed perhaps by his Protestant
readers to be thus shown for the first time will be found in the
three works by Robert Taylor, particularly in his *Devil's Pulpit*.
Other facts are in the works of Dupuis and Volney. Whether
Hislop ever thought that his crushing exposé of Papal claims
could be turned against Christianity as a whole (and this includes his own Protestantism) I do not know; but *The Two
Babylons* makes an excellent work for those Freethinkers who
want Pagan and Christian parallels presented in a handy form.

Hislop has a chapter on "The Sign of the Cross" and it is to his
credit that he does not hesitate to give the truth as far as he
knew it. Here are a few of his admissions:

The same sign of the cross that Rome now worships was used in the Babylonian mysteries, was applied by Paganism to the same magic purposes, was honored with the same honors. That which is now called the Christian cross was originally no Christian emblem at all, but was the mystic Tau of the Chaldeans and Egyptians—the true original form of the letter T—the initial of the name of Tammuz—which in Hebrew is radically the same as ancient Chaldea, as found on coins . . . and in Etrurian and Coptic. That mystic Tau was marked in baptism on the forehead of those initiated in the mysteries and was used in every variety of way as a most sacred symbol. To identify Tammuz with the sun, it was joined sometimes to the circle of the sun; sometimes it was inserted in the circle. . . . The mystic Tau, as the symbol of the great divinity, was called "the sign of life", it was used as an amulet over the heart, it was marked on the official garments of the priests of Rome. . . . The Vestal Virgins of Pagan Rome wore it suspended from their necklaces, as the nuns do now. The Egyptians did the same . . . There is hardly a Pagan tribe where the cross has not been found. The cross was worshiped by the Pagan Celts long before the incarnation and death of Christ. . . . It was worshiped in Mexico for ages before the Roman Catholic missionaries set foot there, large stone crosses being erected, probably to the "god of rain". The cross thus widely worshiped, or regarded as a sacred emblem, was the unequivocal symbol of Bacchus, the Babylonian Messiah . . . (it) is reverenced at this day in all the wide wastes of Tartary, where Buddhism prevails . . .

Hislop makes a point of giving full authorities for all these statements and if they are ever taken to heart by his fellow Protestants, they will cause consternation. It would prove interesting to know what they think of his further remarks:

Surely it cannot be right that the sign of the cross, or emblem of Tammuz, should be used in Christian baptism. At the period of the Revolution, a Royal Commission appointed to enquire into the rites and ceremonies of the Church of England, numbering among its members eight or ten bishops, strongly recommended that the use of the cross, as tending to superstition, should be laid aside. If such a recommendation was given then, and that by such authority as members of the Church of England must respect, how much ought that recommendation to be enforced by the new light which providence has cast on the subject!

Hislop is obviously alluding in the last sentence to his own labors.

Another eminent Christian writer who had no illusions about the Cross was Bishop Colenso who, in his *Pentateuch Examined,* said:

> From the dawn of organized Paganism in the Eastern world, to the final establishment of Christianity in the West, the cross was undoubtedly one of the commonest and most sacred of symbolical monuments . . . it appears to have been the aboriginal possession of every people in antiquity. . . . Of the several varieties of the cross still in vogue, as national and ecclesiastical emblems, and distinguished by the familiar appellations of St. George, St. Andrew, the Maltese, the Greek, the Latin, etc., there is not one amongst them the existence of which may not be traced to the remotest antiquity. They were the common property of the Eastern nations.

If we bear these facts in mind we can perhaps begin to see why the common stake, the *stauros,* was not very acceptable to Pagan converts to Christianity, and why the Cross was artfully substituted as the Christian symbol par excellence. Just as the Day of the Sun—Sunday—was in time substituted for the Jewish Sabbath because it was already venerated by Pagans, so the Cross eventually replaced the stake or pole upon which Jesus was said to have been crucified.

In *Curious Myths of the Middle Ages* the Rev. S. Baring-Gould has a chapter on "The Legend of the Cross". He is obliged to admit that the cross was "a sacred sign among the Gaulish Kelts" and "that it was symbolic among the Irish and British Kelts is more than probable". He adds that Thor's hammer was a cross, and it is still used in Iceland "as a magical sign in connection with storms of wind and rain". There was a cross found in the temple of Serapis when it was demolished by Christians about the year 390 A.D. though it was probably the famous Crux Ansata, the Tau with a handle. This is called the "Cross of Life". Baring-Gould denies that it has any *phallic* significance, which he calls "monstrous". No one, he contends, "knows, and probably no one will ever know, what originated the use of this sign, and gave it such significance". Its use was widespread among the

Egyptians; Horus, Osiris, and other Gods are often seen with it, and it is found on many of their ancient monuments. Colenso also noted that the ancient Egyptians used to put a cross on their sacred cakes just as we do on "hot cross buns".

The Cross was the symbol of the Babylonian God Baal as well as of their principal God Anu. It was adored by the ancient Etruscans, by the Greeks and Romans, and even among the Laplanders. And when missionaries began to arrive in America in the 15th Century, they were astonished to find the Cross was adored by the red Indians.

In his *Atlantis,* Donnelly claims that the reason why the Cross was so venerated in both the Old and the New Worlds was because they were at one time bridged by the lost continent of Atlantis. The cross on a sacred cake dividing it into four parts, so to speak, was symbolical of the Garden of Eden which, according to Josephus, "was watered by one river, which ran down the whole earth and was parted into four parts". "Here", says Donnelly, "in the four parts we see the origin of the Cross, while in the river running around the whole earth we have the wonderful canal of Atlantis, described by Plato."

The Garden of Eden, the Gardens of the Hesperides, the Land of Nod where Cain went after the murder of Abel, the Olympus of the Greeks are all man's memories of the lost Atlantis, the marvelous continent which some mighty convulsion of Nature destroyed nine or ten thousand years ago, which gave rise to the story of the Deluge, and from which, according to Donnelly and other believers in the legend of Atlantis, came so much of our knowledge in the sciences and arts. The reason why the Cross is found in Europe and Asia and in North and South America is because it originated in Atlantis where it was also adored. "We find the emblem of the Cross in pre-Christian times venerated as a holy symbol on both sides of the Atlantic; and we find it explained as a type of the four rivers of the happy island where the civilization of the race originated." Thus Donnelly.

But there appears to be a great deal more in the way the Cross originated than accounted for here. A stick put through a ring and looked at sideways gives us the shape of a cross; and those who believe in the great influence phallicism, or the worship of the sexual organs has had on religion in general, claim that the origin of the Cross is almost certainly phallic. At first it was pillars—representing the lingam—which were erected in towns and villages, and nearly always on some *cross* road. To these, the people used to address prayers for good luck or protection, and this is still done in India.

J. B. Hannay in his *Gods of the Hebrew Bible* and other works puts in a strong claim, which, he says, is admitted by scholars of all ages, that the cross and the phallus are identical; and he adds that putting a man representing Sun-worship upon it definitely joins the two religions, Phallicism and Sun-worship, together.

Certainly, it is a fact that the Pagan Romans had army standards which they carried to war representing a man on a cross. In writing to the Pagans about Christianity, Tertullian said, "The origin of your gods is derived from figures molded on a cross. All those rows of images on your standards are the appendages of crosses; those hangings on your standards and banners are the robes of crosses". This means that at about the date Tertullian wrote (200 A.D.) Jesus was not adored on a Cross. In fact it is one of the most surprising things in the history of the Christian Cross, to find how late he does appear for the first time on a crucifix.

The earliest representations we have of the Crucifixion, according to Mrs. Jameson, date from the eighth century. It appears not to have been at all the subject of early Christianity. There is one picture of this in the Catacombs supposed to be of the 11th Century; and it is interesting to note that before this date and up to the year 680 A.D. the oldest representation of Jesus was generally a lamb though as admitted by Farrar in his *Life of Christ in Art* the fish "was the most frequent and favorite". The fish continued to be so until the time of Constantine. I invite the Historicists to account for this if there had been a real Jesus going about "doing good".

"Early Christian Art", says Mrs. Jameson, "such as it appears in the bas-reliefs on sarcophagi, gave but one solitary incident from the story of our Lord's Passion, and that, as we have had repeated occasion to remark, utterly divested of all circumstances of suffering. Our Lord is represented as young and beautiful, free from bonds, with no 'accursed tree' on his shoulder." This seems to me very remarkable if the Crucifixion had really taken place, and all the circumstances attending the event had been known— as indeed they would be known if the four Gospels were in circulation. Mrs. Jameson is obviously completely bewildered for it need hardly be said that the distinguished authoress was a thorough believer in Christianity. She shows the same perplexity quite a number of times when faced with pictorial evidence that "Gospel" truth is not quite Gospel truth—in Art, at all events.

When did the Cross first appear in connection with Christianity? Mrs. Jameson gives, from "that form of Art which exists in great abundance, namely, coins," an illustration of the simple Cross in a coin issued by Galla Placida who died in 451 A.D., from which time Crosses appear in great numbers. The reader should note the date—long after the famous vision of a Cross in the sky seen by Constantine the Great when with his army in the year 312 A.D. It is Eusebius who, in his life of that monarch, says:

> He (Constantine) said that at mid-day when the sun was beginning to decline he saw with his own eyes the trophy of a cross of light in the heavens, above the Sun, bearing the inscription "By this, conquer"; he himself, and his whole army also, being struck with amazement at this sight.

This cross is supposed to be the Christian cross; but as the Gauls led by Constantine venerated what is known as the Solar Wheel (a circle with a cross in it) this was most likely on their standards. It is never difficult for Christians to insist on a miracle in the sky with Jesus and his Cross as the principal actors. Even as I write, (1944) a crucifix has been seen in the sky by many people in Ipswich, England, and a local vicar took upon himself the investigation of this divine occurrence. It is doubtful whether the facts that he elucidated, that the crucifix was an accidental formation of smoke from an aeroplane, will convince the people who saw it that God had not favored their town with a genuine manifestation of his power; certainly, had we been living in the age of Constantine, the miracle would have been duly recorded and defended.

The story of Constantine goes on to say that "Christ appeared to Constantine when he was asleep, with the same sign of the cross, and directed him to make use of the symbol as his military ensign". Hislop, as a good Protestant, will not deny the miracle altogether. He suggests that what Constantine saw was the name of Christ—a Cross (like an X) with a P through it, the well known "monogram" of Christ, which can still be seen on some of the coins Constantine struck.

Hislop only comes to this conclusion, he says, by assuming that Constantine "acted in good faith as a Christian". But he is not quite sure that Constantine did act in good faith, and suggests that "the X may have been intended to have one meaning for Christians and another for Pagans". He adds "It is certain that the X was the symbol of God Ham in Egypt, and as such, was exhibited on the breast of his image". In any case, we have definite proof that while Constantine was quite sure that Christianity was a good religion for his subjects, he was by no means sure of it for himself, at least, not until he was dying and, as a hoary old sinner, could get no absolution except from Christian priests mindful of the rejoicing in heaven over one such rather than nine and ninety good men. At all events, it is a fact that about twenty years after seeing the Cross of Christ in the heavens he caused a statue to be erected in the Forum of Rome, a statue of the Sun-God Apollo; though it is alleged that this statue was really of himself as a Sun-God.

In his work *The Non-Christian Cross*, Mr. J. D. Parsons, who deals very fully with Constantine, comes to the conclusion "that he was a Christian only insofar as, out of policy or conviction, he acted as if he considered the Christ to be one of many conceptions of the Sun-God". This is an interesting surmise for, as I have already pointed out, the whole contention of Dupuis is that Christ actually was a Sun-God, in common with many others.

But crosses or crucifixes in the sky after Constantine were by no means uncommon, and in 351 A.D. St. Cyril of Jerusalem and all its inhabitants saw a brilliant Cross in the heavens shining like the Sun for several hours. We are told that this is vouched for by Jerome, Socrates (the Church historian) and St. Cyril, among others, and a solemn festival in its memory is still kept by the Greek Church.

The loop or circle on top of a T, the famous symbol of Life known also as the "Cross of Osiris" and undoubtedly a purely phallic symbol, may or may not have been the actual origin of the Cross venerated by Christians. But there can be no doubt of its great antiquity, no doubt that it is "the root symbol of the entire religious philosophy of the old world; and in it Hindoo, Egyptian, and Hebrew alike read the mystery of creation, and the ultimate secret of Eternal Life", as E. H. Jones claims in his *Cross of Life*. He adds:

"And it is noticeable that this emblem of primeval religion is unwittingly employed to this day in the construction of Christian churches, the intersections of the cross on the ground plan being determined by the ovoid lines of the vesica piscis. Thus the cruciform structure of every cathedral stands on the oval ring."

Nothing can get away from the fact that the Crux Ansata consists of the *stauros* representing the male symbol, and the loop or circle representing the female. In his *Aryan Mythology* (p. 352), the Rev. Sir G. W. Cox says, "We recognize the male symbol in the trident of Poseidon or Proteus, and the fylfot or hammer of Thor, which assumes the form of a cross patee in the various legends which turn on the rings of Freya, Holda, Venus, or Aphrodite. In each of these stories the ring is distinctly connected with the goddess who represents the female power in nature". In other words, the Cross of Life recognizes the two principles, male and female, necessary for the production of life, and it is not surprising that in the form of a simple cross it is still adored as the symbol of all symbols.

In early art, Jesus was certainly shown as a young man with a lamb on his shoulders, and so was Mercury, as Mrs. Jameson duly notes. In fact, she complains of the difficulty of ascertaining whether in these pictures it was Jesus or Mercury (Vol. 2, p. 340). Of course, Jesus was not the only good shepherd. Both Horus and Krishna were given, more or less, the same term.

The pictures of Jesus on the Cross generally show him as the suffering God, but this was by no means the case at first. Again

let us go to Mrs. Jameson, whose two volumes on the subject of
Christ in Art are standard authorities, and who is almost a Fundamentalist Christian. No suspicion of heresy can darken her reputation. She gives a number of illustrations showing the Crucifixion
which are very different from the modern and conventional representations. On page 151 of vol. 2 of her work there is a repro-
duction from an M. S. in Brussels showing Jesus on the Cross,
fully clothed, alive, and with his eyes open. There is another on
page 330 which shows the Lord as "young, alive, and upright,
with no wounds, no nails, no footboard, and no sign of suffering,
while the simple and beautiful drapery invests the figure with an
expression of innocence and even gladness". There is an illustration of "an early crucifixion" on page 167 showing the two thieves
bound on a *stauros*—merely a stake—on either side of Jesus, who
is fully clothed, and standing only. In fact, there are all sorts
and conditions of pictures, many completely different from the
modern idea of the Crucifixion.

What does all this prove? The absolute and irrefutable truth
of the Crucifixion story? Or, as I contend, the slow building-up
of a theological myth with Pagan elements gradually added to
suit the wishes of newly acquired converts? I cannot see how
anyone who studies such a work as Mrs. Jameson's can come to
any other conclusion than the one here presented.

Let us turn to a work by another fervent Christian entitled
Monumental Christianity by John P. Lundy, Presbyter. He shows
that up to the year 692 or thereabouts, Jesus was almost always
shown as a Lamb (when he was not a Fish) and that the Church
then began to be afraid that the real story of the Savior "might
eventually be lost or swallowed up in mere symbol and allegory"
(p. 251). And so in the reign of Justinian II, the Council of
Trullo decreed that the man Christ Jesus must be in future substituted for the Lamb. It is our Historicists who must show why
it took nearly 600 years for this to happen if the Crucifixion
had been a fact—for there is no doubt whatever that the idea
at the back of the Crucifixion was long known to the Pagans—
a man with his arms stretched out in a line with his shoulders.

In his *Dialogue with Trypho*, Justin Martyr gets quite lyrical
about it. He instances the case of Moses with his arms stretched

out in the form of a cross during the battle between Israel and
Amalek, and he calls it a "mystic sign, by which some out of all
nations have been turned from idols to God; and by whose
power the enemies of God and unbelievers have been destroyed;
but more especially was the cross a type and a sign erected by
Moses to counteract the serpents which bit Israel, and intended
for the salvation of those who believe that death was declared
to come thereafter on the serpent through Him that would be
crucified. . . ." The Jews indeed have always protested against
the Cross, as for them it was a Pagan symbol; and they get very
angry when Moses with his arms outstretched is put forward as
a type, not only of the Cross, but of the Crucifixion. It is obvious that in Justin's time the Cross was beginning to "infiltrate"
into the new religion from Paganism, and Justin was ready to
see it in almost everything.

As a matter of fact, though Krishna did not actually die on the
Cross (for the Puranas clearly state that he was shot in the heel
by an arrow from a hunter) he has been shown in Indian art
as if he were on a Cross. Lundy gives an illustration of an ancient
bronze relic taken from Creuzer's work on Symbolism which
"has no nail marks in the hands or feet; there is no wood; no
inscription; no crown of thorns, but the turreted coronet of the
Ephesian Diana; no attendants; the ankles are tied together by a
cord; and the dress about the loins is like Krishna's". One authority thinks it may be Buddha but "another most accomplished
Oriental scholar says it is Krishna crucified".

Lundy gives another illustration taken from Moor's *Hindu
Pantheon* "as a most singular monument of the crucifixion". It
actually represents "a crucifixion in space" for it shows a figure
almost exactly as the conventional Christ on a Cross with arms
outstretched but without any wood and with rays from the sun
touching him. Moor tries to show that it might be an early
Christian type, but neither Lundy nor Godfrey Higgins in *Anacalypsis* agrees with him. Lundy says:

> Can it be the Victim—Man, or the Priest and Victim both in
> one, of the Hindu mythology, who offered himself a sacrifice be-
> fore the worlds were? Can it be Plato's second God who im-
> pressed himself on the universe in the form of a cross? Or is it

his divine man who would be scourged, tormented, fettered, have
his eyes burnt out; and lastly, having suffered all manner of
evils, would be *crucified?* Plato learned his theology in Egypt and
the East, and must have known of the crucifixion of Krishna,
Buddha, Mithra, etc. At any rate, the religion of India has its
mythical crucified victim long anterior to Christianity, as the
type of the real one, and I am inclined to think that we have it
in this remarkable plate. I am disposed to believe this to be the
victim described in the Vedas themselves.

The "divine man" who is crucified is described in Plato's *Republic* and is a fact which will astonish most readers, I suspect,
as will Lundy's opinion that Krishna, Buddha, and Mithra were
"crucified". But I shall deal in a later chapter with the remarkable
similarities between these Deities and Jesus.

Higgins claims in his *Anacalypsis* that the crucifix is undoubtedly Hindu, that it is a Wittoba, and Wittoba is really
Krishna, an incarnation of Vishnu. And we must not forget that
though there are some points in the story of Krishna quite re-
pugnant to Christians, there are others—such as the advice to
give the unsmote cheek to an assailant—singularly like that found
in the story of Jesus. At all events Higgins adds, with reference
to the above, that "the crucified body without the cross of wood
reminds me that some of the ancient sects of heretics held Jesus
to have been crucified in the clouds". And "I repeat, I cannot
help suspecting that it is from this Avatar of Cristna that the
sect of Christian heretics got their Christ crucified in the *clouds*".

John M. Robertson thinks Higgins is mistaken in "adopting the
view that Krishna had in an ancient legend been crucified", but
he seems to have overlooked the fact that it is we who call the
representation of a man with arms outstretched on a piece of
wood a "crucifixion". The description could very well represent
"hanged on a tree". Higgins quotes the work of Guigniaut as his
authority and gives the relevant passage in French. I venture to
translate it:

> The death of Crichna is related in many various ways. One
> remarkable and vouched for tradition makes him die on a fatal
> tree to which he was fastened by an arrow and from the height
> of which he predicted the horrors which were going to destroy
> the earth in future ages . . .

The point to note is that even if Higgins calls this a "crucifixion" it is not necessarily so; and it is quite conceivable that Krishna died "nailed" on a tree only in the *imagination* of the writers who relate his many forms of death. As I have already pointed out, the principal tradition followed is that Krishna was killed by an arrow in the foot; and it is Christians who are always ready to use the word "crucifixion" to describe any other god with arms outstretched as, in some way or other, crucified. Not that they will admit that the crucifixion of other gods is like that of Jesus—the point which is always pressed when the "crucifixion" of the other and older gods is produced as proof of a crucifixion tradition in the pagan world.

Osiris, the Egyptian Savior, is said to have been crucified "in the heavens". Horus also suffered the same fate. Prometheus was crucified, so were Ixion and Quetzalcoatl—all three personifications of the Sun—but of course they were not crucified exactly as was Jesus. Behind all these myths will be found one thing fundamental—the death of the Sun in Winter, and his tremendous struggles to come to life again in Spring. But the story is variously told in different countries and in different languages, and other myths have often got entangled in the story. It would be absurd to imagine that the Greeks or Greek Jews responsible for the Gospels would think exactly like the framers of the story of Quetzalcoatl in ancient Mexico, or like the authors of the story of Frey, the Scandinavian deity.

Even the Rosicrucians have as their Crucifix a jewel with a rose on one side and a cross on the other; while the Templars had as their emblem a red rose actually on a cross. The word "crucifixion" can mean almost anything when we come to examine all these allegories and symbols. What does "crucified in spirit" actually mean?

We must not forget, of course, that for Christians there is another idea behind the Cross. It is the redemption of Humanity by the vicarious sacrifice of a God. He becomes, through his death, the "Savior". But it was not a new idea at all as so many Christians fondly think. It was indeed a very old idea, for it is found in ancient Hindu literature, as well as in Egypt; and in most cases the sacrificer was mystically identified with the victim.

Christians are generally horrified at Pagan similarities, and one like Prof. Monier Williams has to plead in his *Hinduism*, when referring to the way in which in the Rig-Veda this idea of sacrifice for the good of humanity is described: "Surely, in these mystical allusions to the sacrifice of a representative man, we may perceive traces of the original institutions of sacrifice as a divinely-appointed ordinance typical of the one great sacrifice of the Son of God for the sins of the world". It always comes as a shock to a Christian to learn that some of the most "typical" doctrines of Christianity were known long before that religion was founded.

Exactly when sacrifices were first made to the gods we do not know, but that of Cain and Abel is no doubt typical of them. Perhaps the fruits of the earth and flowers were first offered as an appeasement to the Deity, and when these failed, the scarcer animals, and then later, human beings. Or perhaps it was the other way round. Jesus Christ is supposed to have taken upon his own shoulders the sins of the world, and is the *final* "Savior". But historians know that human sacrifices were offered long after his supposed Crucifixion; and, in any case, the Church Fathers and historians knew perfectly well that there were in Paganism quite a number of Saviors just as there were "virgin" births. In fact St. Augustine gave the whole show away when he roundly declared that "the same thing which is now called the Christian religion existed among the Ancients. They have begun to call Christian, the true religion which existed before".

The Cross and the Crucifix were known long before Christianity, and they were used in some cases at least for the same reasons given by Christian theology. It is absurd to imagine that events actually took place in Jerusalem which were described by Pagan writers centuries before, the sufferer being a real man. There is no evidence whatever that anybody called Jesus Christ "suffered" under Pontius Pilate by being nailed to a Cross for a crime which Pilate himself declared never happened. And it is for Historicists to prove that the Crucifixion actually took place —when and where.

The ex-Abbé Loisy, perhaps the greatest theologian of our generation, always held firmly to the Crucifixion, recognizing that if that went Christianity was, as a divine religion, finished. On the other hand, Dr. Cheyne, who occupied in England about the same position that Loisy did in France, almost certainly gave up the Crucifixion. His words, quoted by Gilbert T. Sadler in his *Behind the New Testament* are:

> If the Crucifixion is unhistorical—and there is, I fear, consider-able probability that it is. . . . *The Reconciliation of Races and Religion*, page 185.
>
> The myth of a suffering and rising God lies behind Isaiah 53. It is no doubt difficult to see one's way in the Pauline references to the crucifixion. But if the *basis* is elsewhere mythological, one may reasonably conjecture that it is so in the crucifixion. St. Paul, like others of his age, may draw no sharp line between his-tory and myth. Myth has become fact (for him) (May 16, 1913).
>
> Starting from the Virgin narrative it became clear to me that the story of the nativity and that of the Resurrection and Ascen-sion must be of mythic origin, and the myth which bound these stories together must have been the common tradition of the God, friendly to man, who was born (as it seemed) in human form, died and rose again, for man (April 8, 1914).
>
> (Extracts from two personal letters to Mr. Sadler.)

Yet Canon Cheyne died in the bosom of the Church of England!

The part the Cross has played in building up Christianity has been a large one, and perhaps most in the dead figure of Christ on the Cross after an agonizing death. That picture has roused the sympathy of mankind to a tremendous degree, and the wily priest has used to the full an emotion we all under-stand. Jesus must have lived because he died—because, in ad-dition, he died for us. It was not Jesus really, it was God himself on the Cross; and if this be not understood—that is because it is a mystery, a stumbling-block alike for Jews and Gentiles.

But if the reader ponders on what I have written with regard to the Cross, he will perhaps see that the whole fabric of Vi-carious Suffering with its Savior and its Cross is nothing but a huge imposture, that in fact it has literally no meaning. A suffer-ing God is just a Pagan and Gnostic *idea*.

CHAPTER V

The Mother of God

IF JESUS REALLY EXISTED AS A GOD OR AS A MAN
he must have had a mother. It is true that both Mark and
John introduce us first to Jesus as a grown-up Man, and for
Marcion and other Gnostics, that is how he first came on to this
planet. But for most people, all gods except the Jewish one,
had mothers, and some of the most entertaining stories in
Mythology are those relating their *amours*. The picture of Leda
and the Swan is one of many which artists have loved to paint,
and mankind in general simply refuses to take any interest in
a god who has never been moved, if ever so little, by human
passion.

It is therefore not surprising that most of the Gospels—for I
refuse to agree that any are "Apocryphal"—refer to the mother
of Jesus, and that quite a number have given us far more copious
details of her life than are found in the "big four". The Virgin
Mary has certainly captured the hearts and imagination of men,
and indeed writers and artists have vied with one another in pay-
ing her homage.

It need hardly be said, however, that a cold analysis of her
story, divorced from sentiment, reveals that this is really the more

76

or less unconscious homage which the male gives to the female nursing her baby. That is indeed, perhaps, the most beautiful thing in life, and it is not at all surprising that man has nearly always been susceptible to the "mother" influence. At all events, we are not surprised when we find the mother and child motive in other religions, not necessarily *exactly* like that of Mary and Jesus, but sufficiently like to make us recognize the universal idea behind the narrative.

Our own query must be that asked by Robert Taylor in one of his astro-mythological lectures delivered over 100 years ago at the Rotunda in Blackfriars Road. He asked, "Who was Mary? i.e. Who was she when she was at home?" It was a most ungallant question. Considerable experience with all sorts of Freethought literature has failed to produce for me any criticism of Taylor's lecture which he calls "Virgo Paritura"—or indeed any reference to it. Either Bradlaugh, who knew it quite well, or Ingersoll, or for that matter, most of the eminent Freethinkers who succeeded Taylor, did not agree with him, or they thought the question futile, or, as they were nearly all quite certain Jesus did live and must have had a mother they felt that Mary would do just as well as anybody else, and the problem was not worth bothering about. As Howell Smith puts it (p. 52), "If we grant that Jesus may have been an historical person, he may very well have had a father named Joseph". And if a father named Joseph, why not a mother named Mary? It is so much easier to accept the New Testament account than to worry about any underlying myth even if the myth is granted.

Dr. Conybeare, as can well be imagined, pours the whole of his scorn on the attempt J. M. Robertson and other writers make to find out the truth about Mary—"What was she when she was at home"?—which is a fundamental question. He refuses utterly and absolutely to "admit that the cults of Osiris, Dionysius, Apollo, or any other ancient Sun-god are echoed in a single incident narrated in the primitive evangelical tradition that lies before us in Mark and the non-Marcan document used by the authors of the first and third Gospels; I do not believe that any really educated man or woman would for a moment entertain any of the equations propounded by Mr. Robertson. . . ."

We can put aside the "educated" man or woman for the moment,
as they may know nothing whatever of the cult of a Virgin and
yet be quite well read. This kind of angry bluster leads us nowhere. We must still come back to Taylor and to his other queries:

> Why is it, that among all the boasted treatises on the evi-
> dences of Christianity, not one has ever attempted to prove the
> existence of the mother of Christ? And, why is it that in pro-
> portion as the attempt is made to give an historical basis to
> Christianity, all reference to his mother is so carefully avoided?

There is not a line in either Howell Smith's work or in that of
Conybeare which gives the slightest sign of answering these
points; and yet, as Taylor insists, "Are not *these* questions which
a man should ask, and on which he should insist on being satisfied? . . ."

In her introduction to *Legends of the Madonna* Mrs. Jameson
treads very warily indeed on the dangerous ground. As a believing
Christian, it must have gone very much against the grain even
to refer to the worship of a Mother-goddess in the East, and she
feels it incumbent to say at the outset that it is not her intention
"to enter here on that disputed point, the origin of the worship of
the Madonna". But she is forced to add, that just as some "de-
liverers and kings of the Old Testament and even the demi-gods
of heathendom, became accepted types of the person of Christ",—

> So the Eve of the Mosaic history, the Astarte of the Assyrians—
> The mooned Ashtoreth, queen and mother both, the Isis
> nursing Horus of the Egyptians, the Demeter and the Aphrodite
> of the Greeks, the Scythian Freya, have been considered by some
> writers as types of a divine maternity, foreshadowing the Virgin-
> mother of Christ. Others will have it that these scattered, dim,
> mistaken, often perverted ideas which were afterwards gathered
> into the pure dignified, tender image of the Madonna, were but
> as the voice of a mighty prophecy . . .

And Mrs. Jameson finds it "curious" to observe that the worship
of the Virgin "gathered to itself the relics of many an ancient
faith . . . the Madonna, when she assumed the characteristics
of the great Diana of Ephesus, at once the type of fertility, and
the Goddess of Chastity, became, as the impersonation of mother-
hood, all beauty, bounty, and graciousness . . .".

I trust the reader will compare this admission which Mrs.
Jameson was bound to make as a truthful historian with the
bluster of Conybeare who refuses to see a *single* incident in the
story of Mary in Mark and Luke borrowed from other ancient
"Sun-gods".

The truth of course is quite plain. The worship of the Virgin
Mary is, in all relevant details, the same as the worship of the
other Goddesses which was prevalent wherever men and women
worshiped at all. Mary is Isis, or Venus, or Aphrodite, or Semiramis, as seen by various writers, and in different countries. She
is the "Queen of Heaven" or the "Mother of God", or the "Star
of the Sea", or the "Immaculate Virgin", or the whole lot with
many additional epithets. Mary happens to be one of the latest,
but she is exactly what they are, and when Jesus was given a
Mother it was the same old Mother who had done duty for the
same old purpose for centuries, who was chosen. Even her name
Mary—that is, Mariam—was carefully chosen. It could not have
been otherwise.

Both the Mother and Child were worshiped in Babylon, and
everybody knows the names of Isis and Horus from Egypt. We
have in Greece, Ceres as the Great Mother with a babe at her
breast, or Irene with Plutus, and even in China there is Shing
Moo, also with a babe. The Assyrians called their Mother of
God, Mylitta, and her son was named Tammuz the Savior. Another name for Tammuz was Adonis, and according to Firmicus,
who wrote in the reign of Constantine, he rose from the dead.
An account of this is given in Dupuis. The ancient Etruscans
and Italians worshiped the goddess Nutria, who also had a son
in her arms, while Minerva was honored by the title of the Virgin
Queen. So was Juno who was called the "Virgin Queen of
Heaven"; while Diana, though considered a cold and austere
Virgin, actually had the title of "Mother".

Hertha or Ostara, who was fecundated by the "Holy Spirit",
was the Virgin Goddess of the Germans; Disa is the name of a
similar deity in Scandinavia. The mother of the Mexican Savior,
Quetzalcoatl, was considered also a Virgin Goddess, and the
list could be extended.

As Robert Taylor insists, "That the Virgin Mary, the Grecian

Venus, and the Egyptian Isis, are each of them the same as the Virgin of the Zodiac, is a truth borne out, not by one or two, but by a thousand analogies".

It is the Virgin of the Zodiac Virgo who is at the back of all these Virgin Goddesses no matter under what name they are known. It is naturally very unpopular to say this as the easier way is to agree with Dr. Conybeare, accept Mary as the Mother of Christ as he does, and ridicule any attempt to find out the source of the myth by claiming that there is no myth. Mary is the Mother of "Christ", and that simple statement should be accepted.

But it is not accepted by Sir James Frazer who certainly recognized that in Mary we had the old story of the "Queen of Heaven" modernized. Here are his words:

> [Augustine] says that Isis made the discovery of barley. . . . That is why they [Roman writers] identify Isis with Ceres . . . the Greeks conceived of Isis as a corn-goddess for they identified her with Demeter. In a Greek epigram she is described as . . . "the mother of the ears of corn" . . . Accordingly Greek or Roman artists often represented her with ears of corn on her head or in her hand. . . . But the homely features of the clownish goddess could hardly be traced in the refined, the saintly form which, spiritualized by ages of religious evolution, she presented to her worshipers of after days as the true wife, the tender mother, the beneficent queen of nature, encircled with the nimbus of moral purity . . . her worship was one of the most popular at Rome and throughout the Empire. . . . We need not wonder then, that . . . the serene figure of Isis . . . should have roused in their breasts a rapture of devotion not unlike that which was paid in the middle ages to the Virgin Mary. Indeed her stately ritual, with its shaven and tonsured priests, its matins and vespers, its tinkling music, its baptisms and aspersions of holy water, its solemn processions, its jewelled images of the Mother of God, presented many points of similarity to the pomps and ceremonies of Catholicism. The resemblance need not be purely accidental. Ancient Egypt may have contributed its share to the gorgeous symbolism of the Catholic Church as well as to the pale abstractions of her theology. Certainly in art the figure of Isis suckling the infant Horus is so like that of the Madonna and child that it has sometimes received the adoration of ignorant

Christians. And to Isis in her later character of patroness of
mariners the Virgin Mary perhaps owes her beautiful epithet of
Stella Maris "Star of the Sea", under which she is adored by
tempest-tossed sailors. The attributes of a marine deity may have
been bestowed on Isis by the sea-faring Greeks of Alexandria . . .
(*The Golden Bough*, abridged edition, pp. 383-4).

In his almost ignored lecture on the Virgin, Robert Taylor,
nearly 100 years before Frazer wrote the *Golden Bough,* says
many things which prove that he also saw what that great
anthropologist saw. As Isis was really the Virgin of the Zodiac,
it is not surprising that in nearly all the representations of Virgo
she is shown with either corn or barley in her hand. But the
reason why Isis was called Stella Maris was because she was the
Egyptian prototype of the Marine Venus—the Venus arising from
or born of the sea of which so many paintings have been made—
the most famous one being, perhaps, that by Botticelli "the
Birth of Venus".

Now, says Taylor, "The word Mary is, as everybody knows, the
same as the Latin word *Mare,* the Sea; and in its plural form
Maria, pronounced Maria, signifies the Seas, as the adjective
Marina, of or pertaining to the Sea, read without the letter N,
after the ancient manner of writing, is the same word, and was
from the days of an infinitely remote antiquity, one of the names
of the Goddess Venus". Mary is precisely the same name as
Miriam, the sister of Moses, and it, says Taylor, "signifies Myrrh,
of the sea, or Lady or Mistress of the sea. . . . It is none other
than the very name of Myrrha, the mother of the beautiful
Adonis . . ."

The curious thing is that in Vol. I of her *History of Christian
Names*—quite a learned work, by the way, compiled from the
best authorities—Miss Charlotte Yonge says that the name Miriam
or Mary, according to some authorities, comes from the word
Marah (bitterness), "but in the middle ages it was explained as
Myrrh of the Sea, Lady of the Sea, or Star of the Sea, the likeness to the Latin and Teutonic *mar* being probably the guide. Star
of the Sea is the favorite explanation among Roman Catholics,
as the loftiest and most poetical, and it is referred to in many
of their hymns and other devotions".

"The most beautiful hymn of the Roman Catholic service," adds Taylor, "actually bears the title of Ave Maria Stella—hail Mary Star." Why do we find also that a girl whose name happens to be Mary is often called Polly? It comes from the Greek word Pollus, many, and refers to the many waves of the sea.

The truth is that in the Virgin Mary we have a definite example of a myth, the myth of the Mother of God, or the Star of the Sea, or the Goddess of Corn, or the Virgo of the Zodiac. How far we must go back to their common origin it is impossible to say, but the worship and adoration of a Goddess goes back in all probability as far as—or even farther than—that of a God. And the story has come down through the ages in various forms and with many additions and variations. But it is simply inconceivable that, had there been a real Mother of God, the Mother of Jesus, she would have been endowed with all sorts of attributes taken unblushingly from Paganism, the religion of which was so violently opposed by Christians.

Why is "Lady-day" celebrated on March 25? Because, answers the Christian, "our Lord" was born on December 25. But neither date is given in the New Testament, and if we know anything at all it is that there never has been any evidence whatever produced to show that Jesus was born on December 25. Lady-day was held in Rome in honor of Cybele, just as it was in Egypt for Isis, on March 25 or thereabouts.

The festival of the Assumption of Mary is held in the Roman Catholic Church on August 15—the very day, contends Taylor, that the Greeks fixed as the day of the Assumption of the blessed Virgin Astrea; the same day is also "the very crisis of the disappearance or evanescence of the Virgin of the Zodiac". Three weeks later, that is, on September 8, Virgo appears again "emerging out of the Sun's rays"—and, of course, the Church fixed this date for the Nativity of the Virgin.

You will not find the name of the *mother* of Mary given in the New Testament. It will be found in one of the Apocryphal Gospels where it is given as Anna. Why Anna? The word is the feminine of Annus the year—"and thus the Virgin Mary is proved to be none other than the Virgin of the Zodiac, which is 'the Daughter of the Year'", adds Taylor. In fact, he claims that all these dates and many more are purely astronomical—"That the Virgin Mary, the planet Venus, and the Virgin of the Zodiac, are absolutely the same, and consequently that Jesus Christ, the Son of the Virgin Mary, is none other than the same kind of allegorical and imaginary figment, as they were, is demonstrable from the absolute identity of all the epithets and doxologies, prayers and praises ascribed to Venus in the Pagan, and to Mary in the Christian theology".

It is a curious fact, which I leave Historicists to explain, that, carved on the great gate of Notre Dame, the great church in Paris dedicated to "our Lady", there are twelve signs of the Zodiac; but the sixth, that of the Virgin, is occupied by another figure, the Virgin being placed above all "as the Goddess to whom the edifice is dedicated". Surely this proves that the builders of the church knew exactly from where they got the Virgin?

In any case, Notre Dame was built upon the site of a Temple of Jupiter, though nobody seems to know when the change took place. Somewhere in the sixth century, there were two edifices close together which were later merged into one; and though there have been many changes, the original plan seems to have persisted. Many "mutilations" have been practiced on the church, most of them to get rid of pagan associations; and at the time of the French Revolution attempts were made to make it a secular building. The outside statues were threatened, but Chaumette intervened, and with Dupuis at his side, he managed to get the signs of the Zodiac preserved on account of their symbolical significance.

Sufficient has, I hope, been said to show how the story of Mary, the Mother of God and Jesus, is simply a rehash of the stories of other Pagan Goddesses; like them she had no real existence whatever. There is but one reference to her in Acts and she then disappears from "history"—a fact absolutely inconceivable had she really been the Mother of God, and known to the early Christians as the Mother of "our Lord". In Mrs. Jameson's *Legends of the Madonna* will be found many details of how Mary's biography has been "written up". The distinguished authoress was often quite bewildered, and could only very lamely give as an excuse the way in which the world has been enriched by the beautiful works of great artists depicting the legends. She also points out that a great many of the effigies she saw herself, declared to be Mary's, could not possibly have been the Virgin's. "I confess", she adds, "I do not believe in any authentic representation of the Virgin holding the Divine Child older than the sixth century, except when introduced into the groups of the Nativity and the Worship of the Magi." The word "authentic" is quite delightful. All the same, Mrs. Jameson is very perturbed at the extreme attitude of some Protestants who refuse to accept some of the effigies as being, say, of the second century. "It seems to me that nothing could be more likely", she declares, "and that such representations ought to have a deep interest for all Christians, no matter of what denomination—for *all*, in truth, who believe that the Savior of the world had a good Mother, his only earthly parent, who brought him forth, nurtured and loved him." Well, of course, as I have already remarked, if Jesus really lived Mary could quite well have been his mother, just as, in Howell Smith's opinion, Joseph could have been his father.

Joseph naturally comes into the pictures painted of the Virgin, and here again the artists themselves are quite as much puzzled as to how such an illustrious husband should be depicted as is Mrs. Jameson at the way in which they have succeeded in portraying him so differently. Sometimes he is shown as quite decrepit with age and with a crutch,—a support, by the way, which nearly always goes with him as his "symbol". At other times he is shown as a much younger man, say about 40 years old, and even not more than 30. Rarely is he made to look like an old Jew— and, for that matter, Mary is never made to look like a typical Jewess.

As a matter of fact, she is shown as well as the infant Jesus, in many ancient paintings and statues as perfectly black. Godfrey Higgins in the *Anacalypsis* and Dr. Inman in his *Ancient Faiths,* give many particulars of these black Virgins and Child. So does that old 18th century writer, Dr. Conyers Middleton, in his once famous *Letter from Rome.* Many of these black Virgins are representations of Isis, whose worship, in some particulars at least, as shown by Sir James Frazer, was so like that of the Virgin Mary. The mother of Krishna is also depicted as black. "It may be well", says Lundy in his *Monumental Christianity,*"to compare some of the oldest Hindoo representations of the subject with the Romish, and see how complete the resemblance is". And James Bonwick in his *Egyptian Belief* finds it "a little odd that the Virgin Mary copies most honored should not only be black, but have a decided Isis cast of feature". Certainly it is very odd; but if one considers the undoubted fact that it is Pagan mysteries, rites, and symbolism, which are behind Christianity, and that it has not a single original feature which can be considered relevant, the oddity may not be quite so apparent.

In the Gospels are many Marys, and the reader should try to disentangle them, a problem which occupied John M. Robertson a good deal. He came to the conclusion that "the philology of Maria and Mariam is a hopeless problem", but "the central mythological fact is that a Mother Goddess, a 'Madonna' nursing a child, is one of the commonest objects of ancient worship throughout Asia and North Africa". To that plain and clear statement the Historicists have so far given no reply. It is far easier to poke fun at the attempts to find the origin of such words as Mary, Miriam, Mariam, Myrrha, Maria, and other variations of the sound; it is far and away easier to say that if Jesus had a father it might well have been Joseph.

Robert Taylor's query, then, "What was Mary when she was at home?"—what do we know of the Mother of God and Jesus, as a real mother of a household, can now be answered: nothing whatever. We do not know when she was born or where, we know nothing of her girlhood at home, or who were her father and mother; the story of the "Annunciation", with its nonsense about angels, is a pure fairy story, just as that of an angel coming to Joseph in a dream to tell him that God was to be the father of Mary's child. Almost all the details of Mary's life can be found in that of other Mother Goddesses. They were the common heritage of the East. If there has ever been a real Jesus the *Virgin* Mary could never have been his mother. But her story as given in the Gospels—all of them—was necessary to bolster up the myth of Jesus Christ, the Savior, The Son of God and all that title implies.

CHAPTER VI

Jesus and the Witness
of the Jews

IT IS AN EXTRAORDINARY FACT THAT SOME OF
the strongest supporters of the historicity of Jesus are Jews. They
are not concerned in this with his Messiahship at all; that, of
course, they utterly disbelieve. But that there was a Jesus about
whom the stories related in the Gospels arose, they believe with
almost evangelical fervor.

There are two clear reasons for this: the first, Jesus is mentioned in the Talmud; the second, that it ought to be a source
of great pride to all Jews that one of their race—or at least one of
their belief—should be elevated to such a height as the God of
Christendom.

In the past, this second reason was worked for all its worth by
Dr. Claude Montefiore; and his modern successor is Dr. Joseph
Klausner. In his *Jesus of Nazareth,* Dr. Klausner puts all his
scholarship to bear in showing how Jesus was a typical Jew of
the time and how the various details surrounding him of the
customs and localities of the first century Jews are all faithfully
reported in the Gospels. Dr. Klausner believes implicitly in
Mary, for example, and Judas, who was "an educated Judean

with a keen intellect but a cold and calculated heart". And like so many other Historicists, he disregards those texts which he does not like, or which he deems unworthy of his hero, or which he cannot defend. But almost with the enthusiasm of Renan, Klausner hails Jesus as the greatest of Jews, and so long as Christians adore him as their Deity, Klausner's enthusiasm for Jesus will abate not a jot.

In his *Jesus Not a Myth* Howell Smith calls attention to Prof. Charles Guignebert's *Le Problème de Jésus* which he thinks deserves an English translation. So do I—though the worthy professor is a very strong opponent of the Myth theory. His arguments, in a general way, have been dealt with in this book, but I am here concerned for the moment with his express declaration: "Comment se fait-il donc que, dans leur polémiques premières contre les Chrétiens, les Juifs n'aient jamais nié l'existence de Jésus?"—"How is it then that in their first polemics against the Christians, the Jews never denied the existence of Jesus?" (page 148.) Prof. Guignebert adds that this well-founded question encloses such a strong argument that an opponent can do little but remain silent. I am afraid that this opponent, anyway, is not going to remain silent, however unanswerable the "silence of the Jews" may seem to an opponent of the Myth theory.

In the first place I ask, where are these early Jewish polemics against the Christians? Prof. Guignebert speaks so confidently about them—that they do not deny the existence of Jesus—that at least he might have given us some indication of their titles, and where we can read them. Has he read them himself? The answer is very plain. They exist only in the imagination of Prof. Guignebert. He actually gives us, as a proof of his assertion, a reference to the French translation of the report of the debate on the question "Did Jesus Ever Live?" held in Berlin in 1910 between Prof. Arthur Drews and a number of German theologians, which lies before me at the moment. It is the famous Prof. Von Soden who is speaking:

> Thus it is alleged that it is rather astonishing that no Jewish or Greek-Roman contemporary has clearly expressed himself on this question about Jesus. For the Jews the answer is very simple: *we have no Jewish documents of the period in question.* Philo of

Alexandria was a distance away and he was a contemporary whose activities were exercised in quite another direction; and as for Josephus, the historian of this period, he was known as a diplomat and took good care not to play with fire. (Italics mine.)

In other words, Prof. Guignebert tells us that in their early writings against the Christians, the Jews do not deny the existence of Jesus, and sends us to Von Soden for confirmation; and Von Soden calmly tells us that "we have no Jewish documents". Further comment on this point is hardly necessary.

But Guignebert goes farther. He actually mentions the *Dialogue with Trypho* by Justin Martyr as a further proof that the early Jews did not deny the existence of Jesus. It seems incredible that anyone reading this work could make such a statement. It is entirely contrary to the fact. In truth, Justin has reported an astonishing statement which proves that some Jews at least did deny the existence of Jesus—a statement coming from a Christian source, which is the despair of all Historicists.

It would not be unfair to say that the majority of laymen these days are most unlikely to read Justin Martyr. Most of these early Church Fathers are very nearly unreadable, and a good deal of what they say is a hotch-potch of the crudest superstition, credulity, and ignorance. But for the present controversy this *Dialogue* is of supreme importance.

Justin Martyr, who flourished about the first half of the second century, wrote two *Apologies* for Christianity, and the better known *Dialogue with Trypho,* which appeared somewhere between the years 138-161 A.D. He was born in Palestine of heathen (presumably Greek) parents, and in his early years was a disciple of Plato. He shows in the *Dialogue* how he became a Christian through the study of Old Testament prophecy, and was convinced that the Jewish Messiah had come in the person of Jesus Christ. Meeting Trypho and his Jewish companions one day, he had the discussion with them reported at great length in this *Dialogue.* Whether such a discussion actually took place in this way it is quite impossible to say. But Justin's knowledge of the Old Testament, which he must have read in the Septuagint version, proves at least that he had had many talks with those Jews who, like Trypho himself, "came from the last war, and

live now in Greece, but mostly in Corinth". From these discussions which no doubt were even more interminable than modern theological ones are apt to be now, we get what might be
called an epitome of what people like Justin believed about
Christianity and the Old Testament prophecies, and what the
educated Jew thought of this new religion. It is all set down in
an orderly manner, and is especially valuable because what Jews
thought about the year 150 A.D. of Christianity is otherwise difficult to find. This Christian report is, therefore, of vital importance
on the question of the historicity of Jesus. The Jews must have
known all about the Trial, Crucifixion, and Resurrection of the
"simple" teacher who went about "doing good", who gathered
so many disciples and followers, and whose teachings were being
taken up by so many Gentiles as well as by large numbers of
Jews themselves.

And yet almost at the outset, Justin has to report that on the
question of Jesus Christ, the Christ Justin had accepted as his
Lord and Savior, the Christ who, he claimed, was prophesied in
many parts of the Old Testament, and the Christ about whom
he was having these interminable discussions with Jews—this
Christ, in short, Trypho proclaimed a myth. "You have made
him up", roundly declares Trypho; "he is a mere invention on
your part". Here are the words of Trypho as reported by Justin:

> But Christ if he is come, and is anywhere, is unknown, nor
> doth he know himself, nor can he be endued with any power,
> till Elias shall come and anoint him, and make him manifest to
> all men. But you, having got an idle story by the end, do form
> yourself an imaginary Christ, and for his sake you foolishly and
> inconsiderately rush headlong into dangers, and so forfeit all
> pleasures of this life.

And how did Justin answer this charge? Simply by telling
Trypho that the rabbis "do not understand the scriptures", and
that "we do not give heed to vain and idle stories"; in fact
everything but proof that his Christ had ever lived. And there is
one touch in all this protest on the part of Justin which pro-
claims that the *Dialogue* is quite possibly authentic. It is that
Trypho's Jewish companions roared with laughter at some of
Justin's arguments. Those members of the Society for the Con-

version of Jews who have had to proselytize know this laughter very well indeed. It is difficult in fact to describe the contemptuous laughter with which the educated or the instructed Jew receives the arguments of the Christian proselytizer; no wonder that the conversion of Jews has been so difficult. And over and over again, Justin pathetically reports how the companions of Trypho "laughed again" or "behaved themselves very indecently" or "jeered and derided our notions".

The Historicists do not like this passage from Trypho and do their best to explain that by Christ, Justin and Trypho meant some other Christ—not Jesus Christ; or that Trypho merely meant that Christ was not the Jewish Messiah and therefore he did not dispute the question of Jesus as a man. I advise the reader to study the *Dialogue* for himself. If words have any meaning at all I assert here, as plainly as I can, that Trypho disputed the whole argument of Justin including the very existence of his "Christ", a name he uses indifferently for Justin's Jesus. Actually, only on rare occasions, does Justin say anything but "Christ"—here and there we find "Christ Jesus", and "Jesus Christ", but it is principally "Christ".

Trypho suffered under the same difficulty as we all do when debating the problem. I am often obliged to say "But surely Jesus could not have done this or that", thus seeming to imply a Jesus who might have done something else. For example, Trypho says, "But this fellow of yours, who is called Christ, was so inglorious, mean and despicable a wretch, as to fall under the greatest curse in the law of God: for he was crucified". Trypho had already said that Christ was "an imaginery Christ", that his "story" was an idle one and so on; but Justin was not only answering Trypho but all Jews, if possible, and so in Trypho's mouth must be put as many objections as he could gather. He even makes Trypho say, as so many Jews do even at this day: "You are out of your senses to talk at this rate", when Justin was bringing forward one of his particularly silly arguments from the Old Testament. And Justin has to reply by saying, "I am not mad nor out of my senses". The modern Christian proselytizer has had to defend himself in much the same manner when debating with our stubborn Jews.

"Prove now", says Trypho, "that that fellow, who, you say, was crucified and is gone up into heaven, is the Christ of God." Note how Trypho is made to say "who *you say* was crucified". How could he have said this if the Crucifixion had been an historical fact and if all Jews knew that Jesus had been crucified under Pontius Pilate? He was questioning the Crucifixion just as he had at first questioned the whole of the "idle story". And Justin in answer contended that he had already done so to "unprejudiced persons", a reply which I have heard from Christians a thousand times these days when they were challenged in the same way.

It is difficult to read Justin's arguments as a whole without laughing. Over and over again he goes into the most fantastic comparisons such as the lamb which has to be roasted whole according to Exodus "was a type of that punishment of the cross which Christ was to undergo. For a lamb when it is roasting is like the figure of a cross". And the "offering of fine flour, gentlemen, was a type of Eucharistical bread"; and "the twelve bells which were hung upon the High Priest's ephod was a type of the twelve apostles", and so on. Trypho, who appears to have been what we call a gentleman, always listened carefully to the argument, but kept pointing out that it "seems to me incredible, and what cannot be proved", and called the idea that Christ was God who existed from all eternity "not only incredible but absurd".

Justin deals with those "of our profession" who say that Christ "was made Man of Man, with whom I cannot agree". This shows that in his day there were Christians who agreed that Christ was the Messiah, but that he was born of human parents, a position which Trypho thought "credible" for the simple reason that the Jews (we are told) were expecting just such a Messiah. But he wanted proof that this Messiah would be born of a virgin, and though Justin brings forward the familiar text from Isaiah about a virgin conceiving, Trypho knocks out Justin by the modern argument that the prophecy related to Hezekiah, and was then fulfilled. Indeed, I have been quite surprised at the "modernity" of Trypho's objections. He even points out that Justin ought to have more sense than to believe in virgin births which are based

on such "monstrous glaring absurdities" as the birth of Perseus
from the virgin Danaë. And all that Justin can do is to protest at
Trypho's obstinacy and "hardness of heart".

I have dealt rather lengthily with Justin principally because
his testimony as to what Jews thought of Christ about the year
150 A.D. is very valuable, and because he makes Trypho clearly
and unequivocally state that Justin's Christ had been invented by
Christians. I should like to add that the translations of the passage in question vary slightly. The one I have given above is
from that by Henry Browne in *The Christian Fathers,* edited by
the Rev. E. Bickersteth (1838). In the well known Ante-Nicene
Library the passage reads:

> But Christ, *if he has indeed been born* and exists anywhere,
> is *unknown* and does not even know himself and has no power
> until Elias come and make him manifest to all. And you, having
> accepted a *groundless* report, *invent a Christ for yourselves* and
> for his sake are inconsiderately perishing. (Italics mine.)

Trypho here questions his *birth,* and tells Justin that after
accepting a "groundless report" Christians "*invent* a Christ". Yet
in face of this, we get Guignebert telling us that the early Jews
never denied the existence of Jesus Christ; and Howell Smith in
Jesus Not a Myth (p. 19) calmly says that this passage has been
"strangely" misunderstood by "several representatives" of the
Mythicist school. "A more careful scrutiny", he adds quite sol-
emnly, "of the passage, and a better knowledge of Jewish Messianic lore should have made it quite clear what Trypho means".
This pathetic rebuke to those of us who maintain that we do
know something about Jewish Messianic lore and who are certain we have clearly and carefully scrutinized the passage in
question, reminds me very much of Conybeare's more hysterical
outbursts. The idea that John M. Robertson did not understand
the *Dialogue* and Jewish Messianic lore, and that Howell Smith
does, is not borne out by the facts.

So much for Justin Martyr. It is time that we turned to the
Talmud, for it is in that volume that Jewish writers like Dr.
Robert Eisler in the *Messiah Jesus* and their immediate disciples
like Archibald Robertson confidently turn for proof from Jewish

sources that Jesus really existed. I am not going to waste time however in trying to controvert Eisler. He believes that Jesus was the King of the Jews, and at the same time a Robber Chief at the head of 900 brigands, and he claims that the date given for the execution of Jesus is far too late. We are discussing the historicity of the Jesus of the New Testament, and nowhere in that "sacred" volume is there a hint that Jesus was a Robber Chief or even that he was King of the Jews, the title Pilate gave him in contempt in the Gospels.

There is really nothing very mysterious about the Talmud, though often the way Jews speak about it one would imagine it was the greatest book the world has ever seen, containing more wisdom to the page than found in a thousand other books. All the Talmud is supposed to enshrine within its pages is Jewish oral law as distinct from the Law given to Moses to be written down. Jews pretend that this oral law was never to be written down—but there it is, written and printed.

The Talmud is divided into two parts, the Mishna and the Gemara; the first is the text of discussions on all sorts of subjects such as festivals, women, sacred things, and so on; the second is a commentary on these subjects.

The Mishna was *orally* compiled by Rabbi Jehudah about the year 200 A.D., though the actual date is vague and exactly what he did is still more vague. There have been a number of additions made to the Mishna which are not supposed to be incorporated into the body of that work. According to Prof. Graetz, the learned historian of the Jews, the Mishna was finally committed to writing in the year 550 A.D.

The Gemara came into being because of the interminable discussions the rabbis and their pupils had over the precepts in both the oral and written laws. It is really a diffused commentary on the Mishna, and there are two forms known as the Babylonian, and the Jerusalem, Gemara. It is the former which is the more highly esteemed and it is also the longer. Two rabbis, Ashe and Abina, are said to be responsible for putting it in the form—more or less—it is in now, in the fifth century. The Mishna is mostly written in "late" Hebrew with a mixture of Aramaic, Greek, and Latin words; just as modern Hebrew, spoken in Palestine at this

time, has also incorporated many words from European languages
almost in their original sounds, though when written, Hebrew
characters are used. The Gemara is in a corrupt Aramaic, sometimes in dialect form, exceptionally difficult to decipher. There
are no vowel points, and many words are abbreviated, and one
shudders to think of the enormous amount of time and energy
Jews have spent studying it. Exactly what all this has contributed to the Jewish make-up is debatable, though Jews have
always professed the greatest admiration for those among them
who have made a study of the Talmud their life's work.

Although we do not know very much of authentic Jewish
history for some centuries after the rising of Bar Cocheba (about
135 A.D.) it is a fact that small colonies were got together by
surviving rabbis, who made the study of the Law of Moses one
of their principal objects of existence, just as we still have
"cheery" Bible classes up and down the country on Sundays here
in England. It is also easy to see that these surviving Jews must
have met and had many discussions with members of the new
religion, Christianity, as Justin shows so well in his famous *Dialogue*. Yet, with one exception, there is not a line or even a hint
of these discussions in the Mishna. Baring-Gould says in his *Lost
and Hostile Gospels* (p. 51) there is "not the smallest reference
made to the teaching of Jesus nor even any allusion to him personally"; but I think that one reference has been discovered since
he wrote. Surely this is all very strange. It is hard to believe that
if Jesus had really *lived,* if he had gone about for one year (or
three years) "doing good", if he had been crucified under Pontius
Pilate, a mode of execution never practised by the Jews, if so
many of his Jewish followers became convinced that he was the
Messiah predicted in the Old Testament and were thus converted, that not more than one hint should have appeared in the
writing of the oral law of the second century. We know from
Justin that the Jews of his day laughed at his arguments just as
Jews do at Christian arguments these days, and yet we get not
a line about all this in the Mishna. Baring-Gould, of course, gives
what no doubt he considers plausible reasons for this silence: the
teachings of Jesus made no impression on the Jews, they consid-

ered that he belonged to the Essenes, and any other reason which
he thinks might explain away an extraordinary fact.

On the other hand, Jesus *is* mentioned—or it is supposed that
he is mentioned—in both the Jerusalem and the Babylonian Ge-
maras; and this is exactly what we could expect. Christianity had,
in the meantime, captured the Roman world, and was increasingly
powerful, "and the rabbis", adds Baring-Gould, "could hardly
ignore any longer the Founder of the new religion".

But supposing there had never been a Jesus Christ going about
"doing good" and that he was a literary creation slowly built up
in the second century, would not that account for the silence of
the Mishna? Why should the rabbis know anything about these
literary fictions of a Jesus represented so variously by different
communities, each probably with a gospel of its own, and which
were only centuries later separated into the "true" and the "false"
ones?

On the other hand, when the Christian religion becomes all
powerful it was impossible for the small Jewish communities to
ignore it; in fact, it was God help them if they laughed at the new
religion as contemptuously as Trypho's companions laughed at
Justin and his invented Messiah.

There are undoubtedly all sorts of references to Jesus veiled
under different names in the Gemara and many stories about
him. Some of these were omitted in the Talmuds written and
printed in fear of the bitter persecution Jews suffered at the hands
of Christians during and after the Middle Ages. But this is not
surprising. When the Talmud was finally compiled, the story of
Jesus was in some essentials accepted as true by the Jews living
400 years or more after the supposed event. The rabbis, whose
interminable discussions and credulous opinions (to say nothing
of the extraordinary emptiness of many of their arguments) are
recorded in the Talmud, simply had no historic sense. The story
of Jesus, not merely in what we call the Canonical Gospels, but
also in those almost similar productions known as the Apocryphal
Gospels, must have caused them considerable confusion. As they
had records of a number of so-called Messiahs in their own archives (if they had any; if not, they knew of them orally) one
more or less was a matter of no moment. And if his name was

Jesus—the Greek form of Joshua or Jeschu or however the name was pronounced in Hebrew—well, there were a number of Jesuses, anyway, in Jewish history, whose adventures were more or less known.

There was a Jesus or Jehoshua or Jeschu who lived in the reign of Alexander Jannaeus (who died about 79 B.C.). This Jesus lived, then, about 100 years before "Jesus of Nazareth", yet he is often brought forward as a proof that the latter really lived. Baring-Gould points out that "learned Jewish writers have emphatically denied that the Jeschu of the Talmud is the Jesus of the Gospels", but this denial makes no difference to our modern Jews. What they claim to have happened is that the Talmudic rabbis deliberately falsified the date so that the *true* story of Jesus could be known to Jews without bringing them into danger from the ruling religion, Christianity. This "true" story is from the Christian point of view very blasphemous and, unless there really had been a Jeschu, must have been invented early in the history of the Talmud, as it was known in some form, at least, to Celsus in the second century. In any case, the Jerusalem Talmud has the story in a much abbreviated form and without the name Jeschu.

The actual story is a rather thin one. It appears that the King, Jannai (or Jannaeus), ordered the destruction of a number of rabbis, and R. Joshua ben Perachiah took with him his favorite pupil, Jeschu, to Alexandria. Here we have an echo of the persistent idea about Jesus, that he went to Egypt, and almost all Jews, who seem to have combined tremendous admiration for the learning found in Egypt with hatred of the country, always contend that it was there Jesus gained all his "occult" knowledge. On the way, Jeschu appears to have considered the landlady of a "certain inn" rather desirable, and Joshua was terribly shocked that his pupil could think of such things. Later Jeschu in a huff "set up a brickbat and worshiped it". He was rebuked by Joshua who declared that "Jeschu had practised sorcery and had corrupted and misled Israel". That is all, and this story seems to have caused a big commotion inside and outside Judaism.

There are also side by side with various other stories of a Jesus, some about Mary in the Gemara, also terribly confused; and in the Mishna there is the one reference to both Jesus and Mary—

where Simon ben Azzai says, "I found in Jerusalem a book of genealogies; therein was written: That so-and-so is a bastard son of a married woman". "So-and-so is, of course, one of the ways Jesus is referred to in the Talmud; the other is to call him a bastard.

The most bitter opponent of Christianity was the famous Rabbi Akiba who was put to death by the Romans about the year 135 A.D., and it may be he who put into circulation some of these stories about Jesus and his mother in supreme contempt for the gullibility of the early Christians. How little they can be relied upon is shown by the fact that Mary is, in one of the stories, made to be a contemporary of Akiba himself, and in another story the contemporary of a fourth century rabbi. But the point to note in particular is that those who rely on the Talmud for proof that there really lived a Jesus have to face the fact that so thoroughly mixed-up are the accounts, that in one place Jesus is said to have lived about 100 years before, and in another 100 years after, the supposed date given to Jesus of Nazareth.

There are two other names by which Jesus appears in the Gemara. One is as Ben Stada, the other, as Ben Pandera. It seems useless going further into details about them, though actually more will be found about Stada in the Talmud than about Pandera. Stada appears to have had the habit of cutting his flesh and hiding some magic word in it, a regrettable Egyptian custom which gave the possessor of the magic name great "occult" power. In fact, he could fly in the air and the only way in which the rabbis could bring the sorcerer down was to fly a little higher and, using the unmentionable name of God, plus some "fouling" thus bring him down. I have never been able to see what the objection to flying was, but it certainly was held in horror by the rabbis. Perhaps also we get a sort of rehash here of the well known story of Jesus flying with a Devil across Jerusalem to be put down on the pinnacle of the Temple.

The mix-up as to Stada and Pandera was eventually put right by R. Chisda (d. 309 A.D.) in the Gemara, who explained that the husband of Mary was named Stada while it was her lover who was called Pandera, all of which proves how the legend grew and expanded before the Talmud was finally put in writing. In any

case Ben Stada was definitely declared by later Jewish rabbis *not*
to be Jesus of Nazareth, as he was quite unknown before the
beginning of the second century.

Outside the Talmud the name of Ben Pandera is the most popular or perhaps the only one, and in the Jewish Life of Jesus known
as the *Sepher Toldeth Jeschu* it is he who is the hero. This production, in two known varying forms, has been translated into
English a number of times, and a full account is given in Baring-
Gould (*Lost and Hostile Gospels*) and Mead. There are probably
more variations still in manuscript, but fundamentally they are
the same.

Although certain incidents contained in the "Toldeth Jeschu"
can undoubtedly be traced to the Talmud there is little doubt that
in the main it was compiled in the 12th century. If it is contended
that it is a lying libel on the "Savior", the answer must be that it
is at least as truthful as the Gospels, Canonical and Apocryphal.
From these it is quite possible to extract just as much devout
balderdash as will be found in the Jewish production. And it must
be added that the Jewish author, whoever he was, drew on the
Talmud at least for some of his "facts", and the Talmud is called
in as a witness for the historicity of Jesus by unabashed Rationalists like Howell Smith and Archibald Robertson. But as it happens it is not the Ben Stada or the Ben Pandera stories which are
always produced as infallible evidence from the Talmud that
Jesus was an historic character. It is a story about Rabbi Eliezer
ben Hyrcanus who was the teacher of Akiba which, we are confidently assured, settles the question in favor of Jesus for ever.
I give it as found in Mead's *Did Jesus Live 100 B.C.?*

> When R. Eliezer was about to be imprisoned on account of
> heresy (suspected of a leaning towards Christianity) he was
> brought to the court of justice . . . the judge said to him: Does
> a man of mature years like thee busy himself with such nullities?
> Eliezer replied: The Judge is just towards me. The judge thought
> Eliezer was speaking of him; but he thought upon his Father in
> heaven. Then spake the judge: Since I believe thee, thou art
> acquitted. Now when Eliezer came home his disciples presented
> themselves to console him, but he admitted no consolation. Then
> R. Akiba said to him: Permit me to tell thee something of what

thou hast taught me. He answered: Say on. Then said R. Akiba: Perchance thou hast once given ear to a heresy, which pleased thee; on account of which thou wast now about to be imprisoned for heresy. Eliezer replied: Akiba thou remindest me. I was once walking in the upper street of Sephoris (a city in Galilee); there I met with one of the disciples of Jeschu ha-Notzri by name of Jacob of Kephar Sechania, who said to me: It is found in your Law (Deut. xxiii, 19): Thou shalt not bring the hire of a whore . . . into the house of . . . thy God. May a retiring place for the high-priest be made out of such gifts? I knew not what to answer him to this. Then he said to me: Thus Jeschu ha-Notzri taught me: Of the hire of an harlot has she gathered them (A. V. "it"), and unto the hire of an harlot shall they return (Micah i, 7). From offal it has come; to the place of offal shall it go. This explanation pleased me, and on this account have I been impeached for heresy, because I transgressed the Scripture: Remove thy way from her (Prov. v, 8), from her, i.e., from heresy.

There is a variant of the story which is substantially the same —it is given by Mead—but Jesus is there called "Jeschu ben Pandera".

Now if we go by dates, it is as well to remember that Akiba died about the year 135 A.D., at the end of the Bar Cocheba rebellion, that is, about 100 years after the supposed death of Jesus of Nazareth; and it is, of course, possible that the trial of Eliezer took place when Akiba was a very young man and his teacher an old one. Eliezer, therefore, could easily have talked with Jacob who, as a young man, could have known Jesus of Nazareth—if by Jeschu ben Pandera or Jeschu ha-Notzri is meant the Christian deity. Unfortunately for the Historicists, however, we have another story of the *same* Jacob in the Gemara, and not even the most fervent believer in a real Jesus can now say for certain which of these stories is the true one. The best way out for the average believer is to accept the first, and declare the second is the false one. But for the historical investigator, the fact that there are two stories must surely cancel them both. For the second one puts Jacob of Kephar as a *contemporary* of Akiba, and this makes it impossible for him to have spoken to Jesus of Nazareth or ha-Notzri or Ben Pandera or whatever was the real name. It is simply nonsense to imagine that Jacob could be about 130 years old at the time of Akiba.

Here is the second story:

> It happened that Ben Dama, son of R. Ishmael's sister, was bitten by a serpent. Then came Jacob of Kephar Sechania to heal him. But R. Ishmael suffered him not. Ben Dama said: R. Ishmael, my brother, allow me to be healed by him, and I will bring thee a verse from the Torah, showing that it is allowed. But he had not time to complete what he was saying; for his spirit departed from him and he died. Then R. Ishmael exclaimed over him: happy art thou, Ben Dama, that thy body is pure, and that thy spirit has passed away in purity, and that thou hast not transgressed the words of thy companion.

R. Ishmael here is the well known R. Ishmael ben Elisha who was the contemporary of Akiba and therefore Jacob of Kephar, as Mead rightly points out, "cannot possibly have been a personal disciple of Jesus, even according to the canonical tradition of the date. We have to notice also, that according to the rigid legalists of the Talmud, the poison of a serpent was thought to be less noxious than the contact with the magnetism or even thought-sphere of a follower of Jesus". Mead, who as a good Theosophist and therefore a believer that Jesus was an initiate, or a Master, or some reincarnation of a previous Master, or perhaps even a God, could not help trying to identify Jacob, and plays with the idea that he might well stand for James "the Lord's brother". It is an interesting speculation, of course, and like all speculations may be right; only no one knows, and until we get a revelation of some kind nobody can ever know. All I am concerned with here is to show that this story of Jacob meeting Jesus is hopelessly confused, for it is impossible to say how a mistake of at least 100 years could arise and impossible to say when the story was actually written down. That the enormous mass of writing which goes to the making of the Talmud should have been *only* orally handed down for many centuries is quite incredible; and as the Talmud was actually written in the form we have it so many centuries after the date given to Jesus, and Christianity had got such a hold all over Palestine and the Greek and Roman world, anything could have been put into it. In any case, Mead gives up the problem of the two Jacobs as "impossible to give a decided answer". For our purpose one thing does stand out: the two Jacobs do not prove the existence of Jesus as a God or as a Man.

How preconceived ideas may influence a writer can be seen in Baring-Gould's *Lost and Hostile Gospels,* where, in discussing the various Jesuses in the Talmud, he always gives their death as a "crucifixion". As Mead emphatically declares, "Like the Talmud, the Toldoth recensions also know of a stoning and hanging, or of a hanging alone, *but never of a crucifixion".* (My italics.)

The one puzzling factor in all this inquiry is, why should the date of Jesus—whoever this Jesus was—be given with such persistence as about 100 B.C. in nearly all Jewish tradition? We know that the Jewish writers responsible for the Talmud had a very deficient historic sense, yet on this point they seem to be unanimous. And here I must digress a little from the Jewish witness, and go more fully into the strange case of one of the earliest and most respected Christian Fathers, Irenaeus. It is he who first mentions the four Canonical Gospels by name, a strange fact quite unexplained by Christian evidence mongers, for the date given for this is about 180 A.D. If the four Gospels had been in circulation for somewhere near 100 years as apologists maintain, how comes Irenaeus to be the first Christian writer to mention them?

In his work *Against Heresies,* he admits that there were Christians who claimed that it was not Jesus who was executed but Simon of Cyrene, because Jesus had the power to metamorphose himself. And it is interesting to note that the word in Greek translated as "transfigured" in our Bible is in Greek classics translated as "metamorphosed". This gives point to his plain and express statement that Jesus was not executed at the age of thirty or thereabouts, but lived to be an old man. There is nothing in his long paragraph (*Against Heresies,* II., xxii, 4-5) which gives the slightest indication that Jesus was crucified; he simply "came to death itself". If anyone were to read this clear description of Jesus dying as an old man, he would be compelled to come to the conclusion that Jesus died in bed. Irenaeus actually appeals to "the elders, those who were conversant in Asia with John the disciple of the Lord, affirming that John conveyed to them that

information. Some of them, moreover, saw not only John, but the
other apostles also, and heard the very same account from them,
and bear testimony as to the statement".

It is true that in the same work Irenaeus refers to Jesus as being
crucified, but how can one reconcile the two statements? It surely
is obvious that if Irenaeus had the four Gospels in front of him,
he must have known that in them Jesus is shown as about thirty
years of age when he began his "ministry", and all four declare
that he was crucified by Pontius Pilate within three years. But if
Jesus was an old man when he died in bed or by crucifixion, it
could not have been under Pontius Pilate. Was there a Crucifixion at all? If there was not, how did the story come into circulation? In any case, when dealing with the Church Fathers or
nearly any ancient document which has passed through Christian
hands, we are never sure that the text has not been tampered
with. It is quite impossible to imagine that a Christian forger
would have deliberately inserted a statement to the effect that
Jesus died an old man presumably in bed, with the Divine authority of the Gospels *against* him. On the other hand, one can
easily imagine that a forger, horrified at the statement of Irenaeus,
thought it better served the Faith to add a sentence of his own,
that Christ *was* crucified by Pontius Pilate.

I want the reader to settle for himself this question of dates
not only from the Talmud but from such a respected Church
Father as Irenaeus. It is all so confused that the claim that there
is no history whatever in the story of Jesus is confirmed more and
more by all such confusion. If Irenaeus, writing in defense of
Christianity against heresies, did not know the exact details of
the Crucifixion, nay, simply tells us that Jesus died an old man
without reference to the mode of death or the executioner, we
have, I think, sufficient proof that even in his day, towards the
close of the second century, these details were not known or not
well known. And there is nothing in the Talmudic stories which
even hints at a Crucifixion.

As is well known, the most bitter anti-Semites are Jewish converts to Christianity, and it is mostly due to their efforts that the
reigning authorities, kings or popes during the Middle Ages, did
their best to wipe out the Talmud and other Jewish works. The

principal accusation was that the Talmud contained blasphemous attacks on Jesus, and in thousands they were consigned to the flames. How any copies survived at all is one of the marvels of the age. On one occasion (in 1239 A.D.) the French rabbis vigorously tried to defend themselves by pointing out that the references to Jesus *never meant Jesus of Nazareth,* but it was all to no purpose. The Talmuds were destroyed and the work is still on the Roman Catholic "Index".

An interesting sidelight on the way the Christian censors, who eventually allowed the Talmud to be printed by deleting every reference to (a) Jesus and by other "corrections", still function is shown in the case of the very enthusiastic article on the Talmud written by Emanuel Deutsch and published in the "Quarterly" in 1867. Wherever Deutsch wrote "Jesus" the editor altered it to "our Lord", thus giving the impression that Deutsch was a convert. In subsequent editions the word was correctly replaced for Deutsch was never a convert. It is curious that he says not a word about the Jesus stories, but emphatically denies that most of what is known as the teachings of Jesus in the Gospels is original. He claims that nearly all of it, or all, was a commonplace of Talmudic teaching.

And now we can go to the testimony of Josephus, who is always quoted by Jews and Gentiles whenever the question is asked, Where is Jesus mentioned outside the New Testament? Like so many great classics this Jewish historian is known all over the world by name, but few people, I imagine, have read him. The passage in his works generally known is the famous one in which Josephus, always proudly declaring himself a Jew elsewhere, actually calls Jesus, the "Christ", that is, the Messiah, making the historian not a Jew, but a Christian convert.

Born about the year 37 A.D., thus only a few years after the date given for the death of Jesus of Nazareth, Josephus lived throughout one of the most momentous periods of Jewish history. If there had been any truth whatever in the Gospel story he must have heard it a thousand times around him, while his father, Matthias, actually lived through these marvelous days during which (we are told) God's Begotten Son proved that he was the

Messiah foretold in the Jewish Scriptures by performing unheard
of miracles.

Moreover, Matthias appears to have been one of the leading
men in Jewry connected with the priesthood and nobody more
than he could have known better the stupendous events which led
to the Crucifixion in which the High Priest himself played a leading part. It surely is very curious that in the account of his boyhood with his brother in which he lays claim to quick and pre-
cocious learning, Josephus says nothing whatever about his father
telling him of his own experiences and of events of which he was
an eye witness. And more curious still is the description he gives
of joining a religious body of monks of some kind before he was
nineteen, and yet he says nothing whatever of meeting a similar
sect called Christians. Indeed not only does Josephus know nothing about a sect calling themselves Christians or the followers
of Jesus of Nazareth, but he clearly mentions four sects, the
Pharisees, Sadducees, Essenes, and the followers of Judas the
Galilean.

Whether Josephus can be absolutely relied upon as a historian
is difficult to say as we have not his sources of information. In
his history of the Jewish race, he follows the Bible only partly,
and it is remarkable that he appears to know so little of the
Maccabean period, and does not refer to I Maccabees, the official
account, at all. In the *Antiquities* Book 18, he gives an account
of the killing of a Samaritan leader by Pilate for which crime the
Roman chief had to answer to Tiberius. No name is mentioned,
but it is hard to see why this incident should have been related
of an obscure individual, and nothing said except in the one disputed passage about such a being as Jesus of Nazareth, who,
when Josephus was writing, already had a large following in
many parts of the Greek and Roman empires.

In Josephus's *History of the Jewish War* there is no mention
whatever of Christianity or the Christians, yet it deals with the
very time when the new religion was making converts. But in
Jewish Antiquities there is the famous passage known all over the
world, and for most people it is the only passage they have ever
read of Josephus. Here it is, in Whiston's translation (Bk. xviii,
ch. iii, 3):

Now about this time, Jesus, a wise man, if it be lawful to call him a man, for he was a doer of wonderful works, a teacher of such men as receive the truth with pleasure. He drew over to him both many of the Jews, and many of the Gentiles. He was (the) Christ; and when Pilate at the suggestion of the principal men amongst us, had condemned him to the cross, those that loved him at the first did not forsake him, for he appeared to them alive again the third day, as the Divine prophets had foretold these and ten thousand other wonderful things concerning him, and the tribe of Christians, so named from him, are not extinct at this day.

How any reader of this passage, knowing that Josephus was a Jew and proud of his race, could imagine he had written it, is one of the most mysterious puzzles connected with the Jesus problem. The whole paragraph shrieks forgery; it aroused the most scathing contempt from Gibbon, and most Christian theologians, thoroughly ashamed of its unmitigated imposture, have denounced it in no unmeasured terms. They did so because in their day the question of the existence of Jesus was never seriously raised; the Gospels were historical documents with the additional advantage of being "inspired". So there was no need of the testimony of Josephus. Baring-Gould, writing in 1874 in his *Lost and Hostile Gospels*, had hardly patience dealing with it. "One may be, perhaps, accused of killing dead birds, if one examines and discredits the passage", he says, contemptuously.

The early Church Fathers, Justin Martyr, Tertullian, Clement of Alexandria, and Origen, knew nothing about the passage. The first Christian writer to call attention to it was Eusebius (about 320 A.D.) but even later Christians than he ignored it. Eminent modern Christians like Chalmers, Milman, Farrar, Keim, Hooykaas, and numbers of others all rejected it, though some rather shame-facedly claimed that there *may* have been a passage about Jesus which was suppressed by Christians and the present one substituted. Yet in spite of all this wholesale rejection by their own authorities, many Christians never scruple using Josephus as a witness for Jesus outside the Bible whenever they can do so unchallenged.

But the importance of this passage came to be recognized more

and more as the controversy regarding Jesus became more acute.
And this was particularly the case when so many Rationalists,
who had given up Jesus as a God, decided to fight to the death
to keep him as a Man. Every effort was made—and is still being
made—either to show that Josephus wrote the passage as it stands,
or that he wrote some similar passage, or that it has only been
"interpolated". One of the latest examples is Dr. Robert Eisler's
The Messiah Jesus which discusses at length a "Slavonic" Josephus dated about the 12th century which is supposed to be a
correct translation of Josephus's Aramaic original. One can only
marvel that so much ingenuity as Dr. Eisler shows should be so
thoroughly misplaced. The particular passage about Jesus which,
we are confidently told, must be the one dropped out of the version from which ours is translated, is just as big a forgery as the
one here in question. The fact that it attacks Jesus only makes it
all the more suspect.

The reader will find in most of the books dealing with the Jesus
problem lengthy and critical studies of the fraudulent passage in
Josephus. So I pass it here. But there is still another passage in
the *Antiquities* dealing with the death of James who is called
here "the brother of Jesus who was called Christ". This clause is
just as barefaced a forgery as the other passage. In any case, this
death is put seven years before the death of James the Just, who
is considered by the primitive Church to be the "brother" of Jesus.

Baring-Gould is positively shocked at the silence of Josephus,
and devotes nearly thirty pages to a minute examination of its
cause. He comes to the conclusion that the early Christians were
mistaken for Essenes or Nazarenes or even Jews, and therefore
as Jews, Nazarenes, and Essenes were all fully dealt with by
Josephus, it is not surprising that no special mention of the early
Christians and their God was made by the Jewish historian. Moreover, "Nazarene and Pharisee were most closely united in sympathy, sorrow and regret for the past". There is, naturally, not a
scrap of evidence for this, so Baring-Gould is obliged to add, "If
this explanation which I have offered is unsatisfactory, I know not
whither to look for another which can throw light on the strange
silence of Philo, Josephus, and Justus". This Justus (of Tiberius)
was a Jewish historian who wrote a history dealing with the

period of Jesus, which has perished. We know that it was in existence in the ninth century, for then the Christian scholar Photius saw it, and says, "Justus makes not the least mention of the appearance of Christ, of what things happened to him, or of the wonderful works that he did".

And there was still another Jew who knew nothing whatever about the living Jesus of Nazareth who, it is true, wrote a little later than either Josephus or Justus. He is known as the "Jew of Celsus" and a word or two here about him is necessary.

Celsus, who is supposed to have lived late in the second century, wrote a work, attacking Christianity, which is lost. All we have is what Origen, writing a hundred years or so later, quoted from him in *Contra Celsum*. The German theologian, Theodore Keim, claimed that he could almost construct Celsus from Origen's quotations.

Now here is a notable fact—if it is true:

> It is remarkable that Celsus, living in the middle of the second century, and able to make inquiries of aged Jews whose lives had extended from the first century, should have been able to find out next to nothing about Jesus and his disciples, except what he read in the Gospels. This is proof that no traditions concerning Jesus had been preserved by the Jews, apart from those contained in Gospels, Canonical and Apocryphal. (*Lost and Hostile Gospels* p. 45.).

It is strange that such a staggering admission from a Churchman like Baring-Gould should not have attracted more notice, particularly from those of our Historicists who put forward Guignebert as a formidable opponent of the Myth theory. The reader can turn to a former page and see what he said about the Jews never denying the existence of Jesus. If Celsus was unable to contact any Jew who could give him particulars of the wonderful events which marked the governorship of Pontius Pilate, and was obliged to go to the Gospels for the necessary details about Jesus, does not this prove they knew nothing whatever about him?

Celsus's Jew certainly gives some information about Jesus but it is more or less on Talmudic lines and not at all like the "biographies" in the Gospels. Where he got his information is not stated, and no one has so far been able to explain how the tradition of Mary becoming unfaithful with a soldier named Panthera got mixed up with the "facts". Celsus, it is true, declared that he knew a great deal more than he said concerning Jesus, but Origen denied it and said that all he knew, *he got from the Gospels.* After dealing in detail with Celsus, Baring-Gould adds:

> This is most important evidence of the utter ignorance of the Jews in the second century of all that related to the history of our Lord. Justus and Josephus had been silent. There was no written narrative to which the Jew might turn for information; his traditions were silent. The fall of Jerusalem and the dispersion of the Jews had broken the thread of their recollections.

There is one clear reason why the Jews of the second century either knew nothing at all about Jesus Christ or only the ridiculous legends spread by unconverted Jews in the hope of damaging the new religion. Jesus was nothing but a literary creation and never had a real existence. That simple explanation gives the sufficient answer to mystified Christians like Baring-Gould and to Rationalist Historicists.

And, finally, what about Philo? Born about the year 20 B.C. at Alexandria, he belonged to a wealthy Jewish family of priestly descent. We know little about his private life, but in 39 or 40 A.D., he was sent to Rome at the head of an embassy to protest to Caligula against the Roman treatment of Jews in Egypt. He obtained no redress. Philo also visited Palestine, and he therefore must have known all about Jesus either from actual contact with his early followers, or from hearsay. There is not a line in his voluminous writings which shows the slightest acquaintance with the early history of Christianity. He mixed up history with allegory and was much influenced by Plato and the Greek writers generally. For him, therefore, the Bible had an allegorical as well as an historical meaning, but he often denied the historical altogether. He, like John, wrote about the "Logos" from which it has been inferred that the Christian writer simply borrowed the idea turning it into support of Christianity. That is a problem which does not concern us here. What does is, why do we find nothing whatever about Jesus or Christianity in the work of Philo, who

was a contemporary of the Christian God? To that simple question, the Historicist has no answer. May I suggest therefore that
the reply is because there was no Jesus of Nazareth nor any of
his Apostles or disciples in his day. They were not invented till
many years afterwards.

The Jewish "race" has always been called the great witness to
Jesus, for though they have denied his Godhead as well as his
Messiahship, they have not denied his existence as a man. That
is true. But when we examine the basis of this belief by going
back to the earliest possible sources we find either complete
silence as in the cases of Josephus, Justus and Philo and—with
one exception—the Mishna of the Talmud; or we find the taunt
of Trypho the Jew to Justin that the Christians had *invented* the
story of Christ; or we get the hopelessly confused legends of
the Gemara with the most absurd chronological difficulties, and
the express declaration of Jewish rabbis that Jesus of Nazareth
was never meant at all in these legends.

The Jewish witness, in short, strongly supports the Myth
theory.

CHAPTER VII

The Pagan Witnesses

IT IS TIME WE TURNED TO THE THREE ROMAN
writers Tacitus, Pliny the Younger, and Suetonius, who are put
forward as proving the truth of the existence of Jesus with the
same assurance that Josephus is put forward. To begin, there are
these two passages in the life of Nero and the life of Claudius by
Suetonius (77-140 A.D.): "The Christians, a race of men of a
new and villainous superstition, were punished" (Nero); and "He
[Claudius] drove the Jews, who, at the instigation of Chrestus,
were constantly rioting, out of Rome". Apart from the difficulty
of determining who "Chrestus" was, most historians seem also
unable to settle whether the Jews here are meant to be Christians;
and, how in the world, if Chrestus is Christ, he came to be in
Rome leading Jews in riots? It is also noteworthy that while
Suetonius is quoted to prove the existence of Chrestus, that is,
Christus, that is, Jesus Christ, he is never called in to prove that
the early Christians were "a race of men of a new and villainous
superstition". In any case, Suetonius does not give the Historicists
much hope, as can be seen in Howell Smith's *Jesus Not a Myth.*
"Suetonius", he says, "seems to have had some vague notion of
Messianic quarrels between Jews and Christians, the former de-

nying and the latter affirming that Christ had already appeared. The passage in question does not tell us much, but favors the Christian tradition rather than otherwise". This means, if it means anything, that Chrestus was really Christ, and that somehow he turned up in Rome leading the Jews there in riots; or perhaps not. One can take one's choice.

Pliny, born about the year 61 A.D., is said to have written to the emperor Trajan a letter showing how he dealt with Christians in the year 106 A.D., while acting as proconsul in Bithynia. It has been urged that this letter is a forgery, but that is a matter of small moment for it is possible that Christians were in the province in Pliny's time. But Pliny—surely a tolerant Roman—is made to say that "those who were brought before him" had to confess that they were Christians; or if they would not, they were either "punished" or "executed". They admitted that on a certain day "before it was light" they sang hymns to "Christ as to a god". This proves, say the Historicists, that Christ really existed as a man (or Man).

If Pliny had been interviewing the worshipers of Serapis or Apollo they might reasonably have confessed that they sang hymns to Serapis or Apollo, but surely this does not prove that these pagan gods existed as men. All we are entitled to say from Pliny's letter is that there were, when he was in Bithynia, a number of Christians who were worshiping somebody called Christ, not, be it noticed, Jesus; and for my part I see no particular reason to doubt that there were Christians then who worshiped "Christ" just as there were Jews who worshiped "Jehovah". This does not prove that either Christ or Jehovah were real men.

Come we now to Tacitus. Quite a storm has broken over the head of this Roman historian whose famous *Annals* would have been read as we read Livy, for example, but for the fact that it contains a paragraph dealing with the fire at Rome in 64 A.D. under Nero, and the well known Neronian persecution of the Christians for having caused it. This is the last ditch of the Historicists. Take away this passage from Tacitus and the witness of external history to Jesus goes. Every effort is now being made to uphold its genuineness by Christians and Historicists alike and it must be admitted that the discussion has become almost as embittered as that on the Shakespeare problem.

Tacitus was born about 55 A.D. and died about 130 A.D.; his *Annals* were therefore written—if genuine—in the first quarter of the second century, and they contain this passage:

> Nero, in order to stifle the rumor, ascribed it to those people who were abhorred for their crimes and commonly called Christians. These he punished exquisitely. The founder of that name was Christus, who in the reign of Tiberius, was punished as a criminal by the procurator, Pontius Pilate. This pernicious superstition, thus checked for awhile, broke out again; and spread not only over Judea, the source of this evil, but reached the city also; whither flow from all quarters all things vile and shameful, and where they find shelter and encouragement. At first, only those were apprehended who confessed themselves of that sect; afterwards, a vast multitude were detected by them, all of whom were condemned, not so much for their crime of burning the city, as their hatred of mankind. Their execution was so contrived as to expose them to derision and contempt. Some were covered over with the skins of wild beasts, and torn to pieces by dogs; some were crucified. Others, having been daubed over with combustible materials, were set up as lights in the night time, and thus burned to death. . . .

(Translations vary but all give the same sense as the above.)

Although Gibbon claims that this passage is genuine, even his great authority has not been able to stifle doubts about its authenticity by other historians. If there had been a Neronian persecution, why in heaven's name has so remarkably little been found concerning it elsewhere? Even allowing for poetical license, what did Tacitus mean when he declared that there was "a vast multitude" of Christians in Rome about 64 A.D.? Why, there was not a vast multitude in Jerusalem, or even in the whole of Judea at that time. How comes it that such a passage was never quoted by Tertullian (who often quotes Tacitus) or by Eusebius or even by any of the other Christian apologists always ready to enlarge on the terrible sufferings of the early Christians steadfastly acclaiming their faith in Jesus? Why is it, if Christians were being tortured and executed in Rome at this time (64 A.D.), according to Acts xxviii, 30-31, Paul was preaching the Gospel in Rome freely, "no man forbidding him", between 63-65 A.D.?

Paley, in his *Evidences of Christianity*, quite sadly admits that "evidence of the sufferings of the first propagators of Christianity from profane testimony" is lacking. He could only get it "in our own books".

It was not until some centuries later that we find a similar account of the Neronian persecution in the work of Sulpicius Severus (d. 420 A.D.), the idea being, of course, that he used Tacitus as his authority. He was an ecclesiastical historian, and like almost all writers of the early Church history was so utterly credulous that he believed Nero (as the first Roman emperor to persecute Christians) would "live again as Anti-Christ in the millennial kingdom before the end of the world".

Christians have been inordinately proud of these persecutions of the first Christians and have written them up in great detail particularly those under Nero, Domitian, Trajan, Hadrian, Aurelius, Severus, and Maximin. Whether any of them really occurred, or if they did occur, were violently exaggerated, is an historical question not in the scope of this work. Suffice it to say that laws against religions and "heretics" appear to be conspicuous by their absence in Roman history. In fact, one can say with almost certainty, that the Romans never punished anybody because of his religion; but the shrill cry of Christian martyrdom has never ceased to impress people and make them believe almost anything.

Mosheim, who was a very candid Christian historian, was very cautious in admitting the persecutions—in fact, he says that as we have lost so much evidence on the matter, "very much is left wholly to conjecture". As a matter of both fact and interest, it is strange that Acts never mentions any Roman repressive laws against Christians, and certainly never mentions the persecutions under Nero, though Paul was in Rome at the time. And Christian works written admittedly later than Acts, like the Shepherd of Hermas (about 140 A.D.), considered by Origen to be "divinely inspired", appear to mention "Christ" only, never Jesus.

How did Tacitus get his information about the Christians of Nero's day, and whom it was they worshiped? It can be admitted that there were Christians when he wrote, and no doubt he asked them who was their God, and took it for granted that "Christus" had been put to death under Pontius Pilate. Or alternatively, he got the information from the very convenient archives which Christian writers assure us were always handy for him to consult. Drews quotes Dupuis: "Tacitus says what the legend says. Had he been speaking of the Brahmans he would have said in the same way, that they derived their name from a certain Brahma, who had lived in India, as there was a legend about him; yet Brahma would not on that account have lived as a man, as Brahma is merely the name of one of the three manifestations of the personified god-head. When Tacitus spoke thus in his account of Nero and the sect of the Christians, he merely gave the supposed etymology of the name, without caring in the least whether Christ had really existed or whether it was merely the name of the hero of some sacred legend. Such an inquiry was quite foreign to his work."

If Tacitus got the name of Christ from the "archives" how comes it that it is "Christ"? If Pilate, or his secretary—if he had one—or a scribe, had sent a report of the execution of Jesus to Rome, would not the name have been Jesus? Is not Jesus the name Pilate used on the cross? Although the four inscriptions differ from one another, they all use "Jesus" and never "Christ".

But did Tacitus use any archives? Drews points out that in H. Schiller's *History of the Roman Empire under Nero,* he says, "We are accustomed to hearing Tacitus praised as a model historian, and in many respects it may be true; but it does not apply to his criticism of his authorities and his own research, for they were astonishingly poor in Tacitus. *He never studied the archives".* And Drews adds that it is very improbable that any report of the execution of an obscure personage such as Jesus was would have been sent to Rome by Pilate.

All anyone is entitled to infer from the passage in Tacitus is that when he was writing about 110-120 A.D. there was a Christian sect, and that its members told him that they derived the word "Christian" from "Christ" who was put to death under Pontius Pilate. And there is no need to deny this. But what we are entitled to deny is that this constitutes absolute proof of the existence of a *man* called *Jesus.* Even the rest of the passage is under suspicion for critics are by no means so ready now to affirm the Neronian persecutions as they once were. They cannot visualize the "vast multitude" of Christians all of them hating mankind. And were they known then as "Christians"? The disciples were called Christians first at Antioch according to Acts, but the word "Christian" only occurs three times in the New Testament and was never, as far as I have been able to find out, used by Christians of *themselves,* but only by other people. The early Christians called themselves "brethren" or "believers" or "saints". Another point to note is that Tacitus nowhere else refers either to Christ or to Christians. This surely is very strange, as it is the case also with Josephus.

The early Christian Fathers who knew the work of Tacitus never quote this passage; for instance, Clement of Alexandria, who made it his business to quote all passages from profane authors on Christ, never quotes this particular notice. Even Eusebius missed it, though it is generally acknowledged that it was he who forged the passage in Josephus.

Not until the fifteenth century was it known, the century when Poggio Bracciolini first "discovered" the manuscript containing the *Annals*. It was a heaven-sent discovery, of course, for here was a pagan author testifying to *Christ*—not to Jesus as a man, but to Christ the Messiah. And the passage has proved even more of a "God-send" to our Rationalist historicists. They do not, as it happens, believe in Christ, but they do very much in the man Jesus— therefore, when Tacitus speaks of Christ the Messiah, it is excellent proof that he means Jesus the man.

Moreover the testimony of Josephus—also to Christ by the way —has proved fallacious or, at least, it is "suspect". And if you take away Josephus, there is almost nothing whatever left outside the New Testament which even hints at Jesus the man. Tacitus therefore must be held on to at all costs.

Unfortunately for the Historicists there appeared in 1878 a book entitled, *Tacitus and Bracciolini,* by W. J. Ross, in which the author, who was an excellent Latin scholar, tried to bring proof that the *Annals* were forged by Bracciolini. This was too much. Previously it was Robert Taylor in the *Diegesis* who gave weighty reasons why the particular passage in the *Annals* referring to Christ was undoubtedly a forgery; but Taylor was never accepted as an authority, though it may as well be said here that he was a very good one. His university career had been excellent, and he was, besides being an ordained clergyman of the Church of England, a fully qualified surgeon. He had also a great gift of languages, and was far ahead of his time as a Biblical critic. But an "infidel" priest who did three years in prison for blasphemy proved too much for the evangelical Christian England of the early part of the 19th century, and even for the non-believers of his day. Taylor claimed that there never was such a person as Jesus Christ, and thenceforth he was boycotted by all believers and by most unbelievers. But his *Diegesis* is, in spite of that, a very valuable work. One or two attempts were made to reply to it, but they are deservedly forgotten. And when Ross's work appeared, most critics either ignored it or lied about it.

Take as an instance this letter sent by the Rev. Mark Pattison—who in his day enjoyed a considerable reputation—to Prof. Churton Collins (*Life of J. C. C.*, page 77):

> In that absurd Tacitean criticism called, Tacitus and Bracciolini, which came out anonymously about two years ago, it was proved conclusively that the Annals were written by Poggio, in spite of the fact that one of the MSS of the Annals is at least as early as the XI century, a consideration which the critic whose name I forget did not think worth his attention.

Mr. Pattison had never read Ross's work, or if he had, he was deliberately hiding the truth from Collins. For the question of the dates of the MSS of the *Annals* is fully discussed on pp. 27-31 including, of course, the MS mentioned by Pattison. Ross says of it:

> The two oldest (MSS) are the "Second Florence" and the "Buda." It would seem that the "Second Florence", from the note at the end, dates back to the year 395, though the Benedictines in their Nouveau Traité de Diplomatique (Vol. iii, pp. 278-9) thought they recognized in it a Lombard writing of the tenth or eleventh century; Ernesti modified that to the ninth; others again changed it to the seventh and even the sixth; but it will be shown to satisfaction in the course of this treatise that it belongs to the fifteenth century. So with the Buda MS., believed

by Justus Lipsius to be as ancient as the Second Florence (which he thought with the Benedictines was of the tenth or eleventh century) was considered by James Gronovius to be very modern; and very modern it is, being traceable to a little after the same period as the Second Florence, namely, the fifteenth century. The First Florence, which was stated to have been found in the Abbey of Corvey, and which furnished the opening six books of the Annals as first given to the world by Beroaldus, is of an age that has never hitherto been determined; but that age will be shown, towards the close of this work, to be the first quarter of the sixteenth century.

The truth is that when the real existence of the man or God Jesus is in question, it is almost impossible to trust any statement by believers. It will be seen that Mr. Pattison gives no authority for his statement that "one of the MSS of the Annals is at least as early as the XI century"; nor for that matter does Dr. Conybeare who says in *Historical Christ* (p. 162) "that Poggio . . . lived in the fifteenth century, whereas our oldest MS of this part of Tacitus is of the eleventh century; it is now in the Laurentian Library". Perhaps Dr. Conybeare thinks that because the MS is in the Laurentian Library it is of the eleventh century; or perhaps he imagines it is just sufficient to say that the MS is of the eleventh century and he ought to be believed because he says so. We know perfectly well that "authorities" have given dates to the various MSS of the *Annals*; what some of us would like to see is their proofs, not their mere *ipse dixit*.

Let us examine the question a little further.

In the "Literary Guide" for February 1942, A. Robertson, says, it is a "calamity" that Rationalists should take up positions that are "a laughing stock" to the majority of scholars; and he cites as an example, "this matter of the authenticity or otherwise of Tacitus's Annals". He adds,

> The facts are simple, as anyone can discover who turns up the article on Tacitus in the Encyclopedia Britannica by W. J. Brodribb, a well known translator of Tacitus, and A. D. Godley, late Public Orator in Oxford University and editor of Tacitus's works. According to these two classical scholars, "the first six books of the Annals exist nowhere but in the first Medicean MS.,

and an attempt was made in 1878 to prove that the Annals are a forgery by Poggio Bracciolini, an Italian scholar of the fifteenth century, but their genuineness is confirmed by their agreement in various minute details with coins and inscriptions discovered since that period. Add to this the testimony of Jerome that Tacitus wrote in thirty books the lives of the Caesars, and the evidence of style and there can be no doubt that in the Annals we have a genuine work of Tacitus. The authors refer in a footnote to Vol. i of Furneaux's edition of the Annals for fuller discussion of the question.

This proves, according to Mr. Robertson, that "the formidable arguments of Ross and Hochart" have been replied to; and implies that anybody who still holds to the non-authenticity of the Annals is a "laughing stock". Unfortunately, Robertson forgot to point out that in the article on Tacitus in the Encyclopedia Britannica, W. J. Brodribb and A. D. Godley refer the reader to the 1884 edition of Furneaux's Tacitus, an edition that could not have replied to Hochart whose three books on the problem are dated 1885, 1890, and 1897. This omission Mr. Robertson hastily rectified by adding that the second edition of Furneaux was published in 1896—which still makes it impossible to reply to a book published in 1897. In any case, there is no reply whatever to either Ross or Hochart in the E. B. article. Certainly there is no reply to either in Furneaux's Tacitus as any reader can see for himself. In the 1896 edition the editor says,

> It has hitherto not been thought necessary for any editor of this work [the Annals] to establish its genuineness; but the recent attempts to prove it to be a forgery by Poggio Bracciolini in the fifteenth century, while they cannot be said to have found such acceptance as to necessitate a full discussion may make it desirable briefly to subjoin some external evidence to show that it is at least the work of an ancient author.

And in a note is added:

> Those who desire a more full statement and an examination of the first of these works (Ross) may be referred to an article in the Edinburgh Review of October 1878.

Ross is, as seen by these extracts from Furneaux, not answered in any way, for the reader is sent to the "Edinburgh Review" for an examination of his theory. What Furneaux does is to take some names from the *Annals* and to tell us that they are confirmed by coins and inscriptions discovered since Poggio's time: "None of these facts could have been derived from any other literature known to us; all are confirmed by coins and inscriptions of which Bracciolini and his contemporaries must have been ignorant. It seems hardly worth while to pursue this subject further".

Furneaux's "must" in this passage may well be so; but he offers no evidence for it. And as for his impatience with the objectors—"it seems hardly worth while", etc., that surely is a matter of opinion. It certainly is worth while to some of us, and we should much have liked such a scholar to deal, not with an argument untouched by Ross, but with Ross's own arguments.

As I have said, Ross was a fine Latin scholar, and a good deal of his argument is concerned with the subject of *style*. Given the Latin of Tacitus' *Histories*, why is the Latin of the *Annals* so different? Why is it so full of errors no Roman with his Latin background could possibly have made? Over and over again Ross shows how different the style of the *Annals* is from that of the *Histories*, and how often words and phrases are used in the *Annals* which are used by Bracciolini in his works which have come down to us. It is very difficult for a non-Latin reader to follow Ross in all this, but the very full quotations given in his book will enable anyone familiar with Latin to follow the argument. For example:

> Narcissus, addressing Claudius in the eleventh book of the Annals says: "he did not *now* mean to charge him"—that is, Silius, "with adulteries"; "nec *nunc* adulteria objecturum" (XI.30). The language used seems to be very good language. A Roman historian, though, would have written, "nec *tunc*": he could not have fallen into the error of failing to define time in reference to himself when ascribing words to persons, any more than he could have failed to vary the grammar to the accusative and infinitive. This elementary principle in Latin composition is known, (as Lord Macaulay would have said) "to every school boy". It was, certainly, well known to such an accomplished "grammaticus" as Bracciolini; and for the very simple reason that he adheres to it on all other occasions. His neglect of it in this

instance is as strong a proof as any that can be advanced, of his forgery: it makes the forgery the more obvious, his slip not being accidental, but intentional: it is a deliberate violation of a rule that must never be infringed; but as a countryman will sometimes run after a jack-o'-lantern, till running after it he finds himself in a burying ground, so Bracciolini suffered himself to be misled by his literary will-o'-the wisp—alliteration: therefore he preferred writing "*nec nunc*" instead of "*nec tunc;*" he therefore did that which was fatal to the work which he wanted to palm off upon the world as the composition of a Roman, because a Roman would not have done this, because he could not have done it . . . (Ross, op. cit., pp. 283-284).

This is only one of scores of the proofs that Ross brings against the Latin of the *Annals*—a Latin that no Roman could have used, but which was just the kind of thing a forger of the 15th century familiar with the Latin language would have done. An Englishman might be a very good French scholar, for instance, and yet easily make a number of mistakes in French phraseology which no Frenchman could possibly make simply because thinking in that language follows a different set of rules to thinking in English. No Frenchman could write "blanche rose", he would be forced to write "rose blanche".

In this connection, W. B. Smith in his *Ecce Deus* has something to say which, as far as I know, has never been answered by those who believe that the *Annals* are genuine.

He deals lengthily with the one passage regarding "Christ"—Ross deals with the whole of the *Annals*—and Prof. Smith is even prepared to agree it is genuine for "it proves nothing that is worth debate". All the same, "it reads very much like fabrication, or at least emandation, of a Christian hand". And among other criticisms against the passage, he discusses the "vast multitude" of Christians who, according to Tacitus, were in Rome in Nero's time.

Smith says that this is "an exaggeration more than Tacitean, and not at all paralleled by the *iacuit immensa strages* of An., vi, 19, and we should fix attention solely on one purely stylistic consideration, the expression *humani generis*. The whole sentence has sorely vexed the wits of commentators, but especially

these words. Muretus (following Faernus?) boldly strikes out
the word *humani,* and understands by *generis* the Christian race!
Acidalius sees that this cannot be, and accordingly alters *humani*
into *Romani*: they were condemned for hatred of the Roman
race! Indeed, it seems almost impossible that Tacitus should have
written *humani generis. Everywhere* else he writes *generis
humani.* It is in the last degree improbable that such a con-
summate stylist as Tacitus would here just this once deviate from
his lifelong habit, especially as the inverse order produces with
the foregoing word a disagreeable hiatus: *odio humani.* No very
delicate ear is needed to perceive that *odio generis* is a much
pleasanter collocation. Besides the whole weight of Tacitean related usage falls against the inversion . . . we may affirm, then,
with much confidence that the inversion in question of itself
stamps the passage as not probably from the hand of Tacitus."

The interesting thing about this criticism is that it is exactly
on the lines of Ross, and Smith is not inclined in the least to
agree with Ross. I doubt very much if, up to the time of writing
Ecce Deus, he had read *Tacitus and Bracciolini.* At all events,
this question of Tacitean usage and style is certainly at the very
heart of the problem of the authenticity of the *Annals* and it
simply cannot be answered in the offhand way so beloved by
the Historicists.

Moreover, it must not be forgotten that it is not part of the
mythic case to maintain the forgery of the whole of the *Annals.*
All we are concerned with is the one passage mentioning "Christ"
—a passage which could just as easily have been inserted by a
Christian forger as the one inserted into the text of Josephus. Yet,
curiously enough, while the Rationalist who believes in a real
Jesus is prepared to throw over the passage in the Jewish historian, he gets quite angry when the passage in the Roman
historian is called in question.

It was, I think, Robert Taylor in his *Diegesis* who first pointed
out that this part of Tacitus was a forgery "from no disposition",
he adds, "to give offense to those who may have as good reasons,
and probably better, for esteeming it to be unquestionably genuine, from no wish to deduct from Christianity one tittle or
iota of its fair or probable evidence, but from a consideration

solely of *the facts of the case,* which I here subjoin; and which,
if they shall have less weight in the judgment of the reader than
of the author: the reader will reap the advantage of holding the
opposite conclusion, not only in concurrence with the decision of
the wisest and best men in the world, but on that surer ground
of satisfaction with which every conviction is held, after men
have been so faithful to themselves as to weigh the objections
that can be alleged against it".

Taylor enunciates twenty arguments against the authenticity
of the passage in question, the principal ones being that it
would have served the purpose of Christian quotation better
than any other in all the writings of Tacitus; it is not mentioned
by Tertullian, who quotes largely from Tacitus, nor by Clemens
Alexandrinus who made it his business to quote all pagan writers
on Christianity, nor by Eusebius who simply could not have
missed it if it had been in existence in his day, nor by any
writer whatever before the fifteenth century. Nor does Tacitus
anywhere else in his writings ever allude again either to Christ
or Christianity.

It cannot be too strongly urged that the first publication of
"any part of the Annals of Tacitus", says Taylor, "was by Jo-
hannes de Spire, at Venice, in the year 1468. His imprint being
made from a single manuscript, in his own power and possession
only, and purporting to have been written in the eighth century.
From this manuscript, which none but the most learned would
know of, none but the most curious would investigate, and none
but the most interested would transcribe, or be allowed to transcribe; and that too, in an age and country, when and where to
have suggested but a *doubt* against the authenticity of any
document which the authorities had once chosen to adopt as
evidence of Christianity, would have subjected the conscientious
skeptic to the fagot; from *this,* all other manuscripts and printed
copies of the works of Tacitus are derived."

These arguments of Robert Taylor were almost completely ignored for 40 years, when W. J. Ross began his own examination;
and even he would have been also ignored but for the fact that
the advocacy of the myth theory of Jesus has forced defenders
to fight for the authenticity of Tacitus at any price. For if Tacitus

goes, where else in "pagan" contemporary literature can be found any mention whatever of Jesus?

Was Taylor right when he said what he did about the origins of the *Annals* as we now have this work? It is difficult to get clearly from Furneaux exactly what were these origins. But he admits that the manuscript called the Second Medicean is in Lombard characters "generally assigned to the eleventh century, and thought by Ritter to have been one of the many transcripts of works of ancient authors made at that date in the great monastery of Monte Cassino. . . . Nothing appears to have been known of the history of this manuscript until the time of Poggio Bracciolini who received it at Rome in 1427 from Nicola Nicoli at Florence". Furneaux does not, it will be noticed here, give us any names of the people who have "generally assigned" the MS to the eleventh century; we must take his word for it, though some of us at least would have liked just a little more information on the problem. Who have "generally assigned" the MS to the eleventh century? What were their qualifications? Has no one a right to question them?

It appears also that the characters of this manuscript were very faded and indistinct and that "many other MSS of this portion of the works of Tacitus exist, but none of them claims any earlier date than the middle of the fifteenth century. Many are known not to have been direct transcripts of the Medicean and very few are even supposed to be such". The title *Annals* was given no earlier than 1544 A.D. by Rhenanus, and the first intimation that such a work was in existence came from Ruodolphus, "a learned monk" of Falda in Hesse Cassel, writing in the ninth century. All this really means is that a monk, about whom we appear to know very little, and who is called learned, I suppose, because he could write, cites Tacitus as speaking of the Visurgis and "would therefore appear to have known a manuscript containing" the *Annals*—"containing these books", says Furneaux. "The next intimation," he continues, "is from Poggio Bracciolini who writes in 1425 on a communication made to him from Germany respecting some unknown works of Tacitus said to be preserved at Hersfeld, near Fulda. Nothing further is known till 1509." And this kind of "evidence" is considered by our Histori-

cists as absolutely annihilating to the claims of, say, Taylor and
Hochart, and of course, Ross, that the *Annals* are forgeries!

Furneaux has the greatest difficulty in giving a coherent account
of the origin of the *Annals,* and spends very little time or space
on the task; and he fobs off the reader with a reference to the
"Edinburgh Review" article dealing with Ross. Had this article
really contained a devastating reply to Ross, is it conceivable that
Furneaux would not have quoted it? Would he not have tri-
umphantly produced the gist of such a smashing victory over
Ross?

As for Hochart, there is no answer whatever in the whole of
Furneaux's Tacitus to that formidable critic. I invite readers to
get the work for themselves and they will be able to judge how
much truth there is in the claim that the Encyclopedia Britannica
and Furneaux have between them demolished Taylor, Ross, and
Hochart.

In his work, *Jesus the Nazarene—Myth or History,* which is
strongly on the side of the Historicists, Prof. M. Goguel devotes
nearly six pages to Tacitus, and does his utmost to squeeze some
semblance of authority for the disputed passage. He admits that
the famous letter written by Pliny—if genuine—is "evidence of
the cult of Christ, but it does not say explicitly whether He was
conceived to be a personage having lived on earth or a being of
entirely spiritual nature". What Goguel means by the latter I am
by no means clear; but the "testimony" of Tacitus, he declares, is
"more explicit". That may be so, but Goguel finds it exceedingly
difficult to ascertain exactly how Tacitus got his information about
"Christ"—the word "Christ" proving that he could not have got
it from the Jews. And Goguel insists he could not have got it
from the Christians either.

And curious to relate, Goguel also considers that Tacitus could
not have got his information from the (convenient) "archives".
Where did he get it from then? Well, "Goetz has surmised that
Tacitus obtained his information from his friend Pliny the
Younger". As, however, Pliny looked upon Christianity as "an
innocent superstition", while Tacitus "calls it execrable", Goguel does not agree with Goetz. He therefore brings forward his
own explanation. It is based on "a fact" which is "certain". I

should have thought that any fact was certain; but it appears that "Tacitus knew of a document which was neither Jewish nor Christian, which connected Christianity with the Christ crucified by Pontius Pilate. The importance of this observation," gravely adds Goguel, "does not require to be emphasized." I should think not indeed. It is *very* important. For, if Tacitus used an *authentic* document connecting Christianity with Christ crucified by Pontius Pilate there is an end of all argument respecting Jesus. Jesus as a man is proved up to the hilt.

But Goguel, who is most lavish in quoting all sorts of "authorities" even when he does not agree with them, gives no authority whatever for his statement that Tacitus knew of this particular document. The statement comes from Goguel without the shadow of a proof of any kind. It is, so to speak, quietly slipped into his argument, and the reader, if he is lazily indolent in demanding evidence, may quite easily swallow "the importance of this observation". Or to put it in another way, the "observation" is just so much balderdash.

Goguel is obliged in any case to admit that "what the Roman authors say about Jesus and Christianity amounts to very little indeed. Only the testimony of Tacitus is plainly incompatible with the theory of a Christ entirely ideal". But Tacitus, genuine or not, does speak of Christ, and not Jesus, and Christ must be "entirely ideal"—if he is Christ.

I have dealt with Tacitus at length deliberately, for over and over again we, who take up the Mythicist position, are accused of avoiding the testimony of the Roman historian. I deny that there is any testimony at all, even if the passage is genuine. It is obviously only a report from believers in "Christ", who certainly is not shown by Tacitus to have been a "man". Though I am entirely with Ross and his theory that the *Annals* were forged by Bracciolini, my case against Tacitus does not rest on this, but on the fact that the particular passage describing the Neronian persecutions and "Christ" is as clear a forgery as the famous and notorious passage in Josephus.

The late John M. Robertson was always careful in expressing any *definite* opinion on the authenticity or otherwise of the *Annals*, and he sent his readers to Hochart to study the facts of the case. But nothing could exceed his contempt for those who, faced by these formidable arguments and others, refused to deal with them. In *Jesus and Judas* (p. 169) he says,

> Prof. Smith in his *Ecce Deus* advances (as does Prof. Drews) a crushing array of arguments against the authenticity of the passage in Tacitus concerning the burning of Christians by Nero —arguments which no scrupulous historical critic would ignore. But from the latest "biographers" of Jesus there comes no mention of, no attempt at an answer to, the arguments against them. "Theirs not to reason". Their simple task is to asseverate.

It is only fair to add that one "Mythicist", Thomas Whittaker, makes it quite clear that he "does not feel any doubt about any of the writings ascribed to Tacitus. The literary character of those writings is perfectly in accordance with the tradition. The style, only slightly individualized at first, becomes steadily more difficult and 'Tacitean' from the *Dialogue on Orators* which is said to be the earliest, to the *Annals* which is said to be the latest, work. . . . Some details in Tacitus have received unexpected antiquarian corroboration." Whittaker concludes that the famous passage on the Christians "is perfectly consistent". No forger, he thinks, could have assumed the style and tone in which Tacitus describes his contempt as a Roman for the oriental sects invading Rome.

The truth is that Whittaker uses the same kind of argument which the defenders of the forged passage in Josephus have adopted. No one could forge a certain style, everything said appears to be in harmony, unexpected corroboration has been discovered in support, and so on. As a matter of fact Sir Max Beerbohm has shown in his incomparable *Christmas Garland* that it is possible to imitate almost any writer, not only with "authentic" style, but also the way in which the writer *thinks*. And it would have been far more convincing if the "unexpected antiquarian corroboration" had been given in detail. In any case, while it may have convinced Whittaker, it may not have convinced others. He comes again later in his work to the point and admits that knowing what we do know of the age of Bracciolini, "forgery of the *Annals* was a suggestion not quite devoid of plausibility" and he does give "one undesigned coincidence", which seemed to him "altogether beyond the subtlety ascribable to a humanist of the fifteenth century". (page 24, note.) The coincidence noted, however, deals with the impossibility of the forgery of the *Annals* as a whole. This is a matter of small moment to the Mythicist. It is purely of academic interest. The point raised by Robert Taylor and the Mythicists is whether the passage referring to "Christ" is or is not a forgery. What "unexpected antiquarian corroboration" has been discovered about this particular passage? I have not so far been given or seen one such reference. In fact, even Whittaker has to admit the "absolute want of plausibility" of the charge made in the text against the early Christians. Not only that, he says that "to suppose that he [Tacitus] may have derived the information from the 'Roman Archives' is perfectly gratuitous".

Needless to say the "multitude of Christians" does not mean Christians but "Messianic Jews" according to Whittaker. But it does appear to me quite logical to infer that if Tacitus derived his information from the Christians of his time he would have said "Messianic Jews" and not Christians. And if, as Whittaker believed, there was a "pre-Jesus" cult, why should there not have been a "multitude" of Christians in Rome? In fact, I am rather surprised that he throws over "Christians" for "Messianic Jews".

But the point to note is the way in which such a strenuous defender of the authenticity of the passage in Tacitus has to throw overboard what it plainly says, and substitute his own explanations; and that is the position of the Historicists in general. They are acute enough to see that with Tacitus gone there is no authentic reference in non-Christian testimony to the existence of Jesus as a man, let alone as a God; and it is not inexcusable that they want to hold on to the Roman historian at any price—even of logic and common sense.

Prof. Drews closes his discussion of the matter with a characteristic quotation from the German theologian, J. Weiss, a thorough believer in the historicity of Jesus Christ. Weiss says:

> There is no such thing as a convincing witness in profane literature. What could Josephus or Tacitus do for us? They could

at the most merely show that at the end of the first century not only the Christians, but their tradition and Christ-myths, were known at Rome. When it originated, however, and how far it was based on truth, could not be discovered from Tacitus or Josephus.

And Drews quotes also the Pastor Kurt Delbruck, also very orthodox:

What does it matter whether or no Tacitus wrote it? He could only have received the information, a hundred years after the time, from people who told it to others. It matters nothing to us, therefore, whether the passage is genuine or not. The historical personality of Jesus Christ is proved only by the fact that the earliest Christian community recognized its savior in him who had once been alive. *We have no further historical documents.* (page 56.)

Pastor Delbruck would find no favor with our British Historicists.

CHAPTER VIII

Some Sources of the
Jesus Myth

IN THE FOREGOING CHAPTERS I HAVE TRIED TO
show how small is the evidence for the existence of a real Jesus,
but it is necessary now to face the one question: How or why did
the story of Jesus come to be written?

Why should anyone, or any number of persons, deliberately set
down an impossible story of a God basing it on the life of someone who never had an existence? We can understand a Dickens
writing about a Mr. Pickwick or a Cervantes giving us the story
of Don Quixote. They both wrote fiction—fiction partly for en-
tertainment, and partly for didactic reasons. And there never was
the question of a cult of religious Pickwickians or religious followers of Quixote. But in the case of Jesus, do we understand
from unbelievers that his story was deliberately forged to give
power to priests?

It seems to me that those of us who disbelieve in the existence
of the man Jesus have really no need to account for his story, or
the beginnings of the Christian Church, or even to show how
they both originated. We are given a religion called Christianity,
taught us from almost babyhood, and we are told that it is true

and must be implicitly believed, and we are threatened with eternal damnation if we doubt. This religion comes in with our birth, follows us all our life, and does its utmost to be in at our death. It is practically impossible for the average person to escape it. Yet, when some of us ask for evidence for its truth or necessity, every effort is made to fob us off with statements clearly not evidence at all, accompanied with the rather brazen request to account for Jesus and Christianity in any other way than that taught by the Church. In fact, it is suggested that it is *we* who must give a coherent account of the origins of the Christian Church.

I fail to see any reason for this. I disbelieve entirely in the reality of Osiris, Horus, Isis, and Amen Ra, to say nothing of Jupiter, Apollo, and Venus. If the religions associated with their names were prevalent in England, were indeed the State Religions taught us from childhood, and I pointed out that there was not a scrap of evidence that these Gods existed either as deities or plain men and women, why should I be expected to account for them or show how they originated? That is a task for their followers. All I am concerned with is to show that the evidence brought forward to prove that they at one time habited this earth is completely lacking, and belief in them is just crude superstition. I am quite certain that the average Christian priest would resent having to show what were the beginnings of Jupiter and the rest when he protested his utter disbelief in their reality at any time.

I have shown that the Jewish belief in the existence of a great Jew called Jesus is entirely without any support in their own writings; that the Christian gospels are a hopeless conglomeration of sheer superstition and inconsistencies, and were certainly unknown for over a hundred years after the supposed death of their hero; and that there is no evidence worth considering in non-Christian sources. In other words, I claim that the Christian churches and their more or less believing followers, including the Jews, Mohammedans, and Rationalists who believe that Jesus, while not being God Almighty, undoubtedly lived as a man—"doing good"—have been entirely unable to produce any evidence for their beliefs. And I could finish this book here without in any way going into the question of "origins", having concluded my examination of Jesus as a myth.

But to make my work more complete I propose doing what should have been done by believers and indicate, as far as I am able, at least some sources of the myth of Jesus. Coming as it did when, at long last, the impact of Greek and Roman civilization was beginning to have some effect on the beliefs of ordinary people, it was only natural that one story of the gods might emerge from the welter of deities then believed in. It is not easy to account for the fact that eventually the Jesus myth did gain precedence over, say, the Mithra myth, but the causes, whatever they were, are quite understandable in the light of ordinary human history. They required no "Divine" interference—as Gibbon convincingly showed in his immortal work.

Christianity spread, but it never really conquered. It never conquered Buddhism, or Hinduism, or Islam. It never even conquered Judaism. But perhaps one reason for its success is that it quietly absorbed so much "paganism" that it was never particularly difficult to make converts.

In the story of Jesus we have almost an epitome of the lives of other gods. Just as I have shown that in Mary we have much of the characteristics of Pagan Goddesses, so in the story of her "son" we find all sorts of ideas and incidents taken from Paganism—and quite a number from Judaism considered by Christians to be the fulfillment of Old Testament "prophecies".

This does not mean, of course, that the resemblances are absolutely exact. These things must be looked at with a sense of proportion. Obviously, the Babylonians and the Assyrians and the Greeks never worshiped in exactly the same way, but it would not be difficult to show that certain underlying ideas in their religions were the same, however much they appeared to be different in detail.

John M. Robertson, Prof. Drews, Dujardin, and Whittaker, were all certain that there was a pre-Jesus cult. That is, that years before the emergence of Christianity as a fully-formed religion, there was worshiped a "Jesus", possibly a Savior God of some kind, in a "mystery" religion in Palestine. Nearly all religions had their "mysteries"—just as in these days the Freemasons, the Rosicrucians, and Occultists in general, do their utmost to prevent their "secrets" becoming widespread.

Augustine himself was obliged to admit that "the same thing which is now called the Christian religion existed among the Ancients. They have begun to call Christian the true religion which existed before." But one need not go quite as far back for something of the same kind of admission. In *The Bible is True* (1934) by that pious Fundamentalist, Sir Charles Marston, we have, "As knowledge increases, it may prove that Christianity, although connected to the Jewish religion, was actually the fulfillment of far more ancient religions than the one instituted in the days of Moses". And Brodie Sanders, in his translation of Dujardin's *Ancient History of the God Jesus* adds, "And in the context the writer connects such 'ancient religions' with 'the mystery religions practiced six or seven centuries before Christ'". Sir Charles flatters himself on being an archaeologist and excavator, and if his researches in Palestine force him to confess this much, it must be apparent that the thesis of a pre-Jesus cult is at least plausible, however difficult to substantiate with mathematical accuracy.

Whatever may be the ideas of Jesus in the more cultured modern world, throughout the centuries and in official circles Jesus is a Sacrificial God. "He died for humanity" is the glorious creed of Christianity, according to its votaries. He allowed himself to be put to death so that all might be saved. He was God Almighty himself come down on earth to die for us sinners. Jesus, in short, was—and is—the Savior of the World.

But this "Savior" idea permeated the ancient religions. It is one of their greatest characteristics. Primitive man appears always to be sacrificing something to his god, either in appeasement of the divine anger, or as a gift in thanks for blessings received. Altars were loaded with the finest of fruits, vegetables, and flowers; or the most beautiful animals were slaughtered; and it even came to the killing of human beings, and the most loved ones at that. In fact, when things became very bad, such as terrible defeat in war, or a devastating hurricane or flood, even a beloved king would be sacrificed. There is not the slightest doubt that human sacrifices were made all over the world and that the idea at the back of the Christian claim that Jesus is the "Supreme Sacrifice", must be admitted by all impartial readers.

In the Bible the sacrifices of Cain and Abel are typical examples; and one of the most pathetic stories of Abraham is the one in which he was quite prepared to kill his son Isaac, and Isaac was quite prepared to die, just to show their infinite faith in the Almighty. We are so used to the slaughter of animals even to the point of extermination—look at the way in which the bison nearly disappeared in America—that no one gives a thought to the animal substituted for Isaac; but its sacrifice is typical of the terrific toll taken from the animal world to propitiate imaginary gods.

Even at this day, the eldest sons of Jews have to be "redeemed" by cash payment to a priest, as they are on birth "devoted" to God. And in a race like the Japanese, the idea of committing suicide or sacrificing one's life for some imaginary reason connected with their "divine" Emperor, is a mere commonplace.

The supreme sin for Christians was the disobedience of Adam in the Garden of Eden. Had this not been chosen it would have been quite easy to get some other excuse for following the prevalent idea that their God had to be either a Sacrifice, or sacrificed, or both. Dujardin gives an excellent summary of this sacrificial idea and proves that "Christianity derived from a historic event such as a judicial execution, is not a religion. But Christianity derived from the expiatory sacrifice is a religion in the true line of religious evolution". It is impossible to think of Jesus as a mere man because this would furnish "the great religion of the Christ with a god who is not a spiritual being but a man among men" and Jesus, according to Dujardin, was neither a historical nor a mythical being but a "spiritual being". And this is the idea which permeates Paul (or most of the documents attributed to Paul) as well as Gnosticism.

J. M. Robertson insisted that some parts of the Gospel story were manipulated transcripts from a "mystery" drama; and Dujardin so far agrees that he says his task in writing his book was "to establish from the documents that the death of Jesus was originally, not a judicial execution, but an expiatory sacrifice practiced ritually and periodically in a sacred drama". The death of Jesus is then "not a historical assertion" but "a theological doctrine".

Dujardin notes, as so many other writers have noted, that in the documents written before the Gospels—as Christian writers maintain—the Epistles of Paul, though Paul constantly refers to the crucifixion of Jesus, he gives no *details* of this, never refers to the Jews who took part in the "drama", nor to Pilate, the Romans, Herod, or Judas, in fact "there is no trace in St. Paul of the hearings, of the conviction, and of the judicial execution. On the contrary, we find throughout the idea of an expiatory sacrifice . . . (Paul) knew only of a rite of sacrifice—that alone, and nothing else".

Crucifixion, or to put it more accurately "hanging on the tree", is a mode of punishment mentioned often in the Old Testament and was obviously practised as part of the expiatory sacrifice in ancient Palestine. At first, no doubt, the unlucky victim had to die; later a "substitute" was allowed—an echo of which is found in the story of Barabbas. This word in Aramaic means "son of the Father" (or "son of a Father") exactly as Christ was the Son of the Father. J. M. Robertson points out that in Matt. xxvii, 16, 17, the ancient reading was *Jesus* Barabbas, and that the story is "one of those elaborate irrelevancies which leap to the eye in a narrative so destitute of essentials" and "that it carries a curious corroboration to the myth theory". (*The Historical Jesus*, p. 170).

That the story of Barabbas is quite unhistorical is admitted by that great champion of an historical Jesus, the late Abbé Loisy, one of the greatest, if not the greatest of modern theologians. He found it difficult to understand how such a story ever got into the sacred records. But it is easily explainable on the myth theory —"a sane solution" concluded Robertson, "where the historical theory can offer none. . . . The conception of Jesus as sacrificed lies at the core of early Christian cult-propaganda." He is supported by Sir James Frazer in the *Golden Bough*—"The custom of sacrificing the son for the father was common, if not universal, among Semitic peoples". And Frazer admits that the Jewish Passover, which is kept by Jews in commemoration of their bondage in Egypt, was "originally a sacrifice of firstlings, human and animal, the former being probably most prevalent in times of disaster", as Robertson puts it.

The pre-Jesus cult is a problem difficult to solve because it was, as Dujardin says, "a mystery religion, like the religion of the Great Mother and Attis, like that of Adonis, of Osiris, of Demeter, of Dionysus". It had to be secret because it was practised side by side with Judaism, always a most intolerant religion. Adds Dujardin:

> All the mystery religions have a great father-god, and below him a second god who is a son-god. Here the great father-god is the Lord Jahveh who, as at Jerusalem, has become simply "God". And below him, in the body of equivocal monotheism, is a second god who is an ancient Palestinian Baal conquered by Jahveh.

In an interesting excursus on the names given to Jesus such as Christos, the Annointed, the Messiah, the Savior, and others, Dujardin maintains that the title of Messiah was rarely given by the Jewish rabbis to their expected liberator—it is "mainly the Christians who state that the Jews expected 'the Messiah'. The Jewish notion of Messianism attributed to the name of Christ was the main cause of the Judaization of Christianity when, in order to take the place left vacant by Judaism, which appeared to have perished with Jerusalem in the year 70, it sought to make Christianity the heir of 'the New Israel' ".

I have already referred to the fact that Jesus was called Icthus, the Fish. There is no suggestion in the Gospels or in Paul that he ever was considered a Fish, "but the fact that," says Dujardin, "he preserved traces of an animal form is for the historian of religions one of the surest indications of a remote origin". Joshua of the Old Testament was called the "son of Nun" that is the "son of a fish". Jesus is the modern form for the Hebrew Joshua, in Greek always Ihsous, and in Hebrew, in various spellings among which is Ieshou. Now it cannot be repeated too often that almost all the names given to persons in the Old Testament are *artificial*, they were deliberately designed to fit the person to whom they were given. On this point the article on "Names" in the *Encyclopedia Biblica* leaves no doubt whatever. Joshua

means "Savior" or "Salvation" and it is no mere coincidence that
the same name was given to Jesus. It is absurd to imagine that a
real mother should have chosen this name by accident, that
she should have stumbled upon it by sheer luck. Even Prof.
Guignebert (as quoted by Dujardin) has to say, "One must admit
that chance was singularly far-seeing, if it alone bestowed the
name of Succor of God or Savior, on a child who was thirty
years later to reveal the destiny of saving men". And he admits
the possibility that "the name of Jesus was in truth a title of
Christ corresponding to his divine function . . . and not the
name of a man". In other words Guignebert, who is one of the
strongest defenders of Jesus as a man, appears to be quite uncertain as to his real name.

Dujardin gives seven "coincidences"—How came it that Jesus
the Savior-God was given the name of Jesus which means Savior?
Why is this name that of one of the old Palestinian Gods? How
does it happen that Barabbas, who stood before Pilate with Jesus,
was also called "Jesus the Son of the Father"? Why is Jesus called
the "Nazarene", a word which has nothing to do with Nazareth
where he was supposed to be born [except, of course, when his
birthplace is given as Bethlehem in "fulfillment" of an Old Testament prophecy]. Why was Jesus called Icthus the Fish—and the
old god of Palestine, Joshua, the "son of a Fish"? Why was Jesus
crucified at a place called Golgotha which, like Nazareth, was
unknown before being mentioned in the Gospels? Was Golgotha
a form of Gilgal, that is, a megalithic circle called also a cromlech? If Jesus was crucified on a cromlech then we have here
proof of the survival of an ancient cult, for according to Dujardin,
"Joshua the ancient patriarch, appears to have been a Palestinian
god, having his seat at a gilgal".

Was there then an old Palestinian God called Joshua, later
turned into the famous successor to Moses by the compilers of
the Old Testament? It can well be so, but I must confess that
the evidence produced by Dujardin does not seem to me conclusive.

Noting the fact that "the Joshua (Jesus) of the book so named
is quite certainly unhistorical, and that the narrative concerning
him is a late fabrication" (*Pagan Christs,* p. 163), John M.

Robertson "divines" that Joshua is like Samson and Moses, an ancient deity with several attributes of the Sun-God. His celebrated feat of causing the sun to stand still and the moon to stay "until the people had avenged themselves upon their enemies" is paralleled in other religions. Godfrey Higgins in his *Anacalypsis* gives particulars of how Bacchus "arrested the course of the sun and moon", and a Chinese legend has a similar story. The disciples of Buddha were also able to do the same thing.

Whether Joshua's mother was Miriam—that is, Mary—and therefore "Joshua the son of Miriam" is much the same as "Jesus the son of Mary", it is difficult to say with certainty. What is certain, however, is the sacrificial idea which permeates Christianity and which undoubtedly permeated Judaism. The Sacrificed Savior-God, in fact, is a characteristic of dozens of pagan religions, and it is not surprising that it should form such a strong feature of the Christian religion. That human sacrifices were made either to appease a God, or for some "magical" reason supposed to be known only to the priests of the cult, can be seen from a study of the instances given by Robertson in *Pagan Christs* or in the *Golden Bough* of Sir James Frazer. There is no doubt that these things were done up to recent times, and may indeed still be the practice of some savage tribes. How can they be connected with the story of Jesus as the "Supreme Sacrifice", which some of us hold never took place at all? Robertson says:

> Only one hypothesis will meet the whole case. The different narratives testify to the existence of a *ritual or rituals* of crucifixion or quasi-crucifixion, in variants of which there had figured the two procedures of breaking the legs of the victim and giving him a narcotic. . . . We find the psychological clue in the hypothesis of a known ritual of a crucified Savior God, who had for universally-recognized reasons to appear to suffer as a willing victim.

Robertson gives very many details of the practice of various rituals having as their basis the sacrificial idea, and he has little difficulty in showing how the ideas behind the ritual have survived in the Christian story. Just as among the various primitive tribes the victim of the ritual was eaten, so we have the formula, at least, in the words of Jesus: "Take eat, this is my body."; or

"Drink ye all of it for this is my blood"; or "I am the bread of
life . . . the bread which I will give is my flesh, for the life of the
world . . . except ye eat the flesh of the Son of Man and drink
his blood, ye have not the life in yourself. . . . He that eateth
my flesh and drinketh my blood abideth in me and I in him." As
the flesh of Jesus was *not* eaten, according to the Gospel story,
we have bread substituted and the magical ceremony of changing
it into flesh performed by the priest of the ritual these days, the
Roman Catholic priest.

Did the Christians who made up the story of the "Last Supper"
believe that a piece of bread really changed into a "living" Christ,
or did they look upon the story as a "mystery" only to be solved
by a priest; or, if it is looked upon as wholly "mystical", or a
"mystery", or "symbolic", is not the story "gratuitously fantastic"?

Among the Jews there is a feast called Purim held in honor of
Esther the Persian Jewish queen who saved her people from extermination by Haman. It is kept fairly peaceably nowadays, but
there was a time when it was not so kept. The story as given in
the Bible is quite unhistorical—see the article in the *Encyclopedia
Biblica* on Esther. Mordecai certainly is the Babylonian god Marduk or Merodach, while Esther is Astarte or Ishtar. Says Robertson:

> When criticism has done its worst . . . it will be found that
> there remains clearly open the inference that certain details of
> the crucifixion myth are drawn from some old Semitic rite re-
> sembling the Sacaea, not by way of Purim in its evemerised
> Jewish form, but in a simpler form, in which there was no Ishtar
> or Merodach.

Personally I do not think it matters whether in Purim there is
anything analogous to the "sacrifice" of Jesus. All I feel constrained
to show is that there were rites and ceremonies among the Jews
in which some "sacrifice" is clearly indicated. Were not Saul's sons
"sacrificed"? Was not the king of the imaginary city Ai "hanged
on a tree", as well as were other kings? If as Robertson maintains,
"the curse of God" means "devoted to God", and if as Robertson
Smith admits in his *Religion of the Semites,* that "all executions
became sacrificial", we need not be surprised that when the Gos-

pels were being compiled Jesus was made the "Supreme Sacrifice", just as he was made God's Only Begotten Son.

Even in these days, pious Jews "sacrifice" a cock on the eve of the Day of Atonement, just as among the peoples of the Congo we find a similar ceremony. And Robertson devotes a whole chapter to proving "the Eucharist in Orthodox Judaism" in his *Pagan Christs*. The upshot of his investigations and those of Dujardin is simply that if we find the idea of sacrifice and a cult-drama permeating primitive and pagan religions, if the stories of the deaths of Dionysus, Attis, Osiris, Demeter, and other deities, run so much on the same lines, "it could hardly be otherwise with the Passion of Jesus". Concludes Dujardin: "It is therefore evident that most of the episodes of his being put to death, though untenable as history, are perfectly explicable as legendary transpositions of ritual episodes; and what is true of the crucifixion is equally true of the resurrection".

For Dupuis the story of Jesus is but a variant of what is roughly called the Sun-Myth. It had been told before with other gods as the heroes, and under the name of Christianity we get substantially the same adventures of the solar myth with his twelve apostles who were merely personifications of the twelve signs of the Zodiac.

These twelve Apostles were supposed to rule over the twelve tribes of Israel, and if the reader cares to take up his Bible and turn to Genesis, chapter 49, he will find an excellent description of the twelve sons of Jacob mostly in the very terms of the Zodiac. Reuben is the first born, "unstable as water"; surely here Aquarius is indicated. This sign is shown generally as a man with a pitcher of water and its monogram as two zigzag lines.

Simon and Levi are coupled together, just like Pisces, the two fish. And what is meant by "Instruments of cruelty are in their habitations"? Robert Taylor says "the instruments of fishing nets, hooks, spears, and harpoons are necessarily associated with the business of fishing".

Judah "is a lion's whelp", that is, the sign of Leo; and it is in this sign that the sun is at its highest altitude and, therefore, the brothers of Judah are said to bow down before him. Judah still has his famous lion, the Lion of Judah.

"Zebulon shall dwell at the haven of the sea" describes Cancer the Crab very clearly. Here, however, the writers who see the astronomical significance of these descriptions of the sons of Jacob are not altogether in agreement. Taylor thinks that Zebulon is more likely to be Capricornus, as that sign used to be represented as the tail of a fish; and he gives to Issacher the sign of Cancer. Issacher "is a strong ass" and the two stars in Cancer are called "the Asses"; Taylor adds "even that very ass, and the colt, the foal of an ass, upon which Jesus Christ rode in triumph into Jerusalem".

Dan "shall judge his people" and "shall be a serpent by the way".

Scorpio the Scorpion or Serpent is the sign next to Sagittarius the Archer seated upon a horse; and if Dan is Scorpio, he is clearly recognizable as "an adder in the path that biteth the horse's heels, so that his rider shall fall backward". Scorpio is certainly ready to bite the heel of the horse upon which Sagittarius sits. Dan may also be Libra the Balance, the sign used for "justice" and therefore for a judge.

Of Gad we are told "a troop shall overcome him". Taylor says that this is Aries the Ram, which in the heavens is the domicile of Mars, the God of War, or the Lord of Hosts.

"Out of Asher his bread shall be fat", which may refer to Gemini the twins in the delightful month of May when spring is causing the fat of the land to grow. Or it may refer to Virgo who is shown with an ear of corn in her hand. Asher was the God of the Assyrians, and his feminine counterpart was Asherah or Astarte or Ishtar, the goddess of "fruitfulness". Both were undoubtedly phallic deities. The word Asherah is translated "Grove" in the A.V. of the Bible, but that is not the correct translation. Fruitfulness or fertility are well described by "his bread shall be fat".

Naphthali described as a "hind set loose" is difficult to place but both Taylor, and Sir W. Drummond in his *Oedipus Judaicus*, try to show that Virgo is meant.

Joseph is "a fruitful bough" but "his bow abode in strength". There can be no mistake here, for Sagittarius the Archer is very clearly indicated—his bow is bent and the arrow is ready to fly.

Benjamin "shall ravin as a wolf". The Egyptian sign for Capricorn was a goat with a wolf's head, so perhaps it is from this we get Benjamin as a wolf.

It is interesting to note (as Taylor did) that "Levi has no part nor inheritance with his brethren: the Lord is his inheritance". That the sons of Jacob are thus shown in the very words of Holy Writ to be the signs of the Zodiac seems to me to be incontrovertible but, of course, we must not expect the likeness to be in what we know of the Zodiac mathematically exact. We do not know whether our Genesis ch. 49 is in every particular what was originally written. The text we follow is the Massoretic text of the Hebrew, finally settled about the year 600 A.D., and translated into a kind of jargon English considered suitable for a Divine Revelation over 300 years ago, by no means altogether from this Hebrew text. It may well be that, whatever obscurities or inconsistencies are found, they are due to the final or repeated editing of the original text, and the difficulties connected with translating the obscure Hebrew words. But there can be no doubt whatever that astronomical myth played a great part in the Bible stories.

Reuben, Ephraim, Judah, and Dan, represent Winter, Spring, Summer, and Autumn. Their signs, Aquarius for Reuben, the bull or Taurus for Ephraim, the Lion for Judah and the Eagle for Dan were taken over by the four evangelists, Matthew, Mark, Luke, and John. In describing the ornaments worn by Jewish priests Clement of Alexandria says: "The bright emeralds upon the ephod signify the Sun and Moon; and the twelve precious stones arranged in four rows describe to us the Zodiacal circle relatively to the four seasons of the year". And this is confirmed by Josephus: "Whether anyone wish to refer to the twelve stones, to the twelve months, or to the same number of constellations in the circle which the Greeks call the Zodiac, he will not wander far from the real meaning".

The Zodiac is an imaginary belt through which the sun was supposed to go as he journeyed round the heavens, and it was divided into twelve "mansions", possibly because there are twelve moons during the solar year. The year, it is true, is divided into four seasons but, broadly speaking, for the ancients it was divided into summer and winter. The visible signs of "rebirth" in summer of the fruit and flowers which had disappeared for the most part during winter gave rise to countless stories which, retold a thousand times, eventually were so to speak stabilized in the adventures and misadventures of the pagan gods. The misfortunes which they had to face, and their struggles with the power of darkness, gave rise to the death of the gods in various ways and, in most instances, to their resurrection. There was nearly always a tremendous struggle, and at Easter a triumphant return. With the Jews, this was at Passover, with the Christians, at Easter. The "crucifixion" and "resurrection" of Jesus was the old story retold.

There is of course a great deal more in the religion of Christ than just sun-myth, but in its main essentials I do not see how anyone can deny the part played by the pagan myths of the adventures of the sun as it entered each "mansion" of the Zodiac. Jesus himself is made to use the very term employed by astrologers: "In my father's house are many *mansions*".

When Moses found the Israelites in the wilderness worshiping a golden calf he was very angry. The story is supposed to read like a piece of history to us, but to the early Jews, for whom it was written, it may quite conceivably have been a purely symbolic narrative. When the ancient Egyptians worshiped a Bull, the sun at the vernal equinox was in the sign of Taurus, but it had, during the course of years, moved into the sign of Aries the Ram. The change took years before being recognized by the mass of the people, and it is fairly certain that Moses is shown as being angry because Aries the Ram had taken the place of Taurus the Bull when the Pentateuch was compiled, and Jews were still worshiping the Bull. Some of this symbolism can be seen in the story of Abraham substituting a ram for Isaac in his sacrifice to the Lord.

When the story of Jesus was being written up he was endowed with the appellation of "Lamb of God", a title he still holds though the sun had moved into the sign of Pisces by the time Christianity was established. Thus, to the early Christians, Jesus became a Fish, and a fish was his symbol. Also, we get the various stories in the later Gospels about fish and Jesus eating fish— I think he is never represented as eating any animal food but fish.

Tertullian called him "our great Fish". Origen, who had wit enough to notice that the Gospels were for the most part symbolical, insisted that Jesus was "allegorically called the Fish", and even St. Augustine and Jerome among other Fathers spoke of Jesus as a Fish. If there had been a real man called Jesus it is difficult to see how he would have ever been talked about as a Fish. The sun-myth theory is the only rational explanation.

And there is the question of the Devil. He is almost always represented with a barbed tail. Why? The barbed tail comes from the Zodiacal Scorpion and he is the Evil One because his month is October, which ushers in the cold, dread winter.

And still further there is the Sabbath question. Although those Jews converted to Christianity in its early days kept their Jewish Sabbath, it was not long before they followed the other Christians in keeping the first day of the week, and rejecting the seventh day in spite of the solemn commandment in the Old Testament, the only Bible they knew. The first day of the week was devoted to the Sun God, it was the Day of the Sun, and it is still kept as Sun-day. It is not the Sabbath day of the Bible, though habit and custom is so strong that Christians still talk of Saturday as being the Jewish Sunday! Of course it is nothing of the kind.

The Sun God had various names, among them, El, adopted by the Jews as part of the name of Elohim. In Greek, the title of the Sun God is Elios (or Helios), while elsewhere he goes under various names like Amen-Ra, Osiris, Mithra, Apollo, Hercules, Adonis, Bacchus, and Baal. Osiris was also, it must be added, a Moon deity; it is difficult to sort out correctly all the Egyptian gods, they were a strange mixture in which phallicism often prevailed. There is little doubt also that Samson was a solar deity, his story being not unlike that of Hercules. Here is a summary of the history of most solar deities from Dupuis given by Remsberg:

> The god is born about December 25, without sexual intercourse, for the sun, entering the winter solstice, emerges in the sign of Virgo, the heavenly Virgin. His mother remains ever-virgin, since the rays of the sun, passing through the zodiacal sign, leave it intact. His infancy is begirt with dangers, because the new-born sun is feeble in the midst of the winter's fogs and mists, which threaten to devour him; his life is one of toil and

peril, culminating at the spring equinox in a final struggle with
the powers of darkness. At that period the days and nights are
equal, and both fight for the mastery. Though the night veil the
Sun and he seems dead; though he has descended out of sight,
below the earth, yet he rises again triumphant, and he rises in
the sign of the Lamb, and is thus the Lamb of God, carrying
away the darkness and death of the winter months. Henceforth
he triumphs, growing ever stronger and more brilliant. He
ascends unto the zenith, and there he glows, on the right of God,
himself God, the very substance of the Father, the brightness of
his glory, and the express image of his person, upholding all
things by his life-giving power. (*The Christ*, p. 461)

However much the histories of the various Sun-Gods may differ in detail, the fact remains that fundamentally, if we know one,
we know them all. Apply the above summary to Jesus and the
most astonishing similarities instantly appear. Nearly all the solar
deities had a Virgin for a mother; all the ancients meant by a
virgin was that the child born to her was due to a God and not
to a man. The birthday of Jesus, like that of Mithra and other
solar gods, was about December 25, and his twelve Apostles certainly correspond to the twelve signs of the Zodiac. When Jesus
(who was the Sun of Righteousness) was "crucified", the Sun
naturally died; it was eclipsed. And of course, Jesus rose with the
Sun on the day of the Sun. It would have been out of the question for him to have risen on any other day—say on Moon-day.
"Every detail of the Sun Myth", says R. A. Proctor, the famous
writer on astronomy, "is worked into the record of the Galilean
teacher". It could hardly have been otherwise.

Judaism itself, as far as its imagery is concerned, is packed with
Sun worship, most of it quite unknown to its votaries. The Old
Testament can hardly mention Jehovah with praise without referring to his "brightness" or "glory". I do not know how many
times he is shown "as a flame of fire" or a "consuming fire". He
even appeared as, or caused to appear, "cloven tongues like as a
fire" in Apostolic times. The God of "Hosts" in the Bible is certainly the Sun, and the "heavenly host" praising God when Jesus
was born was surely the stars. Jesus is the "light of the Gentiles",
or "the Light of the World", or he "shall give thee light", or the

Lord "shall be an everlasting Light", these and dozens more like phrases beautifully describe the Sun God.

It is also rather curious that Jews, not allowed to pronounce the unpronounceable "IHVH" (which we call Jehovah), are made to say "Adonai" instead, obviously the Sun God Adonis. Moreover, the translators of the Bible actually translate the Hebrew of Adonai into "Lord". Adonis or Tammuz or Chemosh was obviously adored by the Jews in their Sun-worship period, and the only difference between them and Elohim seems to be that Elohim was the greatest of these deities. Whether the Jewish women in Ezekiel's time ever wept for Elohim or Jehovah I am not certain; but the prophet mentions that he saw them weeping for Tammuz. I shall have something to say later about this.

Although the New Testament is so different from the Old, its writers undoubtedly had the Septuagint version before them in compiling it, and they certainly adopted the Jewish God and a great many of his sun-like attributes. If Elohim or Jehovah or Ihvh is a Sun-God, there surely can be nothing surprising in finding Jesus, who is at one with his Father, also a Sun-God. Many of the incidents of his life as described in the Gospels can easily be recognized as part and parcel of Sun-worship, however much we may believe that they contain the human element in them.

Is John the Baptist a historical character? That this kind of religious lunatic existed there can be no doubt. Wherever religions have flourished, the itinerant preacher, the evangelist, the hermit or monk, the hysterical fanatic, or fakir, can always be met with and the faithful are always deluded in believing him to be a "holy" man. There actually is nothing surprising or incredible that "holy" men of the type of Jesus or John should have existed. The real question is, did this particular man live—apart from the scores of his type?

When we come to look at John the Baptist, not with the eyes of faith, but through the medium of Sun-myth it can be seen at once that his story, as given in the Gospels, is as untrue as that of Jesus. Or to put it another way, we can say that the only truth in the Bible story of John is, that he is the representative of so well known a type that his creators simply could not go wrong in describing him, while at the same time endowing him with all sorts of esoteric qualities easily interpreted in terms of myth.

John the Baptist is John the "Dipper"—and there can be little doubt he is based on the "Oannes" of Berosus—a fish-god who is supposed to have come out of the Erythraean Sea. During the day, Oannes is said to have spoken with men, but at night he sunk into the sea, obviously the sun setting or "dipping" and disappearing in the horizon. Dagon (not to be confused with the Hebrew "dagan" which means corn) was a similar fish-god. Oannes is supposed also to have preached "righteousness" just as his namesake Jonah did. Tylor in his *Primitive Culture* claimed that the "widely spread nature myth of the dragon" must be connected with Jonah, in his case probably a sea dragon.

John was born six months before Jesus, at the summer solstice; and the sun then "decreases". The cryptical saying attributed to John the Baptist, "He must increase but I must decrease" (Jn. iii, 30) can only be understood in the light of the Sun Myth. At the same time, other sources than myths have certainly their connection with the name of John, particularly phallicism.

Taylor pokes fun at the way the Baptist is introduced "In those days", and at the "wilderness of Judea". The Greek original says that John "is—beside becoming", that is, "became present" or "made his appearance"—where from is not stated. "He appeared", says Taylor, "the term is not historical, but astronomical".

John the "Dipper" is based on Aquarius the Water Bearer, "who pours his stream of water into the mouth of the great Southern Fish; and hence became Jonas, swallowed by the fish . . ."

The festival of the nativity of John is on June 24 and the sun decreases then until August 29 when we get the festival of the beheading of John. Or as Taylor puts it, the sun "gets his head cut off by the line of the horizon". Therefore, "with most mythological accuracy is the birthday of John the Baptist fixed so near the Sun's highest point of ascension because that point really is not merely figuratively but physically the mountain of the Lord . . ." A great deal more could be said on John but let us turn to Peter.

This famous apostle is introduced to us first in Matthew iv, 18 as if we all knew him, and we discover that he has another name—Simon; it is curious also to learn that he lodged with another Simon, at Joppa, Simon the tanner. Moreover, he is actually called by Jesus, "Simon bar Jonah", that is, Simon the son of Jonah. Jonah or Jonas may be the same as Janus.

Whatever the Roman Church may say about the first Pope Peter, it is a fact that no one has ever produced any evidence whatever for his existence outside the New Testament—not even the testimony of Tacitus. At the same time, as Robert Taylor pointed out, "Rome through all its periods of pagan history was famous for its temple of Janus". This temple of Janus is now known—or the building on the same site—as St. Peter's Church. Janus, like other pagan deities, has his own symbols. He carries a staff (like Peter), there is with him a rock from which comes water, something like a ship is near him, and he carries a key (again like Peter). He is often shown as two-faced. Our January is named after him, and his two faces (one is often old, the other is young) symbolize his looking at the old and new years. Pater, the word so often used for "father", is like that of Peter, who was the first Pope (or Papa). The word Jupiter seems to be IU-Peter. But whatever the name, some analogy to Aquarius, or Janus, or Jacob, Reuben, or Jonah, or even John the Baptist, is certainly there. Taylor claims that the Greek Aesculapius is the same as Janus.

Peter is represented in art also as carrying one or two keys, and he carries a scroll or book, for the legend has it that the Gospel of Mark was written by Mark from Peter's dictation. He also carries the inevitable fish to show his connection with the honorable business of fishing or the sea, just as Janus has a ship with him. And it is curious to note how the disciples (of whom Peter was one) were told to go to the city and "meet a man bearing a pitcher of water"—surely the figure of Aquarius.

It is well known that the Gospel compilers drew many of their "prophecies" from Isaiah, and in chapter xxviii, 16, is seen, perhaps, why Peter is called a "rock"—"I lay in Zion for a foundation a stone, a tried stone, a precious corner stone, a sure foundation".

And what is the sign given to those that seeketh for a sign from heaven—called "an evil and adulterous generation"? Of course, the "sign of the prophet Jonah", again Aquarius.

There seems little doubt therefore that behind the gospel story there is something of the pagan symbolism of what Taylor calls the "natural history of the year", or "of the Sun in passing through the year under the pleasant fiction of an imaginary hero". He is known as Osiris, or Tammuz, or Adonis, or Atys (Attis), or Chrishna, or Apollo, or Christ. And he is there sometimes as a subordinate character. One of these characters is Thomas, "doubting Thomas", of whom very little in the Gospels is said; but in John, he is called "Didymus", the meaning of which is given by Cruden as "a twin". And like Peter himself he is unknown outside the New Testament.

Thomas is from Tammuz, and Tammuz is certainly Apollo whose other name is Didymaeus "the dispenser of twin light or light both, of day or night". He may also be the Gospel interpretation of Gemini, but one must never expect a *literal* rendering of the signs of the Zodiac in any of the various histories of the gods. "The sign in which the sun is", says Taylor, "is at any time identified with the Sun. And the Sun of every year, of every month, and of every day, is spoken of in allegorical astronomy, as a distinct and particular Sun; while yet, there never is or was, but one and the self-same Sun. Thus the *Dii Majores*, or greater Gods of pagan mythology, were but one and the same God—that is, the same Sun, as distinctively considered in the twelve months of the year, as the three Gods or three persons in One God, in the Christian Trinity, are in like manner but one and the self-same God—that is, the productive energy of nature as considered in the three elements of Fire, Water, and Air, which are the original and only Father, Son, and Holy Ghost, 'which was in the beginning, is now, and ever shall be, world without end. *Ammon.*'" (Ammon, the Egyptian Sun God, is the source of the Christian Amen.)

Nothing is easier than to pooh-pooh all the Sun-myth allegories as, of course, it is much easier to believe in the literal meaning of a story than in anything connected with it of an esoteric character. The great Jewish Rabbi Maimonides, who in these days is claimed as a great Jew—like Jesus—by Jews, was in his own day looked upon as a heretic, for he often refused to take only the *letter* of the Law, holding that behind it was a hidden meaning known only to the wise. Anything would do for the "vulgar". He knew perfectly well that the Garden of Eden story was symbolical and never meant to be taken literally. Christians will argue and have argued and are still arguing that the Gospel story is "historical", though when pressed hard over some of the "yarns" in it like Jesus being carried about by the Devil, very reluctantly admit that they are "symbolical". But the very word "Sun-Myth" frightens them, and they nearly always get hysterical in their repudiation of it if it is connected with Jesus, though ready to admit it in the case of Adonis. In this they are supported by a number of eminent Rationalists—like Dr. Conybeare—with the result that the reputation of any Freethinker who insists on following, at least part of the way, in the footsteps of Dupuis and Robert Taylor, is looked upon as "out of date" and ridiculed. "I would ask the reader", says Prof. Drews, in his *Witnesses*, page 313, "not to pass judgment on all this until he has studied the constellations. There are too many who shrug their shoulders at astral mythology and never glance at the heavens or have the least idea about the corresponding speculations of the ancients". To the genuine student really anxious to get at the truth underlying religion in general and Christianity in particular, this advice is not necessary. It is very necessary for those people who still think that behind the Jesus story was a "real" man going about "doing good".

Jesus had twelve disciples who were just allegorical figures representing the twelve "mansions" of the Sun, and the twelve months of the year.

He also had seventy-two other disciples. These are mentioned in Luke x, 1 and 17, where, in the Authorized Version, they are given as seventy in number. The Revised Version is honest enough to admit that "many ancient authorities" give the number as seventy-two. This is the case with the Codex Sinaiticus, the Vaticanus, and many others. (The Teachers' Variorum Bible says that Sinaiticus gives the number as seventy. My facsimile copy of the Sinaiticus gives it as seventy-two.) Seventy-two is the number of years it takes "for the Sun-God, the place of the Sun at the Vernal Equinox, to precess one degree at the celestial circle" says J. D. Parsons in *Our Sun God*. Jesus said the names of these disciples.

would be "written in heaven", which is quite naturally the case; and no one ever heard of them again.

Jesus is taken up to a high mountain and becomes "transfigured". The word "transfigured" is, in the Greek, "transformed" or "metamorphosed". Anyway if his face shone as the Sun, and his raiment was white as the light, we get a very good description of him as the Sun. And I have already shown that when Jesus died on the Cross, the Sun was "eclipsed". It could not have been otherwise.

If Jesus was the "Logos" and therefore "all things were made by him . . . in him was life . . . and the life was the light of men. And the light shineth in darkness; and the darkness comprehended it not . . .", what better description of the Sun could we get?

Did the writer of John really believe literally in the story of Jesus transforming water into wine by a miracle on the spot? I can hardly believe it. But if we take the story as an allegory of the power of the Sun causing rain water to fill the grapes in a vineyard and ripen, to be turned later into wine, the story is full of meaning.

And so with most of the other stories. The reader will find abundant explanations of them in the books detailing Sun and Astral worship, and very few can be understood without this astronomical key. "I am the Light of the World", says Jesus in perhaps his most famous saying. Is he? Is he so considered in the world now or was he so considered at any time? But if Jesus is the Sun . . . ?

One of the collects in the Evening Service says, "Lighten our darkness, we beseech thee, Adonai . . ." and in the Nicene Creed we have, "God of God, light of light, very God of very God".

The Rev. J. P. Lundy in his *Monumental Christianity*, finding Sun and Astral worship almost everywhere in the books and pictures he was dealing with, considered that the Sun was a *type* of the true Son of Righteousness. "If Apollo was adopted by early . Christian art", he says (page 177), "as a type of the Good Shepherd of the New Testament, then this interpretation of the sun-god among all nations must be the solution of the universal mythos, or what other solution can it have? To what other historical personage but Christ can it apply? If the mythos has no spiritual meaning, then all religion becomes mere idolatry, or the worship of material things." Lundy was obliged to admit the "idolatry" in Egypt, India, Persia, and other countries, but it was all meant to be a type of the true Son of Righteousness, not "Sun" but "Son", the Son of God, or God himself. So does religion befog a believer.

The only explanation that can be given for the halo round the head of Jesus whenever he is pictorially portrayed is the astronomical one; needless to say, almost all the Sun-gods were thus depicted, or were shown with golden locks of hair. This was the case with both Indra and Mithra; with Samson, and Izdubar the Chaldean God; with Buddha and Serapis. Serapis indeed could be taken for Jesus, just as the early Christians were called worshipers of Serapis.

Helios the Sun was yellow haired, Perseus was called the Golden Child, Baldur had golden locks, as had Ixion and Theseus; and of course Jesus is generally depicted as a fair Aryan with golden hair. It was the obvious way that the Sun's rays could be symbolically rendered. Yet it is very doubtful that the Greeks were golden haired, and if Jesus had been a living Jew, he would have had dark colored skin and almost certainly black hair.

The only way in which the Historicist can avoid the plain fact that the history of Jesus is riddled with Sun-worship is to say that solar legends were tacked on to the true history of a real man. They themselves throw overboard these accretions and remain faithful to the "common sense" point of view of a "living Jesus" shorn of his solar attributes; but they rarely indicate to us exactly how much is left after the shearing process.

With Sun-worship goes Astral worship, the two together being so closely intertwined, that it is often impossible to separate them. It gave us the "science" of Astrology, and it plays a prominent part in the Bible.

Cruden in his famous *Concordance* devotes a very long note to the stars, admitting that the "idolatrous" Israelites called the sun and moon, the king and queen of heaven, and the stars their army or militia. "The sacred books", he says, "sometimes seem to ascribe knowledge to the sun, moon, and stars". But such expressions, "which are merely popular are not to be understood literally". Cruden tries very hard to show what must or must not be taken literally, and how we are to understand expressions which commentators have found very difficult to explain.

He himself takes the story of the Magi "following a star", the "Star of Bethlehem", very literally though he is quite puzzled how to explain it. And he admits that, "by stars are sometimes meant the princes and nobles of a kingdom", and that by "day-star (2 Peter i, 19) is meant either a more full clear and explicit knowledge of Christ . . . or that full and perfect knowledge which believers shall have, when in heaven they shall see God face to face". The Historicist can take his choice.

Stars are mentioned a great number of times in the Bible, the most obviously astrological references being found in Revelation. In this sacred work, Jesus not only calls himself "the bright and morning star" but he "had in his right hand seven stars". And of course the Second Coming of Christ will be heralded by "signs in the sun, the moon, and the stars". The Apocalypse is a mine of astral worship, as a glance at W. G. Collingwood's *Astrology in the Apocalypse* would prove.

Traces of nature worship abound in the Bible though the final editors tried hard to eradicate them. I have shown how Jehovah (or Jhvh) is likened to fire; and he seems often to have fire with him, or in his surroundings. He "spake out of the midst of fire", or he was "a pillar of fire", or he answered David "from heaven by fire", or "there went up a smoke out of his nostrils and fire out of his mouth devoured; coals were kindled by it". There are many texts like these in the Old Testament and there can be no doubt that the Jews were strongly influenced by fire. Even at this day a light must be kept burning day and night before the Ark in the Jewish synagogue, and candles must be lit to usher in the Sabbath day or a festival.

As for Jesus he, unlike John the Baptist, used fire, not water, to baptize his disciples. "He shall baptize you with the Holy Ghost and with fire", said John (Matt. iii, 11). Jesus, who is always described as being "gentle", and who asked *us* "to love our enemies" never hesitated to consign his own enemies to Hell, which he called "a furnace of fire". A typical curse of Jesus is

"Depart from me, ye cursed, into everlasting fire". Hell fire was for Jesus, "not quenched" and his faithful followers, not to be outdone in similar ferocity, when they saw that the Samaritans were by no means ready to receive him, said, "Lord, wilt thou that we command fire to come down from heaven and consume them?" (Luke ix, 53, 54).

Trees, animals, and serpents were also worshiped by the ancients and the Bible has many references to them. Everybody knows the Tree of the Knowledge of Good and Evil which stood in the Garden of Eden and which, with the Serpent, was the cause of the "Fall of Man". Frazer, in his *Golden Bough,* deals very lengthily with Tree worship, which he claims formed an important part in the religious history of the Aryan race in Europe. And he comments, "Nothing could be more natural".

The Druids certainly worshiped the oak tree, and the Greeks and Italians "associated the tree with their highest God, Zeus or Jupiter, the divinity of the sky, the rain and the thunder". Worship of trees, or the divinities in trees, used sometimes to take place in "groves". The Bible mentions some of these groves, but it is much more likely that they contained a phallic idol than a tree.

The ancients probably endowed trees with "animation", and treated them as sexual beings. Certainly some savage races claimed that trees were inhabited by spirits, and they had sorcerers who pretended that they could speak with these spirits and would threaten to cut down any tree refusing to bear fruit.

Frazer gives evidence to show how, in India, neither the owner of, say, a grove of mangos nor his wife dares taste the fruit until one of the trees is "formally married to a tree of a different sort". All this tree worship has to do with "vegetation" gods, the gods responsible so much for the corns and the fruit; some of them were even believed to have the power also of making women fruitful.

Frazer points out that our Maypole is probably a relic of tree worship, the "intention" of the customs surrounding the games and festivals associated at midsummer with the Maypole being to make the people aware of "the blessings which the tree spirit has in its power to bestow". Needless to say, the Puritans looked upon these holiday festivities with great disgust and called them "heathenish"—but that may have been because they gave pleasure and happiness.

Dionysus (or Bacchus) was worshiped as a god of trees in general, and of the vine in particular. He was considered in Boeotia as being actually in the tree. Frazer says:

> The ivy and the fig tree were specially associated with him. . . . Further there are indications . . . that Dionysus was conceived as a deity of agriculture and the corn. . . . In the land of the Bisaltae . . . a bright light shone forth at night as a token of abundant harvest. . . . Like other gods of vegetation Dionysus was believed to have died a violent death, but to have been brought to life again; and his sufferings, death, and resurrection were enacted in his sacred rites. . . . (*The Golden Bough*, abr. edition, chap. xliii)

Dionysus is nearly always shown as a "bull" god, often with horns, and bull-shaped; he is probably one of the gods associated with Taurus in the Zodiac. But when the Sun moved into the sign of the Ram, Dionysus became more and more like a Goat. His worshipers would "rend in pieces a live goat, devour it raw, and believe that they were eating the body and blood of the god". When one recognizes that this custom of tearing in pieces and devouring the bodies of both animals and men used to be a religious rite, and is still practised by savages, there should be no difficulty in seeing the origin of the Eucharist. Catholics still believe that they eat the body and drink the blood of Jesus at the ceremony of the Eucharist; Protestants say it is only a symbol. But both perform the ceremony for exactly the same reason that the worshipers of Bacchus did; there is not a particle of difference, whatever reasons are given by Christians.

Frazer shows how the custom of killing the god in animal form was a very early one. The vegetation god soon lost his plant and animal attributes and became more and more anthropomorphic, though the plants and animals still retained a vague connection with the god grown out of them; and many various stories were then invented to account for all kinds of differences. The sacred animal was slain, or spared, for example, and often in the end we find out that it is the god who eats his own flesh. "The goat-god

Dionysus is represented as eating raw goat's blood; and the bull-god Dionysus is called 'eater of bulls' ". And so we find that the animal victim was once the god himself.

An understanding of Frazer on these points will show the reader how close is the connection between the stories of the pagan gods he recounts and Christianity, the consecration and oblation of the host in the Eucharist in particular. And one therefore must not be surprised to find a "tree" story connected with Jesus; nor that the Gospel writers got hold of different versions.

According to Matthew, Jesus cursed a fig tree because it had no fruit *after* he had purged the temple a few days before his death. (It should be added that John puts this purging at the beginning of his ministry, causing Origen to look upon the whole story as a mere allegory.) Mark puts the cursing *before* the purging. His disciples discovered the tree had withered as soon as it was cursed, according to Matthew. For Mark, it was not until the next morning. In any case, it does not seem a very edifying spectacle for a god to curse a tree for not bearing fruit when, according to Mark, "the time of figs was not yet". That such a story should be religiously preserved, to the disgust of many commentators who are quite unable to account for it—proves that it must have some real significance other than a literal reading gives it.

Among the population of some islands near Australia, the fig-tree is considered sacred. These people also consider that it is the Sun, as the male principle, which fertilizes the earth, the female principle. Once a year, says Frazer,

> at the beginning of the rainy reason, Mr. Sun comes down into the holy fig tree to fertilize the earth . . . on this occasion pigs and dogs are sacrificed . . . men and women alike indulge in a saturnalia; and the mystic union of the sun and earth is dramatically represented in public, amid song and dance, by the real union of the sexes. The object of the festival, we are told, is to procure rain, plenty of food and drink, abundance of cattle and children and riches from grandfather Sun.

Frazer has a deal to say of the "sacred" fig tree, and I think it not unfair to maintain that something of the fertility rites he describes are at the back of the story of Jesus and *his* fig tree. Be that as it may, the above extract will show how strongly inter-

twined is the Sun Myth with phallic or sex worship. However
varied are the stories connected with the adventures of the Sun,
and however far away seems this connection, there can be no
doubt that at the back of them all is the idea of the life-giving
energy of the Sun, his fertilizing power, the fact that he represents the productivity of Nature, and that through his beneficent
rays, fruits and crops abound. This meant something more perhaps to primitive man than to us, as he was dependent on agri-
culture for life itself without our means of intensive culture and
transportation.

I have dealt with Phallicism in my *Short History of Sex Worship* and can only deal with the subject briefly here. Just as the
Sun was looked upon as the great life-giver with the earth as
the mother bearing the fruits for man to consume, so the sexual
organs of man and beast were recognized as also the great life-
givers, for it was they which produced the flocks which provided
us with meat to eat, and with men to cultivate the fields, and
rear the beasts. Sex worship may have been at first "symbolical",
but it gradually degenerated into lust and licence.

The bull, the goat, and the serpent, soon became symbols of
this worship as they are all "lustful"; and other symbols were
discovered and made into objects of veneration, even if their connection with sex was of the slightest, until sex-worship appeared
in almost every country in the world: Egypt, India, Australia,
Dahomey, Mexico—one can find traces of it almost everywhere;
and of course it can be found in Christianity.

Although Baring-Gould in his *Curious Myths of the Middle
Ages* is constrained to deny it, the Cross is undoubtedly a phallic
symbol. It is found in various forms all over the world. The evidence for this is overwhelming, and with this evidence is the plain
fact that it was used as the symbol *par excellence* of generation
and regeneration.

Inman in his *Ancient Faiths Embodied in Ancient Names* gives
many examples of the Cross and where it can be found, treating
the question more from the phallic side than I have done in a
previous chapter. He quotes R. Payne Knight, one of the principal
authorities, who deals fully with phallicism in his *Worship of
Priapus*, as saying:

The male organs of generation are sometimes represented by signs which might properly be called the symbol of symbols. One of the most remarkable of these is a cross in the form of the letter T, which thus served as the emblem of creation and generation, before the Church adopted it as a sign of salvation.

Inman claims that the Cross was a phallic symbol among the Etruscans, that it was associated with the female emblem among the Egyptians—the Crux Ansata—and that it was the sign mentioned in Ezekiel (ch. ix, 4). There can be also no doubt that the Swastika in its original form was purely phallic.

Allied to all this, phallic symbolism was the worship of the Serpent. There is, according to *The Serpent in Paradise,* an anonymous pamphlet published by Thomas Scott, a mummy case in the Egyptian collection in the Louvre in Paris on which is painted very realistically the temptation of Adam by Eve and the Serpent which is unmistakably phallic. And the writer claims that even the great Jewish commentator, the thoroughly orthodox Aben Ezra, admits that the Temptation story in Genesis consists of phallic symbols.

The Serpent was really the Devil and the sin was sexual desire. It was the Devil who seduced Eve; and in the apocryphal Gospel of James (the Protevangelium) one finds the then current belief about the Genesis story. When Joseph who had been away from home comes back to find Mary pregnant, he says, "Who hath done this evil in my house and defiled the virgin? Is not the history of Adam repeated in me? For just as Adam was at the hour of his thanksgiving, and the serpent came and found Eve alone and deceived her, so also hath it befallen me."

In some shape or form, our story of Adam and Eve is found in other and older religions, particularly in Zoroastrianism; and Serpent worship, almost always associated with phallicism, was the religion of ancient Mexico as well as of ancient Egypt and India. The cobra is depicted on the crowns of the Pharaohs of Egypt, yet it is an Indian reptile (there is a species also in Africa, though), and there is no doubt that the serpent generally was used in primitive times as a symbol for "sexual desire".

Without the "Fall of Man" brought about by the Serpent, there could have been no Christianity which depends on a "Savior" and on a "redemption". At one time—and indeed in some quarters even now—the story of Adam and Eve in the Garden of Eden was taken literally as, of course, it should be by Christians. But with the growth of knowledge, and the advancement of science, and the investigations of anthropologists, the Serpent myths have been so thoroughly exposed that it is very difficult to explain away the connection between the seduction of Eve by a Serpent and the redemption of mankind by Jesus except on the grounds that the one, equally with the other, is just myth. Even Christians nowadays prefer to champion their God as going about "doing good" rather than to attempt to prove that the Garden of Eden story is true. A Serpent speaking pure Biblical Hebrew is a little too much for even a bishop to swallow.

What is known as the "Monogram" of Christ, an X with a P through it, is nothing but the monogram of Osiris (or Jupiter Ammon). This is admitted by the Rev. J. P. Lundy in his *Monumental Christianity*. It has been found on coins of the Ptolemies and of Herod the Great struck at least 40 years before our era. Monograms of this kind accompanied many pagan deities. For example that of Mercury was a cross; that of Saturn and Jupiter was a cross and a ram's horn; and that of Venus was a cross and a circle, just like that of the Phenician Astarte and of Freya, Holda, and Aphrodite.

The monogram "I.H.S." has been specially adopted by Christians who tell us it stands for "Jesu Hominum Salvator". Actually the three letters are Y.E.S. which is simply the monogram of Bacchus, and means "Bacchus our Savior". They form part of the Eleusinian "mysteries"; what are known as the Greater and Lesser Mysteries appear to be part of many of the ancient religions. We have their counterpart in our Freemasonry, and the "inner" circle of Theosophy.

The triangle is another symbol which has been taken over by Christianity from Paganism. It can be seen in the Pyramids of Egypt and on many Greek monuments; it was used in the "mysteries" of India, and I believe is part of modern Freemasonry. Two equilateral triangles joined together are known as the Jewish symbol of David. Whether originally the triangle had some sexual significance it may be impossible to say, but it is a fact that in

Egyptian theology, as Bonwick says in his *Egyptian Belief* (p. 213), the triangle "was the type of the Holy Trinity", "three in one". We use it today as a symbol of our "Holy" Trinity.

The "three making one" has always been a mystery, especially to mathematicians, and our Holy Trinity is no exception. With the Egyptians a trefoil leaf adorned the head of Osiris, and it was used by Hindus to represent Brahma, Vishnu, and Siva. In passing, it should be noted that Vishnu was a Fish God like Jesus and like Buddha, who was called Dag-Po or the Fish-Po. Lundy says (p. 133) that in the Talmud the Messiah is called a Fish, and the question must be faced, why is it that Vishnu, Buddha, Jesus, and the Jewish Messiah are all Fish Gods? Is not the principal reason because it represents "fecundity"?

And so with the Serpent. The Buddhist worshiped the Serpent as God in very early times "as is proved from the sculptures of oldest topes where worshipers are represented as so doing", say the authors of *Ancient Symbol Worship*. As for the ancient Egyptians their sculptures and bas reliefs prove how wide spread was its worship. In Chaldea, and among the Phenicians, the Serpent was venerated, and both Apollo and Aesculapius were worshiped in the form of a Serpent. The Serpent is still the emblem of medical art.

The Serpent was for long also an emblem of the Sun. With its tail in its mouth it forms a circle, and standing on its tail the serpent is the Erect One, the lingam, the source of fruitfulness, like the Sun. And with such widespread veneration we need not be surprised that one of the Gnostic sects, the Ophites, venerated the reptile as an emblem of Christ Jesus—the Serpent, they said, brought Wisdom into the world and so did Jesus; could a more glorious connection between the two be better exemplified?

Even in Mexico, we find the same extraordinary belief in the Serpent, for the virgin-born Lord and Savior Quetzalcoatl, appears as a Serpent; though this God really represented the Sun.

I have dealt very briefly with the Serpent, but I hope sufficiently, to show that its worship was bound to influence the literary representation of Jesus Christ. And so with other symbols like the Dove, for instance. As Lundy admits, the Dove seems to have symbolized the "Holy Spirit" among all religious and civilized nations. It is found in Buddhism, it was sacred to Venus as well as to Astarte, Cybele, and Isis. J. B. Hannay points out that the landing place of the priest who first brought the Christian religion to Scotland is "Iona"—the Greek for Dove; the name of the priest was Columba, the Latin for Dove, and both names are still associated with Scotland.

It is impossible to study the history of ancient religions without seeing the enormous part played in all of them by symbols, and when these are traced to their source it will be found, in most instances, that behind them is the idea of *fertility* in some shape or form. Hence the connection in so many religions between Sun-worship and sex-worship; hence the continuous preoccupation of most religions with the sexual question. The recitals in pagan-ism of the love adventures of various gods should occasion no surprise if this fact is borne in mind. It would be easy to mul-tiply instances, but here I am concerned only with the Jesus myth, though I have been obliged, in the interests of clarity, to stray every now and then a little from my proper path.

How do fertility rites and customs affect the story of Jesus? It cannot be too strongly emphasized that one must not expect any of these to be taken bodily and literally over and found in the Christian religion exactly as found in paganism. They have been modified or altered to suit the times and conditions of another era.

When the Sun was supposed to be in Taurus at the vernal equinox, we had Bull-gods and calf-gods predominating; we see them all over ancient Egypt, Assyria, Babylonia and in such a cult as that of Mithra. When in the course of centuries, it was found that the Sun was in Aries, the Lamb, the Ram, the Goat, gradually replaced the Bull; and as far as the fertility motive is concerned there is very little difference between the way Apis the Bull and Mendes the Goat were adored. We should cer-tainly call the rites in which they were the principal objects very indecent. Now that the Sun is in Pisces, it is not at all surprising that the predominating God Jesus is called a Fish. Where and how can we apply the fertility motive to the Christian deity? The answer is found in Matt. xiv, 15-17 in the well known story of Jesus feeding the multitude with five loaves and two fishes. Not

even the Historicists can swallow this miracle, and even orthodox
Christians are not in these days too inclined to press such a
ridiculous story. For my own part I have never believed that the
writer of Matthew himself believed it literally as written. Be that
as it may, I claim that the only explanation which will fit the
facts and common sense is the one I suggest. Feeding the multi-
tudes in this way brings in the fertility motive and the Zodiacal
Fish. If this is denied, then I suggest that Historicists should
set out to explain why we find Jesus deliberately making so much
of his "teaching" so obscure?

For example, when his parents lost Jesus as a boy and found
him in the temple, he said, "Wist ye not that I must be about
my Father's business?" And we are told that "they understood
not the saying which he spake unto them". (Luke ii, 49-50). It
is the same with the Samaritan lady who came to draw water
from the well, and was so surprised when Jesus asked her for a
drink from her pitcher. She was even more surprised when he
started talking to her about "living water", and added, "Whosoever drinketh of this water shall thirst again; but whosoever
drinketh of the water that I shall give him shall never thirst; but
the water that I shall give him shall be in him a well of water
springing up into everlasting life". A lot more of the same kind
of rigmarole puzzled the lady even further—as indeed it puzzles
most, if not all, orthodox commentators—and Jesus seems to have
used similar unintelligible "teaching" in most of the Gospel of
John. He told Nicodemus that he could not see the Kingdom of
God unless "he be born again", which led to the question, "How
can a man be born when he is old?" and it all becomes even
more obscure directly Jesus tries to explain what he means. "That
which is born of the flesh is flesh", says Jesus, "and that which is
born of the spirit is spirit." The word which we translate "spirit"
is "pneuma" which means *wind* and I should like Historicists to
make the whole passage "literally" intelligible, bearing the word
"wind" in mind. In any case, John actually admits that the hearers
of Jesus failed to understand him. "Why do ye not understand
my speech?" asks Jesus. Even when he was talking about the
"temple" they did not understand he meant "the temple of his
body". As for his disciples, we are told that "they understood

none of these things; and the saying was hid from them; neither knew they the things which were spoken" (Luke xviii, 31-34). If we therefore accept the fact that a good deal of the teaching of Jesus has a "hidden" meaning, an "occult" significance, as Origen insisted, is it not reasonable to suppose that many of his "miracles" were never meant to be miracles in the literal sense at all? Whether we have the *right* explanation when we dismiss the literal one, is another matter.

Bacchus or Dionysus was a wine-god and so we find Jesus saying, "I am the true vine, and my Father is the husbandman". The Bible refers to the vine and to vineyards over and over again and the meaning is quite plain in most of the cases; but unless one accepts some allegorical meanings, how is one to interpret Jesus changing water into wine? Surely the writer of John could never have believed such a story literally.

In a number of works dealing with phallic worship, their author, J. B. Hannay, deals very fully indeed with the phallic symbolism which he claims permeates the Old Testament. He takes the letter I or the figure I as symbolical of the male, and the letter O or U as symbolical of the female. There was no J in English till about the 16th century, and so we find IO or IU running through the Bible. IU can be pronounced Jew, and in any case we have IesU—Jesu—showing how Jesus retains the double sex signification which we find in the word Jehovah, which should really be IhVh. IO can be found in many Biblical names such as IOnathen, IOhn, IOseph and others. The *Encyclopedia Biblica* in its article on "Names" is obliged to admit that they are purely artificial, and "originally had some special meaning", which really means that the names were invented to suit the story which the Bible writers had to tell. Otherwise how can it be explained that such names as Abraham, Isaac, Jacob, and Moses, appear only once in the history of the Jewish race told over a period of 1000 years?

Words, phrases, and ideas, in the Bible are full of phallic significance and there is little doubt that the final editors of the Old Testament did their best to gloss over gross sexual meanings and indeed tried in the end to wean away from their phallic idols their "stiff-necked" people. It became a struggle as to whether phallic-worship, plain and unashamed, should prevail, or whether it could be sufficiently hidden under the form of Sun-worship; in the case of Christianity, it is mostly Sun-worship; but phallicism could not even there always be concealed. If the reader wishes for further details he should consult the special books on the question, some of which I give in the Bibliography.

A word here should be said about the Messianic idea which the Hebrews later began to develop, particularly when they were fighting for existence against the invader, and when they were hoping for the return of "David" and the glories of his reign. The idea of a Messiah was not wholly Jewish, it has affinities in Zoroastrianism; but when Christians pressed the claims of Jesus as the Jewish Savior, the long-expected Messiah, if there had been even a modicum of truth in the claim, Judaism might have perished, or at least might have been absorbed by Christianity. The fact that the Jews have always rejected Jesus as their Messiah, that they have denied him as David or a son of David, and have vigorously contested the so-called prophecies respecting him in the Bible, proves that they at least have never been impressed with the Christian claims. In trying to connect Jesus with the Jewish Messiah, the Old Testament was raked through by the Gospel writers, and anything which looked like applying to him was written up and called a "prophecy". Renan puts it this way (as quoted by Remsberg): "Sometimes the Evangelists reasoned thus: The Messiah ought to do such a thing; now Jesus is the Messiah, therefore Jesus has done such a thing. At other times, by an inverse process, it was said: Such a thing has happened to Jesus; now Jesus is the Messiah; therefore such a thing was to happen to the Messiah."

There is no "prophecy" whatever regarding Jesus in the Old Testament. All the chapter headings given in our Authorized Version of the Bible were added by the translators, and all the various number computations and dates given in Daniel and other prophetic books, have no more to do with the coming of Jesus than with the phases of the moon. It would be useless to labor this point, but apart from some of the strange evangelical sects we hear of every now and then, the only people who, these days, produce Old Testament prophecies of the coming Messiah

as referring to Jesus, are those engaged by the Society for con-
verting Jews, who still imagine after nearly 2000 years of almost
hopeless failure that it is the correct card to play. Those Jews
who do get converted are scarcely influenced, if at all, by Messianic prophecies.

It is time now to examine some of the other "Christs" or
"Saviors" whose names are well known, but who are looked upon
as Pagan deities who never had a real existence, by all Christendom. The parallels between them and Jesus are often astonishing
and they are worth a detailed study.

CHAPTER IX

Pagan Saviors

IT CANNOT BE TOO STRONGLY URGED THAT ONE must not expect a Pagan "Christ" to be *exactly* the same as Jesus "Christ". I have already pointed this out, but it is a fact that directly the Mythicist mentions the story of Krishna (or Chrishna) or Buddha or Horus as having in many features extraordinary parallels with Jesus, not only Christian writers but Rationalists cry out in protest, and claim that we are mistaken, or we grossly exaggerate, or the parallels are not parallels. The principal idea seems to be to prove that, in the case of Jesus, we have something unique, and that if there is a *faint* likeness between Jesus and say, Horus, it is stretched beyond the bounds of fairness. Indeed, we are often implored, with almost tearful supplications, not to make ourselves a laughing stock with "historians". And if an encyclopedic writer like John M. Robertson is caught making one slip in a book containing thousands of references, a cry of joy is wafted aloft, as if the case for the non-historicity of Jesus has received a mortal blow.

One has only to study, without bias as far as possible, the stories and legends surrounding Krishna, Buddha, Horus, Zoroaster, Persius, Bacchus, Adonis, and Pythagoras, to see that we are in the presence of a kind of universal mythos, the details of which only vary because they may have been composed in different ages and in different countries.

We do not claim that everything in the story of Jesus is exactly like that of Horus, for instance; we do claim that there are features of the Horus legend which are so like those of the legend of Jesus, and for that matter of Krishna and Buddha, that they are obviously from a common source.

How far back we must go for the invention of the Zodiac it is impossible to say, but it is obvious that not only must there have been a high standard of civilization to evolve such a marvel of astronomical imagination, but that already stories and legends were being composed in which the "gods" were the heroes or villains.

Story-telling has always fascinated human-kind; and in the eternal conflict between winter and summer, or day and night, or the good and the bad, we have first-class material for spinning a yarn. Behind nearly all the stories of gods, however much they are disguised, is that fight to the death between the Sun with his life-giving rays, his beneficent power of raising crops and fruits, and giving joy and happiness to all living things, and that dreadful Winter which brings cold and misery and extinction to man and beast and the fruits of the earth. Perhaps memories of the devastation caused by the Ice Ages and their floods have made their mark on humanity in its days of slow evolution; or perhaps man could never get away from the immediate peril of cold and hunger and the black night of Winter. Whichever it was, he has preserved in his stories of Gods the eternal struggle between the Good and the Bad, a story which, in essence, forms still the plot of nearly all our fiction. The God Osiris struggling with the Devil Set, Chrishna killed by Angada, Jesus betrayed by Judas, or even Sherlock Holmes' terrific fight against the arch-criminal Moriarty, are they not all just winter and summer, or day and night at war for the mastery of good against evil?

"Ah," says the Christian apologist, "but it's quite different with our Jesus." "The 'cult' god 'died' and 'rose' annually; but Jesus 'rose once for all' ".—*The Historical Jesus* by the Rev. J. T. Thorburn, (p. 44). This is a typical "apology" by Christians; and it is so silly that one wonders how it ever could have been written. The "cult" god did *not* die and rise annually. A festival took place in which believers took part every year and they mourned the death of their god—like the women who wept at the death of Tammuz—following this up with joy at the glad tidings of his "resurrection" expressed in feasts and processions. Exactly the same thing happens today in Christian churches all over the world. Sorrow at the death of the "Savior" regularly takes place on Good Friday, followed by the glad tidings that "the Savior is arisen" on Easter Sunday, and the celebration of Easter Monday. Of course, the birth of Spring appears to have always been celebrated, and the custom of eating hot cross buns and easter eggs is a reminder of the fertility rites which regularly took place when Nature began to shower, at this time, her benefits on man. Christianity absorbed these customs just as it had to absorb so many other pagan customs.

Let us begin with Krishna, who was an incarnation of Vishnu, and who is considered the great Hindu "Savior". Needless to say, Christians have been so struck with the similarities between the two Gods that they have been obliged to urge the priority of the Jesus legend so as to make out the Hindu writers as copyists.

The whole question has been so thoroughly thrashed out by John M. Robertson in his *Christ and Krishna* which now forms part of his *Christianity and Mythology,* that there is no need for me to cover the ground again even in brief form. Robertson shows that the *names* Christ and Krishna owe nothing to each other, and that the Krishna legend in some form or other "is proved by documentary evidence to have flourished in India before the Christian era, though it has developed somewhat and gained much ground since". He also claims that myth elements in the legend of Krishna are found "strikingly paralleled in the pre-Christian mythology of Greece and Egypt", and leading elements of the myth "are inexplicable save on the view that the cultus is ancient". In fact we find Christianity "to be wholly manufactured from pre-existent material within historic times: Krishnaism we have seen to have had a pre-historic existence".

Bearing this in mind, we find Krishna to have been born of the *virgin* Devaki, and his birth announced by a *star*, spirits and nymphs danced and sang (Luke ii, 13), he was born in a cave (like Jesus in the Apocryphal Protevangelium, and cp. Farrar's *Life of Christ*) he was adored by shepherds, though lowly born he was of royal descent, and the ruler of the country where he was born tried to destroy him and ordered the massacre of the innocents.

Sir William Jones, one of our greatest Sanscrit scholars, in his *Asiatic Researches* says on this point that the birth of Krishna "was concealed through the fear of the reigning tyrant Kansa, who, at the time of his birth, ordered all new born males to be slain, yet this wonderful babe was preserved". It should be noted that Sir William also said that "the name of Chrishna, and the general outline of his story, were long anterior to the birth of our Savior, and probably to the time of Homer, we know very certainly" (*Asiatic Researches*, i, 274).

One of Krishna's first miracles was curing a leper; and a lame woman came with a vessel full of sweet scented oils, made a sign on his forehead, and poured the ointment on his head. His death took place while he was "hanging on a tree", with his arms outstretched, and it brought a number of calamities. The sun was darkened, the sky rained fire, and spirits were seen on all sides. (Compare the Jewish saints who came out of their graves when Jesus was crucified.) Krishna was pierced with an arrow—Jesus with a spear; Krishna said to the hunter who shot him, "Go hunter, through my favor to heaven, the abode of the gods". Jesus said to the thief, "This day thou shalt be with me in paradise". Krishna descended into hell—like Jesus—and also like Jesus rose from the dead. Moreover he ascended into heaven, and many persons witnessed his ascent. There will be a second coming of Krishna, and when this happens, the sun and the moon will darken, the earth will tremble, and the stars will fall from the skies. Krishna had a beloved disciple, he was "transfigured", he was meek, he preached nobly, he washed the feet of Brahmins, he was the "Alpha and Omega", he said "Give to the poor", also, "I am the light in the Sun and Moon", and among his titles are "The Redeemer", "the Mediator", "The Good Shepherd", as well as "The Savior", and "The Holy One". Added to all this is that Krishna was the second Person of the Hindu Trinity (for he was

the incarnation of Vishnu, in fact, Vishnu in human form) the
Trinity being Brahma, Vishnu, and Siva, and one can see enough
resemblances between the two gods to prove at least their common origin.

We can admit that some of the stories relating to Krishna are
comparatively late, later perhaps than was at first thought, but,
as is admitted by the Rev. G. W. Cox in his *Aryan Mythology*:

> It is true that these myths have been crystallized around the
> name of Chrishna in ages subsequent to the period in which the
> earliest Vedic literature came into existence; but the myths them-
> selves are found in this older literature associated with other gods
> and not always in germ. . . . Practically the myths of Chrishna
> seem to have been fully developed in the days of Megasthenes
> (fourth century B.C.) who identifies him with the Greek Hercules.

There is no need to argue that the early Christian writers actually borrowed from Hindu mythology or vice versa. What we are
entitled to infer is that stories of the "sons of God" were told in
many lands. There were "Redeemers" or "Saviors" as well as
Gods themselves, and it would have been very surprising if the
details regarding their exploits were completely different.

Look how many of the details in the life of Buddha approxi-
mate those of Jesus—and of Krishna for that matter. Buddha's
mother was the Virgin Maya, and he was an incarnation of Vishnu
through the "Holy Ghost", and the usual "star" announced his
birth, which also took place on Dec. 25. Just as in the (so-called)
Apocryphal Gospel of Infancy Jesus spoke to his mother from
the cradle saying, "I am Jesus the Son of God", so Buddha, as
an infant just born, said to his mother, "I am the greatest among
men". King Bimbasara, advised that the newly born child was
"dangerous", threatened to destroy him; and like Jesus, when
twelve years old, he was "teaching" in the temple. Buddha's
genealogy showed his descent from the "first monarch of the
world, Maha Sammata", and just as Jesus was "tempted" by the
Devil when he first went preaching, so, when Buddha was about
to adopt a religious life, he was tempted by Mara, i.e., "the
Author of Evil", or "the King of Death".

The "Spirit of God" was present when Buddha was baptized
(by water) and when he went on a mountain in Ceylon, he was

"transfigured". Needless to add to all this, Buddha performed many miracles; and when he died he was wafted to the "celestial regions" exactly as Jesus ascended to heaven.

Buddha was the "Alpha and Omega"—as was Jesus—he asked that all sins should fall on him "that the world may be delivered", and he taught that one's good deeds should be hidden. He even asked a woman at a well for a drink of water. His disciples had to renounce the world for a life of poverty, and he himself had to establish a "Kingdom of Heaven".

Buddha believed in the same kind of ascetic doctrine as did Jesus and Paul, for he insisted that "a wise man should avoid married life as if it were a burning pit of live coals. One who is not able to live in a state of celibacy should not commit adultery." In fact, as Rhys Davids says in his *Buddhism*, "Gautama (Buddha) was very early regarded as omniscient and absolutely sinless. . . . From his perfect wisdom . . . his sinlessness would follow as a matter of course."

It must be added that there appear to have been several Buddhas, twenty-four of them appearing before *the* Buddha—Gautama—who is said to have died in 543 B.C. Whether there ever was a real historical personage called Gautama or Sakya-Muni is a question I have no need to discuss; but his "romantic" biography has been translated by Prof. S. Beal from the translation made into Chinese about 70 A.D. The original is considered by Beal to have been in circulation before this date, and parts of it were sung even before the original story was compiled. He does not profess to account for the striking resemblances between the stories of Buddha and Jesus; and if it is true that the history of Buddha was in circulation before our era, then it is obvious that the Buddhist writers could not have copied from the Christians.

Two of the Christian writers who have had to face the same difficulties, Bunsen in his *Angel Messiah,* and Rhys Davids in his *Buddhism,* were well aware of the implications in the history of Buddha. "The most ancient of the Buddhistic records known to us contain statements", says Bunsen, "about the life and the doctrines of Gautama Buddha which correspond in a remarkable manner, and impossibly by mere chance, with the traditions recorded in the Gospels about the life and doctrines of Jesus

Christ." While Davids says, "It is true that none of the books of
the Three Pitakas can at present be satisfactorily traced back
before the Council of Asoka held at Patna, about 250 B.C., that
is to say, at least one hundred years after the death of the
teacher; but they undoubtedly contain a great deal of much
older matter".

Prof. Max Muller in his *Science of Religion* is just as puzzled
as his fellow Christians. "Between the language of Buddha", he
says, "and his disciples, and the language of Christ and his
apostles, there are strange coincidences. Even some of the Buddhist legends and parables sound as if taken from the New Testament; though we know that many of them existed before the
beginning of the Christian era."

The fact that King Asoka about 250 B.C. was a "Buddhist" and
that it was therefore an established system then, proves Buddhism as anterior to Christianity; but it does not prove that there
was a real historical Buddha. Readers who wish to pursue that
interesting problem will find in John M. Robertson's *Pagan
Christs* a very lucid examination of the Buddha Myth and he
may reach the conclusion so apposite to my own query re Jesus,
"No Buddha made the Buddhists—the Buddhists made Buddha."
As Robertson concludes:

> It is here submitted that the traditional figure of the Buddha
> in its most plausibly rationalized form, is as unhistoric as the
> figure of the Gospel Jesus has been separately shown to be.
> Each figure simply stands for the mythopoeic action of the re-
> ligious mind in a period in which primary God-making had
> given way to secondary God-making, and in particular to the
> craving for a Teaching God who should originate religious and
> moral ideas as the other Gods had been held to originate agri-
> culture, art, medicine, normal law and civilization.

And now what about Horus? Whatever were the influences, if
any, of the Orient on the Christian legend, no one who reads
about Christian origins can doubt for a moment the immense part
played by Egypt in shaping Christianity. The (so-called) prophecy, "Out of Egypt have I called my son", could be in some
measure justified, for indeed the parallels between Horus and
Jesus are really astonishing. They are not very well known, and

the one book which deals in great detail with the question of the legends of Horus and Jesus is more or less boycotted—*Ancient Egypt* by Gerald Massey. Massey is not mentioned in John M. Robertson's *History of Freethought* or in his *Courses of Study* (1932), though in the edition of 1908, Massey's two earlier works, *Book of the Beginnings* and *Natural Genesis* are noted with "they must be used with caution". *Ancient Egypt* was Massey's last work and embodied his final investigations which carry ever further than his better known and widely circulated lecture, the *Historical Jesus and Mythical Christ*.

Massey claims (*Gnostic and Historic Christianity*, p. 1) "that the original mythos and *gnosis* of Christianity were primarily derived from Egypt on various lines of descent, Hebrew, Persian, and Greek, Alexandrian, Essenian, and Nazarene, and that these converged in Rome, where the history was manufactured mainly from the identifiable matter of the Mythos recorded in the ancient Books of Wisdom, illustrated by Gnostic Art and orally preserved amongst the secrets of the Mysteries".

To follow Massey is impossible in the confines of a work like this, for, with great patience, he has amassed, in his *Ancient Egypt*, hundreds of pages of verifiable facts—and no doubt a good deal of speculation—in proof of his thesis, which simply refuse to be reduced to a page or two. He admits parallels with Buddhism, but "Christianity whether considered to be mystical or historical, was not derived from Buddhism at any time. They have some things in common, because there is a Beyond to both". Again, "Unfortunately you cannot prove anything, or, still more unfortunately, you *can* prove anything from the Gospels! You must first catch your Jesus, before you pretend to tell us what he was personally, and what were his own individual teachings. These 'sayings of mine' cannot be judged as *his* if they were pre-existent, and can be proved to be anyone's sayings, or may be identified as ancient sayings, whether Buddhist, Nazarene, Apocryphal, or Egyptian."

What is true in Historic Christianity, declares Massey, is not new, and what is new is not true. "It is not new, because it represents the ancient Mythos under an intended disguise. It is not

true because it is not genuine history. The supposed human original, set forth in the Gospels, is but the mundane shadow of the
Gnostic Christ."

But for Massey, it is to Horus and all his "mysteries" that we
must go to find "the Christian Christ". And he points out that in
the Epistle of James, "the brother of the Lord", who is said to
have died about 60 A.D. "there is not one single line of Christianity". He knows nothing of Jesus of Nazareth, nor salvation
through the atoning blood, nor the death, resurrection, and
ascension of a personal Christ. No wonder Luther called James
an Epistle of straw and wanted it thrown out of the Canon.

"It is certain", says Massey, "that the Lord or Christ of Marcion
is entirely non-historical. He has no genealogy or Jewish line of
descent, no earthly mother, no father, no mundane birthplace or
human birth." I hope to say something further on this when I
come to Dr. Couchoud's work, *The Creation of Christ,* which
deals fully with Marcion and his Gospel—noting here only how
Massey had preceded him with the same idea.

In *Ancient Egypt* Massey provides in an Appendix the parallels he claims exist between Horus and Jesus. I have space only
for a few out of the large number he has collected:

Egyptian	*Christian*
The Mysteries.	The Miracles.
The sayings of Iu or Iu-em-hetep.	The sayings of Jesus.
Ra the Holy Spirit.	The Holy Ghost.
The Trinity of Atum (or Osiris), the father, Horus (or Iu) the son, and Ra, the holy spirit.	The Trinity of the Father, Son, and Holy Spirit.
Isis, the virgin mother of Iu, her Su or son.	Mary, the virgin mother of Jesus.
Seb, the earth father, as consort to the virgin Isis.	Joseph the father on earth, as putative hus-band to the Virgin Mary.
Seb the builder of the house, the carpenter.	Joseph the carpenter.
Sut and Horus the twin opponents.	Satan and Jesus the twin opponents.
Sut and Horus contending on the Ben-Ben or pyramidion.	Satan and Jesus contending on the pinnacle.

Egyptian	*Christian*
The Petar or Petra by name in Egyptian as revealer to Horus.	Peter the revealer to the Christ.
Asar or Osiris.	Lazarus.
Osiris who slept in the tomb at Annu.	Lazarus who slept in the tomb at Bethany.
Anup the Baptizer.	John the Baptist.
Mati the registrar.	Matthew the clerk.
Child Horus with the head of Ra (i.e. the Sun God).	Child Jesus with the solar glory round his head.
Horus the Good Shepherd with the crook upon his shoulder.	Jesus the Good Shepherd with the lamb or kid upon his shoulder.
Isis commanded to take her child down into Egypt for safety.	Mary instructed to take her Child down into Egypt for safety.
Horus as the typical fish.	Jesus as Icthus the fish.
Sebek the father of the fishers.	Zebedee the father of the fishers.
Horus made a man of thirty at his baptism.	Jesus the man of thirty years in his baptism.
The blind mummy made to see by Horus.	The blind man given sight by Jesus.
Seven loaves of Horus for feeding the multitude reposing in the green fields of Annu.	Seven loaves of Jesus for feeding the multitude reclining on the grass.
Twelve followers of Har-Khuti.	Twelve followers of Jesus as the twelve disciples.
Horus ascending to heaven from Bakhu the mount of the olive tree.	Jesus ascending to heaven from Mount Olivet.

There are dozens more of close parallels between Horus and the Egyptian story and Jesus. Massey discusses them all in great detail and the reader should turn to his book if he wants authorities. And it is quite amusing to see how puzzled are Christian authorities when face to face with the likeness between the Egyptian and the Palestinian Savior. In trying to explain the story of Lazarus and his mummy-like burial, Lundy in *Monumental Christianity* asks, what does it mean? "Only that the dead man may be like Horus, to whose care he was committed; or rather like Him whom Horus typifies, the Son of God, who alone has the power

of life and death. Horus is thus represented as a cross-like young
mummy figure, because he is the lifegiving power of the sun,
using his cross to produce life and joy; and he is thus a type of
Christ, in his greater conflict with sin, Satan and death, and his
triumph through the Cross." This picture of Horus—and for that
matter other "Saviors"—being a "type" of Christ is about the only
explanation Christian apologists can offer, so great is their be-
wilderment at the parallels. Justin Martyr in his *Dialogue with
Trypho* explains away the parallels by claiming that it was "the
Devil, to imitate the truth, who invented the stories of Bacchus,
Hercules, and Esculapius". Justin hardly denies the story that
Bacchus was torn to pieces and killed and that he rose again;
that Hercules was a mighty man the son of Jove and Alcmene
"and that after his death he ascended into heaven"; or that
Esculapius cured diseases and made people rise from the dead.
These things happened in imitation of the prophecies concern-
ing Christ, declared Justin (sec. lxix). And I think later apologists
took the same line, among them, Eusebius.

Even such a sane and broadminded Churchman as Baring-
Gould, quite confounded at the way that the Cross forms part
of ancient Paganism, uses the same argument. How can he account, he asks in *Curious Myths of the Middle Ages* (p. 385, edition 1888) for the truth "that the Cross was a sacred sign long
before Christ died upon it?" And his answer is, "I see no difficulty in believing it formed part of the primeval religion, traces
of which exist over the whole world, among every people; that
trust in the Cross was a part of the ancient faith which taught
men to believe in a Trinity, in a War in Heaven, a Paradise from
which man fell, a Flood and a Babel; a faith which was deeply
impressed with a conviction that a Virgin should conceive and
bear a son, ... it is more than a coincidence that Osiris by the Cross
should give life eternal to the Spirits of the Just . . ." and so on.

This suggestion or belief on the part of the orthodox that God
sent "types" of (more or less) Virgin-born Saviors to precede
Jesus, the only true Savior, and that somewhat similar "types"
of belief also preceded Christianity to make people ready for the
one true religion sent by the Almighty, no doubt convinced the

majority of the faithful; but it can hardly now be so convincing to students of Anthropology and Comparative Religion. Those who contend for a real Jesus have never been able to explain away the remarkable coincidences between Jesus and Pagan Deities, or give convincing reasons why a real man, even if deified by a host of credulous followers, should take on so many characteristics from other Gods. Why—I keep on asking the question—should a real living hero be called within a comparatively short time after his death, a "Fish"? Augustus Caesar was deified, but was he ever called a Fish?

Howell Smith in his *Jesus Not a Myth* makes no attempt, of course, to explain Jesus as a Fish. He is "uncertain" whether "the fish of early Christian art is only a symbol or was really eaten occasionally in the Eucharist", and appears to suggest only that a fish was a religious symbol like a dove. But why were these two, dove and fish, used as symbols? Howell Smith does not know— the origins of these symbols "are not always easy to discover", and "all sorts of theories are debatable". Just so; but at least the fact that the Sun is now in Pisces after being in Aries for over 2000 years is surely something on which we can build. As J. M. Robertson says in *Pagan Christs* (p. 302), "There is no more plausible explanation than the zodiacal one of the early Christian habit of calling Jesus Christ the Fish". And Robertson, who has no use for Gerald Massey in his *History of Freethought,* cites Massey as his authority for Horus as a Fish.

As a matter of fact, Horus is actually called "Icthus" the Fish, in spite of the fact that the letters in the word Icthus are an early (Christian) acrostic, the initials of the five Greek words meaning "Jesus Christ of God Son Savior". Massey says:

> The fish remained as an emblem of Icthus or of Icthon, that savior of the world who came to it first in Africa by water as the fish. We have already seen that the mystical emblem called the "Vesica Pisces" as a frame and aureole for the virgin and her child, is a living witness to the birth of Jesus from the fish's mouth, as it was in the beginning for Iusa or Horus of the Inundation. This will also explain why Icthus the fish, is a title of Jesus in Rome; why the Christian religion was founded on the fish; why the primitive Christians were called Pisciculi, and why

the fish is still eaten as the sacrificial food on Friday and at Easter (*Ancient Egypt,* p. 734).

So much for Horus, though I have hardly touched the fringe of the extraordinary parallels between him and Jesus. The reader must go to Massey for the minute and elaborate details of the resemblances.

What about Mithra—was he also just a "type" of Jesus? It is a fact that Mithraism was a strong rival to Christianity for centuries and it might easily have succeeded in the struggle for supremacy. As it was, Christianity triumphed but was obliged to absorb a great deal of Mithraism; and it is curious to note that the founder of the Christian sect known as the Manicheans— Mani or Manes— according to Mosheim, taught that "Christ is the glorious intelligence which the Persians call Mithras. . . . His residence is the sun." Mithraists, like Christians, were baptized, confirmed and, says Cumont, in his *Mysteries of Mithra,* "expected from a Lord's supper salvation of body and soul". Sunday was their sacred day, and the birth of the Sun, that is, Mithra himself, was on Dec. 25. Mithraists believed in a Heaven habited by the "saved", in Hell peopled by Demons; also in a Flood and a Revelation, in the immortality of the soul, in a last judgment, and the resurrection of the dead. There are plenty more resemblances, indeed so many, that Christian writers have been forced to claim that it was Mithraism which borrowed from Christianity. But the reader should turn to Robertson's *Pagan Christs* for an account of the cult, and the number of parallels with its successful rival; then to the work entitled, *Mythic Christs and the True* by the Rev. W. St. Clair Tisdall, which sets out to demolish Mr. Robertson, and to the latter's reply in the Appendix to *Pagan Christs.* Dr. Tisdall, while bitterly impugning any attempt to show parallelisms between Mithra and Jesus, concedes that "'one unceasing purpose runs' a Divine plan for the education of the human race" through religion—in other words, that if resemblances to Christianity are found in other religions, these are the "preparations" or the "types". But the fact that Mithra died, contends Tisdall, and Christ "lives on", proves how utterly insufficient was Mithra to satisfy man's need for a

Savior. For me and for other Mythicists, Mithra joins the other Pagan Christs as one of the sources from which Jesus was undoubtedly manufactured.

There are "types" like Adonis, Attis, Apollo, Perseus, Prometheus, Pythagoras, Bacchus, and a number of others. It is possible to fill a huge volume with extracts from writers who are thoroughly orthodox, and who would be horrified if they thought that any of their admissions regarding Pagan deities could be construed as helping the awful heresy of maintaining that Jesus never lived at all. But I have, I hope, given sufficient evidence, not that Christianity blatantly borrowed from other religions without acknowledgment, but that similar stories of Christs, Saviors, Messiahs, Virgin Births, Angels, Devils, Temptations, Resurrections, Crosses, and many other supposedly unique features of Christianity, were commonplaces of Paganism and that Christianity is just one more Oriental religion, and no more a "revelation" than is Mormonism.

There is still one method, however, of interpreting the Christian story which requires attention and to that we must devote a fresh chapter.

CHAPTER X

Christianity and
Allegory

MOST STUDENTS OF ANCIENT RELIGIONS WILL
soon come across the word "mysteries", a word which is supposed
to describe or hide the secret religious ceremonies known only
to their priests or initiates. The "vulgar", that is, the ordinary
people, were never admitted to these "holy of holies", and it was
mostly because of this that a priest managed to persuade believers that he was in touch with God and that he had power to
put other initiates also in touch with the Deity. We have in our
own day similar nonsense with what the Christian Church calls
laying on of hands or "apostolic succession", by which means the
priesthood is perpetuated. And in the Church, there have always
been secret communities which pretended to the world, or deluded themselves, that they represented something higher in
God's eyes than the ordinary Christian believer.

In Bacon's *Wisdom of the Ancients* will be found interpretations of stories of the Pagan Gods, which are quite different from
their meaning "on the surface". Bacon called these stories
"poetical fables"; he declared that "religion delights in shadows
and disguises"; and he was convinced that "a concealed instruc-

tion and allegory was originally intended in many of the ancient fables". He gives many examples of incidents in pagan mythology —such as Typhon cutting out and carrying away Jupiter's sinews —which, taken literally, make rubbish, but when properly understood are full of meaning. The relators of these myths "drew from the common stock of ancient tradition", and Bacon looked upon them, not as the invention of poets, "but as sacred relics", and refused to discuss the matter with anyone who insisted that the esoteric meanings were not there, but "were imposed upon the ancient fables" by such as he.

That behind the story of Jesus in the Gospels lies another meaning, an allegorical meaning, has been the convinced attitude of many great Christians, among them, for example, Origen. He did not deny, except in some cases, the literal meaning, but he held very firmly to the allegorical or mystical sense of the Scriptures. Thus, although it was he who championed the Church against Celsus, one of its most formidable opponents—Celsus, by the way, looked upon the Christian Church as a secret society— Origen was by no means considered fully orthodox, and in some Christian quarters he was considered one of the worst of heretics.

There appears to have been always Christians ready to interpret the New Testament in a mystical sense, though for almost the whole body of believers it is the other way. When Thomas Woolston (1669-1733) in his *Six Discourses* claimed Origen as a great believer in Christianity who saw beneath the surface, it was in justification of his own attack on the miracles of "our Lord". Woolston ridiculed the literal interpretation of the Gospel story as unworthy of God, and brought forward a supposed Jewish rabbi to speak for him, as he himself said (or pretended) that he venerated Jesus too much to attack him. "Some of them [the miracles]", says the rabbi, "are absurd tales, others foolish facts, others unjust actions, others ludicrous pranks, others juggling tricks, others magical enchantments." And the only way to get rid of these stupid miracles is by denying that they ever occurred, that in fact, there was another meaning to them. Woolston himself deals with the miracle of curing a sick man of palsy which he considered "the most monstrously absurd, improbable, and incredible of any. There is not one miracle related of Jesus that does not labor under more or less absurdities . . . but this for number and greatness of absurdities surpasses them all."

Over and over again his disciples admitted that they could not understand Jesus—"But they understood not that saying and were afraid to ask him", Mark ix, 32, is typical—which shows that the authors of the Gospels knew perfectly well that the "vulgar" would take their recitals literally, never understanding the mystical or "spiritual" significance behind the words or actions attributed to Jesus.

To save the Bible then from attacks of those Atheists who ridicule its history as nonsense or absurd myths, some Christian writers felt it necessary to stress its mystical or spiritual meaning. This is what Swedenborg did, giving a special sense to many "key" words, and of course making it difficult to attack the Bible on purely materialistic grounds. Every story in the New Testament is history, literal history, cries the fervent Christian, until he is driven into a corner. When he is asked to explain how a Devil managed to carry Jesus, the Son of God, through the air and put him on the pinnacle of the temple, and nobody in the whole of Jerusalem saw it, or if anybody did see it no account outside the New Testament has ever been recorded, the answer is that the story is "allegorical". It never took place. But if one can pick and choose as to what is or is not symbolical or allegorical in a narrative "inspired" by God, of Himself or His own Son (it is not clear which), where and how are we to stop? Who is to say? On what grounds is one story symbolical, and another not?

Moreover, one would like to know who made the symbolism in the first place? Was it God or man made? How can anyone tell unless the Atheistic position is taken and God ruled out?

We are told that "the story in the canonical Gospels is, from the symbolical point of view, a dramatization of the evolution of the human soul" (*The Gospel Drama*, G. A. Gaskell, p. 5). The author contends that "the deep meanings of the scriptures have always been recognized in some degree by a few meditative thinkers through interior illumination of the mind", and "people may often subjectively perceive true ideas which they cannot objectively understand and express; and this intuitive perception makes them fasten upon all kinds of fantastic interpretations of scripture . . . no independent writings, and no formal system of thought, can give the entire meaning embodied in Divinely inspired scriptures."

In another mystical work called *The Coming Christ* by "Johanna", we find the writer insists that "the Virgin, the miraculous Birth, the Baptism and the Baptist are conditions of the soul and spiritual experiences . . . they, together with the Temptation, Passion, Burial, Resurrection, and Ascension, constitute Acts in the mysteries of the soul, and they are to be understood, not as occurring to one individual only, but to any and every son of man who becomes a son of God . . . the teaching regarding the mystical Christ Jesus within the soul is that which constitutes the new gospel." And when we get such a thorough orthodox Christian as Dr. Sanday in *Hasting's Dictionary*, v. 2, p. 612, to admit that "the narratives of the Temptation are upon the face of them symbolical", we are obliged to conclude that there may be "something in it".

But though so many orthodox Christians are willing to admit a symbolism in the New Testament to a more or less degree, very few of them part with the "historic" figure of Jesus. Every story concerning him may be symbolic, or allegory, but he undoubtedly existed if only for the purpose of going about "doing good". Even if it were proved from such texts as Hebrews v. 9-10, vi, 19-20, vii. 26, viii. 4, that Jesus was victim, sacrifice, priest, altar, God, man, king, high priest, sheep, lamb, and perhaps many more things, he would still for them exist. But there are a few "mystics" who see the absurdity of this like Mr. Gilbert Sadler, M.A., who in his *The Inner Meaning of the Four Gospels* and *Behind the New Testament* has been forced to recognize the non-historicity of the Christian Deity.

He claims that "the compilers of the four Gospels . . . used material which arose from an earlier gnostic, mystic circle, perhaps in Alexandria. In that circle, the 'Christ' was a divine figure in Jewish minds, and he was set forth in the Book of Enoch (B.C. 70) as One eternally with God. The Gnostics added the term and the Figure to their idea of the Logos or Primal Man, who had descended to earth, being 'crucified' in so doing, and had risen to lift men to eternal life. The Cross to the Gnostics, meant the boundary between the eternal and phenomenal: and in it the Son of God was fixed."

There is a deal more of this kind of explanation as to how the Gospels came into being bringing with them the message of re-birth in "Christ", which eventually so influenced Greeks, Jews, Syrians, and others, that in time the stories in them were re-edited so that the "ideal" being became a "real" man who once lived on earth, and his death, instead of being the death of the old, bad "soul", was looked upon as an historical occurrence. It may be as well to give a specimen or two of the way Sadler and Gaskell interpret some of the Gospel incidents.

Jesus taught in the Jewish synagogue "as one having authority and not as the scribes" (Mt. vii, 29). "The teaching of the Spirit within comes with authority since it is direct revelation to the soul of the things of eternal life. The teaching of history and the letter of scripture, is of uncertainties and illusions." *Gaskell.*

"And in the synagogue there was a man which had a spirit of an unclean devil, and cried out with a loud voice . . . I know thee who thou art; the Holy One of God, etc." (Lk. iv, 33-34). "The 'devils' are the lowest conditions of the natural man, and even these are instinctively aware of the Higher nature. The 'casting out of a devil' is the transformation affected by the Spirit's response to the soul's active recognition of the Higher." *Gaskell.*

"And then shall many stumble, and shall deliver up one another, and shall hate one another." (Mt. xxiv, 10). "This means that the lower nature is full of strife, and is at cross purpose with itself." *Gaskell.*

"And as Jesus passed by, he saw a man which was blind from his birth." (Jn. ix, 1). "This man is a symbol of the Gentiles. Not only can Christ heal the Jews and Samaritans, but the Gentiles also. They were born blind, i.e., have never had the spiritual light. That the sight referred to here is spiritual is clear from verses 39, 40 where the Pharisees say: 'Are *we* also blind?' So the healing was not history. It was a parable of the Christ's power, re-set as if a miracle had happened. . . . The Inner Ideal Life can save all men." *Sadler.*

"A certain woman named Martha received him into her house. And she had a sister called Mary." (Lk. x, 38-39). "Martha and Mary seem to be allegorical characters. Martha meant 'Kuria' mistress, a giver of laws. Therefore she represents the Law, while Mary by her eagerness represented the teachable Christian, the humble life, the life of the Ptokoi or meek ones. Only that one thing is needed. The Church calls here for Catchumens, initiates." *Sadler.*

Both Sadler and Gaskell proceed on the lines above and explain what look to an ordinary reader, ordinary teachings and ordinary incidents; as a "re-birth" or "renewal" of the soul in its fight against evil. It is the old struggle—in my opinion—of the battle between the Sun God and his enemies, Night, Darkness, Winter, or Death, placed into Man's inner consciousness, or in his "spiritual" being. It is just Gnosticism made "alive" in the shape of a story easily understood. But it knocks out all idea that there ever was a real Christ or a real Jesus, whether "doing good" or not.

Even Theosophists are agreed that behind the Gospel story there is an inner meaning. In his book *The Christian Creed,* C. W. Leadbeater claims that the *true* meaning of the Apostle's Creed and the Nicene Creed, if known at all, is known to very few Christians. Well before many of the ecclesiastical councils had edited and authorized these Creeds, Leadbeater thinks that the true signification had been lost.

Let us take a phrase like "And was incarnate by the Holy Ghost of the Virgin Mary." Leadbeater says this should read "and was incarnate of the Holy Ghost *and* the Virgin Mary" and his explanation is,

> That is to say, the monadic essence, having already "come down from heaven" as mentioned in the previous clause, materializes itself by assuming a garment of the visible and tangible matter already prepared for its reception by the action of the Logos in His Third Aspect upon what without that action would have been virgin, or unproductive, matter. . . . Here again the materializing tendency has introduced a totally different idea by a very trifling alteration—in fact, by the insertion of a single letter, for in the earliest form the name was not Maria, but Maia, meaning simply mother. It would be tempting to speculate as to

whether there could possibly be any traditional connection between this strangely suggestive word and the Sanskrit Maya, which is so often used to express this same illusory veil of matter which the Logos draws round Him in His descent; but all that can be said at present is that no such connection has yet been traced.

Leadbeater then does not exactly believe in the Virgin Mary, though he certainly does believe in Jesus Christ who was "a young man of wondrous devotion and surpassing purity" and "had been fully instructed in the secret teachings which were the real fount of life among the Essenes"—to quote Mrs. Besant's *Esoteric Christianity*. He did not believe that the words translated "Pontius Pilate" were ever meant to be the name of the notorious governor of Judea and claims that the Greek words were corrupted. At all events, he translates them as "a compressed or intensified sea" and therefore instead of "suffered under Pontius Pilate" we should read, "He endured the dense sea —"that is to say, for us men and for our salvation, he allowed himself to be for the time limited by, and imprisoned in, astral matter".

As for the Crucifixion, he calls this a misinterpretation of "an almost universal misunderstanding whose proportions have been colossal and its results most disastrous". It is really "a perfectly reasonable allegory" which has been turned into "an absolutely impossible biography". Both the Crucifixion and the Resurrection "clearly belong to the Christ-allegory". Yet all this misunderstanding and wrong interpretation of the Creed does not in any way whatever prove that Jesus never lived. Theosophists are quite firm on that point.

All this brings me to Prof. W. B. Smith's famous *Ecce Deus* which also stands by its allegorical thesis. For him, as for other defenders of the Myth theory, there was a pre-Jesus cult, but I am not concerned with that as much as what he says about symbolism. He scores—in my opinion—many points against the literalists. He quotes, for example, I Cor. x, 14-22 ". . . The cup of blessing which we bless, is it not communion of the blood of Christ? The bread that we break, is it not communion of the body of Christ?" And Smith quotes quite a number of passages

about the "body" of Christ: "But ye are Christ's body," "Because
we are members of his body," "And he is the head of the body,
the Church," "Which is the shadow of things to come, but the
body is the Christ's", and so on. "What is this 'body' of the
'Christ' "? asks Smith scornfully. Of course, it is the Church
"symbolized". And throughout Paul, one gets such symbolism,
which the Church certainly accepts as symbolism.

The trouble with some of the instances given in *Ecce Deus* is
that one can argue both ways, that is, that the passage is symbolical, and that it is not. This is what Howell Smith shows in his
examination of them; it is symbolism, it is not symbolism, it
could have happened, or it might be just a story. For example,
he says (p. 97), "The story of the widow's two mites (Mk. xii,
41-44; Lk. xxi, 1-4) is not a piece of symbolism, or an allegory;
but it *may* have been originally an edifying tale told by Jesus,
like the parable of the Good Samaritan, and been changed into
an episode in the life of Jesus. . . . A similar tale occurs in the
Talmud. . . . Both the Talmudic and the Gospel anecdotes are
probably versions of a very old and far-traveled story, whose
original *may* or *may not* have been true of some actual person."
(Italics mine.)

By arguing in this way, the Historicist has no difficulty in saving Jesus as a real person. One of the stories recorded of Jesus
may, or *may not*, be "history"; it *may* have been just "an edifying
tale", and somebody *may* have "changed" it into an episode in
his life; and anyway, similar stories are found elsewhere, in the
Talmud for example (though here it is as well to point out that
the Talmud was compiled centuries after the Gospels.) Anyway,
the story "*may* or *may not*" have been true of an actual person;
and Jesus is saved again.

Howell Smith also examines the case of "symbolism" in the
Gospels given in *Ecce Deus* of the curious text in Mark xiv, 51-52,
about the young man who fled naked leaving a linen cloth. This
has never "been satisfactorily explained by the commentators" he
admits. The commentary on the passage given in the volume devoted to the Gospels issued by the Society for Promoting Christian Knowledge says, "It has been thought by many that this
young man may be St. Mark himself . . . if not St. Mark, it was

probably someone well known to the readers of St. Mark's Gospel." It was St. Mark, or it was not; and the reader can take his choice, so long as the incident in Christian eyes is considered historical. Needless to say, some commentators never keep their eagle eyes far from the Old Testament whenever they sense difficulties in a text in the New, and so they consider the story was "inspired" by Amos ii, 16, a conclusion to which the Jewish writer, Dr. Claude Montefiore, assents. And if this is so, the story is *not* historical.

In the Concordant Version of the New Testament to which I have already referred, the translator, a staunch Fundamentalist, has this note, "Linen, used as clothing, typifies righteousness. No one could fly from Him in His hour of need without exposing his own shame and utter lack of righteousness". Here then we have an unashamed literalist admitting the symbolism in the story.

Howell Smith works all around the account with all sorts of suggestions trying to find some reason for not giving it up. "Why not accept this episode", he asks finally, "as a plain record of fact? Our hesitation arises from its apparent pointlessness. . . ." And we are left in the dark again as to what his position really is.

But there is no hesitation in *Ecce Deus* which gives strong reasons why the whole episode is "pointless" if considered literally, and full of symbolism otherwise. Mr. Sadler adds, "But the idea of the linen garment seems to be a Gnostic one—for in the mysteries, linen garments were used—so that the story may be symbolic, using the Amos passage as material to set forth a symbol".

Prof. W. B. Smith analyzes, among other examples, the story of the Barren Fig Tree in Mark xi, 12-14, 20-21. "Surely," he says, "no one can for a moment understand this quite literally. To curse a fig tree, to blast it and wither it, because it did not bear figs out of season is inconceivable in any rational being, much more in a perfect man or a man-god." He does not find it easy to explain the symbolism, but he quotes with approval various writers who show how the whole atmosphere surrounding the writers of Bible "history" was soaked in allegory and hidden meanings and concludes, "*So it appears that such symbolism as*

we find in the Gospels was not merely a native plant, it was a
rank growth in the soil from which they sprung".

Whether the interpretation given by Prof. Smith is one which
will appeal to the reader, or is in fact the only reasonable interpretation, is another question altogether. Personally, I cannot
follow him in all his conclusions. But his book is packed with
suggestive material and is highly original; and he makes some
startling points to be considered very seriously. As for example:

> Once more we repeat that there is *not a single distinctly human*
> *trait ascribed by Mark to the Jesus.* . . . There is, in fact, in
> this earliest extant evangelic story not a distinctive human fea-
> ture; it is hardly even in any guise of man, but openly and
> unambiguously as God, that the Lion of the tribe of Judah strides
> through this Gospel. Who will overturn this universal negative
> by producing a single affirmative instance?

Prof. Smith naturally is aware that in all the Gospel allegories
or symbols "certain details are introduced merely for artistic
effect . . . but it seems really surprising how accurately the symbolism is carried out, and how vividly the general situation is
delineated". And he is ready to admit that "occasionally some
ancient mythical motive may have been active, or some historical
reminiscence (*not* of Jesus); yet it is astonishing how large a
fraction of the Gospel total urgently invites symbolic interpretation".

I cannot boil down in a page, or even in a few, Prof. Smith's
closely reasoned argument, and the reader should study for himself the position he so ably maintains in *Ecce Deus*. That he may
be wrong here and there can be admitted without in any way
condemning his whole thesis; and it should be added he had
very great admiration for the early Christians and propagandists
who "were very great men", who conceived "noble and beautiful
and attractive ideas", and who had among them "striking, powerful, and imposing personalities".

Lest anyone after reading *Ecce Deus* still be in doubt about
the symbolism of the Gospels, Prof. Smith asks him to consider
"that a large portion of the Gospels consists of such avowed
metaphors, and that it is expressly said by Mark: 'Without a
parable spake He not unto them' ". Moreover he points out that

the story of Sarah and Hagar which "seems to us to be as plainly, simply, and unequivocally historical as anything in literature" is referred to in Gal. iv, 24, "Which things are allegorical". There are, in short, "no texts in the Gospels that indicate that the Jesus was a man".

Just another word on Judas. Prof. Smith sees in the whole story, and in the deliberate choosing of the name—Judas Iscariot—very clever symbolism, and he devotes many pages to a careful discussion of the "traitor". His conclusion is, "That Judas Iscariot typifies the Jewish people in its rejection of the Jesus cult seems so obvious, it seems to meet us so close to the threshold of the inner sense of the New Testament, that it may move our wonder that anyone should overlook it. However, the ablest, and even the boldest, the most lynx eyed, critics have passed it by". Yes, and for Conybeare and other stout defenders of Jesus—as a man—and even many Rationalists, the Judas story is perfect history!

There is still another kind of symbolism in connection with the Bible to be considered. It is what is known as the Symbolism of Numbers. It may seem strange that in this scientific age anybody would really believe that there was "something" in numbers, something hidden, "esoteric" or occult, something which tells us our fortunes or our fate, yet there it is, for vast numbers of people certainly believe in number symbolism, and there is always a market for a new book giving further details or even repeating the old ideas. Every letter has its number, as indeed was the case with Hebrew and Greek; and every number has its occult signification when reduced to its simplest form. So one's name added to the birth date, and again added to in special ways, gives a particular number which is one's own; or perhaps this same number belongs to famous persons, and therefore all have the same characteristics. My own special number, I believe, is like that of Charles Dickens, though I have never been able to trace any resemblance whatever between myself and that great genius—but then perhaps my calculations may be miles out.

But whatever present day people may or may not believe about numbers, it is a fact that the "mystery" religions had great faith in them. Gnostic and Kabbalistic literature is full of number symbolism and it certainly produces some extraordinary results.

Take the number seven as a first example. The Bible is full of it, and no one can study the cases given without becoming convinced that it was all deliberately designed.

Gen. i, 1 consists of seven words and 28 (4x7) letters—in Hebrew of course. God rested on the seventh day and therefore seven is a perfect number. God gives in Gen. xii, 2-3, a seven-fold blessing to Abraham, and another seven-fold blessing to Israel in Exod. vi, 6-8, beginning with "I will bring you out of Egypt". Seven sprinklings had to be given on the Day of Atonement (see *Number in Scripture* by the Rev. E. W. Bullinger, page 171, etc., for these and other references). There are 126 (7x18) Psalms which have titles, and there are seven names given as authors of these Psalms. David is also mentioned seven times as the author of Psalms, in the New Testament. During his life, the Angels appeared seven times to Jesus. (Before his birth they came along three times which makes ten altogether. 10, says Bullinger, "completes the perfection of Divine order". This may be so, but all the same, the symbol of 10 is *phallic* representing the male and female elements.)

The numbers four and three—that is, seven—play a big part in the Bible, and most of the instances are duly recorded by the industrious Mr. Bullinger. So do the numbers six and seven. Let me quote again, and the reader must decide for himself if there is or is not symbolism in the examples given.

Why are there two genealogies of Jesus? Well, in Matthew, God says to us, "Behold thy King". (Zech. ix, 9). In Mark he says, "Behold my servant". (Isa. xl, 1). In Luke He says, "Behold the Man". (Zech. vi, 12). In John He says, "Behold your God". (Isa. xl, 9). Bullinger says:

> Now a *servant* need not produce his genealogy; neither can *God* have one. It is a *King* who must have one, and a *Man* who should have one. Therefore it is that we have two genealogies and not more than two. And that is why we have one in Matthew giving the *Royal* genealogy of Jesus as King; and one in Luke giving the *Human* genealogy of Jesus as Man. Hence also Matthew's is a *descending* genealogy, while Luke's is an *ascending* one. For *kings* must trace their *descent* . . . and man must trace

his *ascent*. Matthew's therefore, begins with Abraham and comes down to Joseph, the son of Heli; while Luke's starts from Joseph, and goes up to Adam and God.

After more of this kind of exegesis, Bullinger says, "Now the wonderful fact is that we have in the genealogy of Luke iii exactly 77 names, with God at the one end, and Jesus at the other. This is indeed stamping it with the number of *spiritual* perfection". So much for Luke. What about Matthew? Note that, although the number 42 (7x6) generations are given in chapter i, only 41 *names* are actually shown. According to Kings and Chronicles, however, four names are omitted, three between Jehoram and Uzziah and one between Josiah and Jeconiah. Add these four and also the twenty-one (3x7) names before Abraham (from Luke iii) and you get 41 plus 4 plus 21 which make 66 names. "When we remember," says Bullinger, "that *six* is the human number, and *seven* the Divine, can we doubt that we are thus pointed to the fact that Jesus was both Son of God and Son of Man?"

Needless to say, the same symbolism can be found in his name —in Greek of course. Jesus (his name as a man) has six letters, "Ihsous", while Christ (his Divine title as the Son of God) has seven letters, "Cristos". Forty-one names are given in the genealogy in Matthew, when there should be forty-two. This genealogy is divided into three groups, 14 plus 14 plus 13. Why 13? Because it is in this group that the name of Jesus occurs, and so you have 6 plus 7, the human and divine numbers, and Jesus was, of course, both Man and God. (*Six* is the human number because it was on the *sixth* day that man was created, and it was God who rested on the *seventh*.)

In addition we must not forget two other instances of six associated with Jesus, as a Man. His birth was announced in the sixth month (Lk. i. 26); and he was crucified at the sixth hour (Mt. xxvii, 45; Mk. xv, 33; Lk. xxiii, 44).

The truth is, of course, that the Bible is packed with symbolism of all kinds but the "vulgar"—which means ordinary persons like you, the reader, and me—were never permitted to understand it. They were told a plain story, the sweet simple story of Jesus going about "doing good", which they understood literally, and from which it is almost impossible to get people to depart; and this includes many of our most learned Rationalists. Yet the symbolism is there, and it was put there deliberately; and to imagine that these various numbers were really accidental, and that names and circumstances were all not carefully chosen, is to show a credulity even more stupid and naive than that so unblushingly affirmed by our Salvation Army lassies.

It would be possible to go more fully into all the "mysteries" connected with the Christian Church—mysteries very well known to those students who have studied Christian Gnosticism with its "incarnations", "redemptions", "means of Grace", "Meditorial Purposes", "Outer and Inner Circles", "the Elect", "Advents and Avatars", and so on. If the reader wants to see what all this terminology means—I have never been able to find out myself—he should read the *Pistis Sophia* which Massey quotes a good deal, or consult such books as *Progressive Redemption* and *Progressive Creation* by the Rev. H. E. Sampson. He will find therein "mysteries" enough to take him a lifetime to solve.

"Mysteries" always have their "initiates" and naturally Jesus was the greatest of all "initiates", and also perhaps the last one. According to Sampson and Edouard Schuré in his *Jesus the Last Great Initiate*, Jesus was an Essene—as Robert Taylor insisted in his *Diegesis*—who, after being initiated, "lived, practised, healed, and preached, according to the teaching and power attained by the disciplines of the Order. He made Disciples, and initiated them in the esoteric Truth of the Mysteries, and he preached exoterically the same Truth, to the multitude; that is to say by 'parables' and symbolical language". And Schuré has an easy way of accounting for the resemblances to other religions in Christianity. After Jesus had been initiated, and sworn to eternal secrecy, he was "instructed in the doctrine of the Divine Word (Logos) already taught by Krishna in India, by the priests of Osiris, by Orpheus and Pythagoras, in Greece; and known to the prophets under the name of the Mysteries of the Son of Man and the Son of God".

It would be useless to say to these good people that all this "esoteric" stuff is mere "words, words and words", and that almost all of it is completely devoid of meaning; for the answer of the "initiates" would naturally be that it is quite impossible for the "vulgar" to understand such things just as it is impossible for them to understand the meaning of the terminology used in the higher mathematics. We must leave it at that; and the reader must decide for himself on the evidence exactly how much truth there is in the "esoteric" side of Christianity. It is not easy to decide. It was not easy, for example, for Mrs. Besant to decide at first, but good Atheist as she was, she went bodily over to the "symbolists" in the end, and became a thorough believer in Theosophy, the modern version of the "Secret Doctrine". For myself, it was the study of all this which finally made me a convinced believer in the non-historicity of Jesus.

CHAPTER XI

The Myth Theory
and Its Critics

WHEN DUPUIS AND VOLNEY IN FRANCE, AND ROB-
ert Taylor in England, first broached their theory of the non-
existence of Jesus, the scholars and intellectuals of the period
shrugged their shoulders with a smile which often turned into a
guffaw. Infidels would have their little joke, but such a theory
was so utterly silly that no one could expect a reasoned argument against it. It was quite on a par with the flat earth theory
and it was not even a case of answering a fool according to his
folly.

The Sun Myth theory may account for Bacchus, or Hercules,
or Attis, but really to suggest that "*our* Lord" never existed wasn't
even funny—though we had to laugh at it; it was just pure
lunacy. Why, you could apply the theory to anybody—to Napoleon, if you insisted on a famous man. Let us see if Napoleon is
not just a Sun Myth.

It was a Frenchman called Perez who, early last century, decided to annihilate the Sun Myth as applied to Jesus. He wrote
a pamphlet which is often quoted; I mean by this that the pamphlet is mentioned as being a complete answer to the Mythicists,

but few persons appear to have read it. Here then are some of the points it makes: First of all take the word Napoleon. It is practically the same as Apollon or Apollo, but if we take the spelling of his name as it appears on the column in the Place Vendôme, Néapoléo, the prefix "Ne", which in Greek is a participle of affirmation, shows that Napoleon is the *true* Apollo or the Sun. Bonaparte, his other name, really is "bon part", that is, the good part of the day—the sun giving us the good part, or Daylight, and the moon and stars, the bad part—the Night or Darkness.

Apollo was born on Delos, in the Mediterranean, while Napoleon was also born on a Mediterranean island, Corsica. Apollo was an Egyptian deity, so, of course, we can understand Napoleon going to Egypt and being received with homage and admiration.

Napoleon's mother was called Letitia, which means "joy", that is, joy at the dawn of light, or the break of day when the Sun rises or is "born"; but also note that Apollo's mother was called Leto, which is very much like Letitia. Apollo had three sisters called the Graces; Napoleon had three sisters, also famed for their beauty. He also had four brothers—who, of course, represent the four seasons of the year. Three of these brothers were kings,—Spring, reigning over flowers, Summer, reigning over the harvest, and Autumn, holding sway over fruits. And just as the three kings held their authority through Napoleon, so the three seasons get theirs from the Sun. And why was one of Napoleon's brothers not a King? Because he represents Winter, which does not reign over anything.

It may be asserted that at least Winter had an "empire", over cold and waste. Well, Napoleon's brother was invested with a principality when the Emperor's power was declining—as the Sun's does in Winter. It was called Canino, a word derived from *Cani*, which means the "whitened hair of old age"—that is, Winter.

Napoleon had two wives; so had Apollo. Apollo was given the Earth and the Moon. By the Moon, he had Horus. Napoleon also had just one son.

Napoleon had twelve Marshals, obviously the twelve signs of

the Zodiac; he, like the Sun, after being victorious in the South
where it represents its highest power, had to go North. Here he
had to retreat, that is, the Sun is driven back upon his traces,
"following the sign of Cancer, a sign which represents the retro-
gression of the sun in that portion of the sphere". It surely is
clear that the story of Napoleon's march into Russia and his
retreat is based on the Sun being driven back as explained above.

Finally the Sun rises in the East and sets in the West. What
more beautiful proof could be given of Napoleon coming from
his Eastern isle in the Mediterranean and setting (dying) in the
West on the island of St. Helena? It was not until the foregoing
was written that I found Baring-Gould in his *Curious Myths of
the Middle Ages* had given much the same resume of Perez as "a
curiosity and a caution". He warns the Myth believers against
accepting too extravagant interpretations but is quite prepared
"to admit the premises upon which mythologists construct their
theories".

Another pamphlet which is supposed to have annihilated the
Myth theory was written by Archbishop Whately, *Historic
Doubts Relative to Napoleon Buonaparte*, which is sometimes
confused with that of Perez. As a matter of fact, it deals with
Hume's *Essay on Miracles,* and laboriously attempts to show that
if Hume's objections are carried to their logical conclusions, it
would be possible to prove that Napoleon never existed. It is, in
my opinion, a very poor performance, and all that Henry Morley,
who republished it in his *Universal Library,* could say about it
was that it was designed as a "reduction to the absurd of the too
skeptical spirit of inquiry. . . ." Whately was always ready to be
broadminded and skeptical on everything but Christianity. There
he was almost a Fundamentalist.

As for Perez, the plain and sufficient answer is that the "iconography" of Napoleon, and the copious accounts of his contemporaries, prove his existence; while in nothing related of him is
there a semblance of a "miracle". No doubt one could find some
coincidences in "Pickwick" of gods and myths. It would be possible to point to Sam Weller and say that here we have the
Hebrew prophet Samuel—Sam, and in his name Weller is cleverly
hidden God's name "El" as it is in Samu-el. It could even be

urged that the great man himself, "Samuel" Pickwick, was really a re-incarnation of the Old Testament prophet. This kind of argument leads nowhere, while it can be shown that in hundreds of small details the stories of the pagan Gods agree to an astonishing degree. And there are no stories of Gods without many "miracles".

Although thousands of books have been written in defence of Christianity as a credible religion, actually there have not been many first class works specially dealing with the question of the existence of Jesus as a man. Paine, Strauss, and Renan, though quite ready to admit the strong mythical element in the Gospels, were all bitterly opposed to such views as those enunciated by Dupuis, Volney, and Robert Taylor. Strauss, indeed, though discrediting the miracles of Jesus yet could say quite sincerely that "the essence of the Christian faith is perfectly independent of his [Strauss'] criticism. The supernatural birth of Christ, his miracles, his resurrection and ascension, remain as historical truths, whatever doubts may be cast on their reality as historical facts." [Preface.] No doubt, some poetic interpretation of the "eternal truths" appealed to Strauss, though what exactly it was I have not the least idea. He certainly was aware that quite a number of writers had already agreed that whatever was or was not the essence of the Christian faith there was no evidence that Jesus had ever lived. Strauss mentions that "in 1799 was published an anonymous work concerning Revelation and Mythology. The writer contends that the whole life of Jesus, all that he should and would do, had an ideal existence in the Jewish mind long prior to his birth". And of course he was bound to notice Woolston, though without in any way answering him. Strauss is, as one might expect, very thorough, and does his best to labor the differences between "negative" and "positive" myths. But he certainly believed in Jesus.

So did Renan and Paine and Ingersoll; and Bradlaugh, whatever his private opinion may have been, never denied Jesus as he denied "God"—when he was defined. He was very cautious in expressing any opinion, and seems to me to have been rather afraid of the Myth theory, or any theory which took up the allegorizing or the symbolical side of the Gospels.

Not until John M. Robertson took up the case and bent his encyclopedic mind on the problem did we get a modern approach, armed with the immense advance in such sciences as Anthropology and Psychology, as well as the study of Comparative Religions, which the past hundred years have given us.

Robertson wrote six books on the problem of Jesus (if we add his *Short History of Christianity*) and he certainly aroused great opposition. Naturally, he was pooh-poohed by superior Christians and various attempts were made to answer him. Many of these so-called replies he dealt with, but it surely is very amusing to compare, let us say Dr. St. Clair Tisdall's *Mythic Christs and the True*, or the Rev. T. J. Thorburn's *The Historical Jesus*, both still in the pamphlet stage, with such massive productions as *Christianity and Mythology* and *Pagan Christs*. These two works are packed with very close reasoning and authorities, and the evidence is marshalled with marvelous skill. The principal idea of Tisdall and Thorburn is to go through the two books with one idea only: to catch Robertson tripping over his authorities.

It is, as I have already pointed out, an old idea worked by Bentley against Anthony Collins. It has been used by almost every Christian controversialist since and, needless to say, Tisdall felt it was his duty to follow the same road, especially if by doing so his own reputation as a scholar would be enhanced. All I need say here is that it is difficult to imagine that Thorburn and Tisdall really believed they had completely upset the Mythic case by such infantile productions as theirs.

Thorburn dismisses everything in Robertson by saying that "the actual historical existence of Jesus for Josephus is conclusively proved by the second reference" ("the brother of *Jesus who is called Christ*, whose name was James")—the first reference, with very bad grace, Thorburn admits is at least suspect or, in his own words, "The position taken by the present writer is to regard the value of the passage as uncertain, and accordingly to lean no great weight upon it". He admits that several "prominent" scholars hold that this first passage is "interpolated", the polite word used by Christian apologists for barefaced forgery; but though this may be true, it is not true of the second passage.

Christians admittedly forged the first passage but we are made to understand that they did not touch the second passage!

The authority given is that of Origen and Eusebius. Naturally the latter, who is, by the way, suspected of the first "interpolation" in Josephus, and who was writing nearly 300 years after the events, was obliged to follow *his* authority, Hegesippus. And who was Hegesippus?

It is when you track down some of the statements made by Christian and Rationalist believers in Christ (or Jesus) that the fun commences. We find out in this case, for example, that all we know of Hegesippus is that he is quoted by Eusebius, who tells us almost nothing whatever about him. He is supposed to have written something in the second century, and what we know of the end of James the Just comes from a passage quoted by Eusebius; and they both call James "the brother of the Lord". We know so very little about Hegesippus that if it were not for the fact that some such authority must be found by theologians for early Church history by hook or by crook, I doubt whether anything he said, or Eusebius said he said, would be even glanced at by reputable historians. The notice given of him in the orthodox Schaff-Herzog Encyclopedia almost dismisses Hegesippus with contempt.

The fact is that, if Christians admit the first reference to "Christ" in Josephus is a forgery, the second must be equally a forgery, however much they may indulge in wishful thinking.

Thorburn points out that Josephus' reference to John the Baptist is "undoubtedly genuine". But it is one of those mysteries, which Christians hate to solve, that John is never mentioned in the Epistles of Paul though, as baptism *is* mentioned, one would think that the great Forerunner would have been credited with some hand in the ceremony.

Thorburn fails to point out that the "undoubtedly genuine reference" is hopelessly at variance with the Gospel story. Each contradicts the other, as any reader can discover in five minutes. Herod, according to Josephus, imprisoned John because he was afraid that the Baptist's great influence with the people might lead them to rebellion. In the Gospels, John was imprisoned to please Herodias, and he was beheaded to please the daughter of

Herodias, though Herod was sorry to do this, as he liked John and considered him a just and holy man. John, according to Josephus, was imprisoned in Machaerus, which was at least a hundred miles from Galilee where lay Herod's government. But the Gospel account surely indicates that John was beheaded close at hand. It seems extraordinary also that nowhere does Josephus mention the followers of John, who certainly must have numbered many, if he ever lived.

The fact is that as Josephus was copied by Christian monks, it was quite easy to insert here and there clumsy forgeries, and the reference to John equals in veracity those to "Christ".

It is amusing to find Mr. Thorburn advising his readers to verify references, as "the references given to various authorities, ancient and modern, are not always to be trusted". I quite agree with him, and he provides one with a case in point. He refers to Whately's essay on Napoleon (about which I said a few words above) to show how easy it is to make up "plausible" arguments on the Mythic side. Whately, we are told, "cleverly demonstrates that Napoleon was merely a 'sun-myth'". The answer is that Whately does nothing of the kind; in fact, I think I am right in categorically stating that the word "sun-myth" does not occur in the whole of the essay. Whately was attacking the argument in Hume's *Essay on Miracles,* and Thorburn's statement proves that he never read Whately's essay, but confused it with that of Perez, which he obviously, also, had never read.

For the rest one gets the usual objections to the myth theory offered as if they had never been analyzed by, say, Robertson or Drews, and repeated *ad nauseam* as if the criticisms had never been made. As an example we are told that "the actual historicity of Jesus Christ . . . has never been doubted by the Jews". (p. 38). It is astonishing how often one finds this term, "the Jews", used without the slightest hint that as "the Jews" include members of various races—they are black, brown, yellow, and white— it is simply nonsense to lump them together and say "the Jews" said something it is utterly impossible to prove "they" said. The way Thorburn quotes the Talmud is exactly the way Christian apologists quote Eusebius; that is, he uses it as if what it put down about 500 or 600 A.D. is incontrovertible evidence of something which happened four or five centuries previously. When one analyzes the various statements about Jesus in the Talmud, as I have already shown, the result is many confused accounts, each utterly incredible (Thorburn admits that the *Sepher Toldeth Jeshua* contains "foolish and pointless miracles performed by the aid of magic", but, query, does he believe them?), yet he actually tells his readers that this mass of "cumulative evidence" confirms the "more accurate and historical Gospel narratives in a manner which might most reasonably be termed providential". Note the words, the "more accurate and historical" Gospels—as if there was the slightest truth in the absurd stories of Jesus being carried about by a Devil, or his stopping a storm by word of command, or the wholesale resurrection of Jewish "saints" when Jesus was "crucified".

We know from Justin's *Dialogue* that some Jews about the year 150 A.D. *did* deny the historicity of Jesus in no uncertain terms, which brings me to that semi-Rationalist apologist Dr. F. C. Conybeare again. Naturally, he is always quoted with glee by Christians, and, for that matter, even by such an uncompromising Rationalist as Joseph McCabe.

Yet I find it difficult to read him with patience, difficult to understand how any man with his reputation as a classical scholar could write what we find on so many pages of his *Historical Christ*.

He claims that when Trypho said that the Christians had "invented" Christ, that meant *another* Christ—someone the Jews expected as a Messiah. That is, although the whole argument of Justin was to show that Christ, *his* Christ, Jesus Christ, the Jesus of Nazareth of the New Testament, was prophesied in the Old, and therefore that Jews should accept him, yet when Trypho said, "You have invented this Christ", he really meant "exactly the opposite". (p. 109). I have rarely read such an "argument" even in the crudest apologetics. I have dealt with the whole question in a previous chapter. Here I can only express my astonishment again that Conybeare could have imagined that he had effectively disposed of the problem. It is impossible in this book to deal with him page by page. The reader will find in John M. Robertson's *The Jesus Problem* a number of points dealt

with, but the *Historical Christ* reeks with so many absurd statements and "objections" that it would require a whole volume to
deal adequately with them.

It is time now to turn to a more modern work, though I have
already discussed some of its arguments—*Jesus Not a Myth* by
A. D. Howell Smith. Like many other objectors to the Myth
theory, Howell Smith appears to think that if some of J. M.
Robertson's "speculations" as to the origins of the Christ Myth
can be proved to be based on very unsound premises, there must
have been a Jesus. For example, Robertson may be wrong in
assuming that a "Joshua cult" had been long in Palestine, and that
its members later became Christians; yet surely the fact of making
erroneous assumptions on the very difficult problem of Christian
origins is no argument whatever for an historical Jesus.

Actually, we are as much in the dark as to the historicity of
Joshua as we are of Jesus. The *Encyclopedia Biblica*, as Howell
Smith points out, is very skeptical about Joshua and even his
name, and is—rather surprising for the E. B.—disposed to agree
on "a solar mythical origin" for the Jewish leader. But though
according to the E. B., Joshua may be mythical or legendary
there may be, says Howell Smith, an "historical nucleus"; and he
cites Prof. Garstang's excavations on the site of Jericho as appearing to prove "the partial overthrow of the walls of the
Canaanite city by earthquake", and this as an "historical nucleus".
I fail to see what all this has to do with the evidence for Jesus
as a man. In any case, what does Prof. Garstang actually say?
On page 144 of his book *Joshua and Judges* he says, "Theoreti-
cally then, the possibility of the walls of Jericho having been
damaged or destroyed by earthquakes is to be admitted. But
an examination of the walls themselves hardly substantiates the
suggestion". The fact is you can take your choice: the walls *may*
have been damaged by earthquakes, or they *may not* have been.
This kind of reasoning does not seem to me to have much to
do with either Joshua or the Joshua cult.

My own examination of the theories put forward by Robertson
and Dujardin on the possibilities of a Joshua cult in Palestine
before Jesus, and the reply made by Howell Smith, leave me
quite neutral, particularly as speculations on both sides do not

prove anything. They are mere inferences. I can visualize a Joshua cult, and a Jacob cult, and a Jesus cult, all existing side by side, just as we have an "Eddy" cult (Christian Science) and a "Mormon" cult existing with official Christianity, and all three drawing from the same roots. Cults spring up and die in all civilizations. What has become of the once flourishing Essenes, for example?

While I am ready to admit that one can make any theory look extravagant, I do feel we ought to take an author's thesis as a whole in criticizing it and not just a word or a sentence. That is why I deprecate all these attempts to pick out a mistake here, and another there, as if everything else goes when a single error is discovered. As an instance, take Howell Smith's treatment of Niemojewski's thesis that in the story of Christianity we get the old sun and astral myths "humanized". I have to confess that I have not read his book. All I know about it is from what Drews says. Howell Smith may have read it, but that is not apparent from his criticism of Niemojewski's attempt to identify Pontius Pilate with the constellation of Orion as the "javelin man"— *pilatus*. Howell Smith states that the Latin word *pilatus* "has no connection with *pilum*", though in the Latin dictionary before me, (Cassell's) it says "Pilatus,—*Armed with the* Pilum *or javelin* (Verg)." He adds that *pilatus* means "pealed, bald, serried". The dictionary says, "Bald head, *calvitum*; bald place, *glabreta*; serried, *densus, confertus*". Perhaps Mr. Smith has consulted a dictionary unknown to most persons; but the reader can rest assured that the above definitions are correct. He can also see why it is necessary to check *every* statement coming from a defender of the "Jesus as a Man" theory; and why I am quite unhappy when I have to refer to a book like Niemojewski's when I have not read it.

Unlike most of his Christian supporters, Howell Smith does admit "genuine parallels to Christianity in pre-Christian cults and myths" (p. 10), which seems to me to be a fairly big concession. What does it matter if we cannot call a Christian forerunner Joshua with certainty when we agree that there were pre-Christian cults and myths in which are "genuine parallels"? When we are given "Zimmern's tablet" in which there is a "remarkable

parallel to 1 Peter iii, 19", and are assured that the eminent
Assyriologist, Prof. S. Langdon, "believes that the Marduk Passion myth has some bearing on the problem of Christian origins",
and we date the tablet about the ninth century B. C., I think that
Howell Smith's agreement with us in this instance is thoroughly
justified.

The real difficulty in dealing with such a work as *Jesus is Not a
Myth* is that over and over again we find all sorts of statements
made which are now, and have been in the past, questions of
almost interminable discussion. "Jesus," says Howell Smith, "did
not belong to the category of wine gods or bread gods." Yet in
Jn. vi, 35, Jesus says, "I am the bread of life: he that cometh to
me shall never hunger". In Jn. vii, 37, he says, "If any man thirst
let him come unto me and drink". In fact, no one protested more
than Jesus that he actually was "that bread of life", that he was
the "living bread which came down from heaven", and that the
"bread that I will give is my flesh." (Jn. vi, 48-58). So strong were
his protestations, that the Jews "strove among themselves", and
asked "How can this man give us *his* flesh to eat?" If this does
not make Jesus a bread God, then I cannot imagine what would.

As for not being a wine God, Jesus says in Mk. xiv, 22-24—
after handing out some bread which he blessed—"Take eat: this
is my body". "And he took the cup, and when he had given
thanks, he gave it to them: and they all drank of it. And he said
unto them, This is my blood of the new testament, which is
shed for many. Verily I say unto you, I will drink no more of
the fruit of the vine, until that day that I drink it new in the
kingdom of God." And in Jn. xv, 1, Jesus says, "I am the true
vine"—a declaration which makes him surely, as the "true" vine,
the greatest of wine Gods. Finally, there is that awful text which
has given Christian temperance orators more headaches than any
other: "The Son of Man is come eating and drinking; and ye
say, Behold a gluttonous man and a winebibber, a friend of pub-
licans and sinners!" (Lk. vii, 34).

I agree, of course, that whether Jesus was or was not a wine
or a bread God does not actually prove his historicity or otherwise, but I cite this statement from Howell Smith as an example
of the way in which one can slip in all sorts of assumptions for

which there is not a particle of justification—in the vain hope, I suppose, that a mere *ipse dixit* is sufficient to upset the Myth theory. You have an example in the statement that "However much mythology may have colored the evangelical records, sun lore seems to have found very little scope there". (p. 33). If I say that the evangelical records are packed with sun and astral lore, and that this has been demonstrated to the full by Dupuis and Robert Taylor, it is only putting their case against his; and in the end the reader must decide for himself. And even Mr. Smith gives a large number of examples as "probably" solar features—like the manger in which Jesus was cradled (though with due reverence, Jesus is called "the Babe of Bethlehem").

The author of the fourth Gospel is called "a Judaic mystic" (p. 43), on what grounds is not, of course, stated. We know *nothing whatever* of the author of John, and there is not the slightest justification for saying that he "or indeed any writer of the New Testament would go, directly or mediately, to Egyptian statuary for literary material is highly improbable". The New Testament is packed with allusions taken from Egyptian sources, and these sources might just as well have been from statuary as anything else.

Those of us who are not Greek scholars must naturally rely on Greek lexicons, and it is not always easy to follow Mr. Smith in Greek, or indeed other Christian apologists, for that matter, whenever they feel obliged to question the translations given in our Bibles. A case to point—it is only a little matter but it shows how easy it is to slip one in, so to speak—is his effort to show how wrong Robertson is in the Passion story.

The Greek word *apechei* is translated "it is enough" in our A.V., but Howell Smith suggests it ought to be "far from it". Yet Liddell and Scott give "it sufficeth, it is enough". The exact equivalent in the Sinaiticus Codex is "it-is-from-having came". Even Parkhurst gives, "it is enough". But once again, it is very difficult to find out exactly from this and other comments what conclusion Mr. Smith has come to with regard to the Passion being a transcript of a sacred drama as J. M. Robertson claims.

On this question of a sacred drama, Joseph McCabe contends in his *Sources of the Morality of the Gospels* that, "It would be

singular if the historical Jesus had crystallized out of a Jewish
myth in the first century, and not a single Rabbi in the fierce controversies of the second century knows anything about the myth,
cult or drama of his own race which would make an end of the
hated schism". (p. 21). I am not sure whether Robertson ever
took any notice of this criticism, but I would not be surprised if
he passed it in silence as he did much of Christian criticism. It
is—for me—difficult to understand how such a vigorous and
splendid Freethought advocate as Mr. McCabe has proved himself to be could ever have penned it. We simply do not know
anything about the "fierce controversies" of the second century
the evidence for which could in any way be relied on, from
Jewish quarters; for the Talmud, as we have it at this day and
upon which we have to rely for Jewish history of the first and
second centuries, was not compiled until 500-600 A.D. But we
do get a little of the controversy from Christian sources in Justin's
Dialogue, and in that Trypho the Jew bluntly tells the Christian
advocate that Christians had "invented" their Jesus Christ. Moreover, it has never been contended that the sacred drama which
the writers of the Gospels may have used as a basis for the
Passion story was Jewish any more than the story of a Virgin-
born Savior was Jewish—unless, of course, Mr. McCabe believes
that the prophecy in Isaiah referred to Jesus Christ, and that
there never were other Virgin-born Saviors. He adds that he
"finds it easier to believe" that Christ [note that he says "Christ"]
was a religious teacher "in Judaea"—and I am quite certain that
for him it is easier so to believe. It is indeed easier to believe
in the existence of "Christ", than worry about any myth theory;
and if John M. Robertson had so believed, or Robert Taylor, we
would never have had some of the finest of our Freethought
works.

In the same way, no doubt, Howell Smith finds it "easier" to
believe in the historicity of Joshua and his father than not. (p.
69). Yet we would, I think, like to have his commentary on Zech.
iii, 1-8, where the prophet saw "Joshua the high priest standing
before the angel of the Lord and Satan standing at his right
hand to resist him . . ." Is this "historical"?

The problem as to who was "James the brother of the Lord"

is also "faced" by Mr. Smith, and again it is utterly impossible to say whether he finds it "easier" to believe that he really was a true brother of "the Lord" or not. Eusebius obviously thought he was, and he quotes the shadowy Hegesippus making James, when about to suffer martyrdom, say, "Why ask me concerning Jesus the Son of Man? He is now sitting in the heavens, on the right hand of great power, and is about to come in the clouds of heaven". Whether this means that James was talking about his real brother is difficult to say, but in John vii, 5, we are told that "neither did his brethren believe in him". So if James really believed his brother was the "Son of Man", whatever that was, and that he was then in heaven but was about to come "on the clouds" —it sounds suspiciously like another variation of the story of the Sun—he certainly had changed in his belief. Catholics, of course, do not believe that James was a true brother of Jesus, and it appears to me that he only becomes so when the historicity of Jesus is denied. How can you account for his "brethren"? we are asked. But the uncertainty of these "brethren" as being "true" brethren is still being discussed in the Church.

When Howell Smith comes to discuss the "exorcists" using the name of Jesus to cast out devils—whatever this means—he admits that the episode described in Mk. ix, 38, "can hardly be historic". And so this becomes one of the "most plausible pieces [sic] of evidence in favor of a pre-Christian cult". Of course. If the "Lord Jesus", who could exorcise evil spirits and had already become the property of "certain vagabond Jews", was not the historical Jesus Paul was preaching, who was he? Even Mr. Smith has to say of the passage in Acts, xix, 13, that "the words 'whom Paul preacheth' are probably a gloss" (that is, an impudent forgery). And he has to admit that "it is incredible that opponents of Christianity should so use it until the memory of Jesus as an historic figure had long vanished, for only then could his name pass into general currency as efficacious in the mouths of sorcerers". So what? We have here again the uncertainty as to what is, or is not, what may be, or may not be, probable.

"The knowledge of a true incident in the life of Jesus may indeed have reached Buddhist circles" (p. 98) or it may not have; or it "may well have originated independently of the two great

Asiatic religions". Exactly how a "*true* incident in the life of
Jesus" could have *originated* independently of the two religions
I cannot see; but no doubt if it did, Jesus is once again saved
from being a myth.

Finally, we have Mr. Smith's admission that "the Gospels are
not biographies . . . myth, historical facts (often distorted),
symbolism, and didactic fiction are so blended that we can sel-
dom, if ever, be sure of what was said or done by the Founder
of the world's greatest religion". Yet in spite of this almost complete uncertainty of what the "Founder" (reverently supplied
with a capital F) said or did, there simply *must* have been a
"Founder" who "was very kind to the poor"—a variant of the
usual "going about doing good", who, *of course,* "aroused the
hatred of the Jewish hierarchy"—for which there is not the slightest evidence—and who was crucified as "a rebel"—again not a
particle of evidence is given—by Pontius Pilate. Naturally (p.
179), "much more" may be true "of the Master" (who again is
reverently provided with a capital letter) so that it is with pained
surprise that I find Mr. Smith *not* quoting John xxi, 25,—"And
there are also many other things which Jesus did, the which, if
they should be written every one, I suppose that even the world
itself could not contain the books that should be written."

If a good deal of this analysis of *Jesus Not a Myth* appears to
be trivial, I trust that I shall be forgiven. I can only say that I
have not seen in this book any attempt to provide an enquiring
reader with *evidence* which proves Jesus not a myth, but only
discussions of what Robertson or Drews or Dujardin said or im-
plied, and with plenty of "probables" or "may have beens" in
trying to explain them away. What picture of Jesus has Howell
Smith given us? Somebody who went about "doing good" and
was crucified by Pontius Pilate? We all knew this picture very
well. But what was Jesus like—tall, short, big, small, dark, fair,
robust, delicate, handsome, ugly,—what? I can only say that when
I had finished reading *Jesus Not a Myth,* I could fashion for
myself nothing tangible whatever.

Renan did attempt a portrait, at least a romantic, amiable
visionary, perhaps based on himself, as has been pointed out
more than once. But from the modern defenders we get nothing.

And this brings me to Joseph McCabe's pamphlet, *How Christianity Grew Out of Paganism*, published recently in America; and let me say right here that he has a perfect right to his opinions and to express them. It is only when he descends to personalities and not arguments that some of us feel the right to demur. Mr. McCabe has had the same opinions, no doubt, all his life, and in his *Sources of the Morality of the Gospels* he gives his views clearly and unequivocally.

Howell Smith thinks that Jesus was put to death as a rebel; Mr. McCabe, following the "official" records says (p. 22) he was "probably put to death at Jerusalem on a correct charge (from the Jewish point of view) of blasphemy". The reader can take his choice. He adds, "The hypothesis that a real life is the nucleus round which the legends gathered seems to me more plausible and more consonant with the history of religions than any other hypothesis. The insistence of the Pauline letters on a crucified Jesus is not plausibly explained away; and the fact that the Jews always admitted the historicity of Christ and know nothing of a drama or cult which might be the source of the Christian story, is very important". Poor Robertson! He had dealt with every point raised here but it was no use. Mr. McCabe repeats the same old boring objections as if the word criticism never existed, and as if he were enunciating new arguments. You will notice that Mr. McCabe says, "the Jews always admitted the historicity of *Christ*" without, of course, giving the slightest evidence or authority for this utterly absurd statement. But in his pamphlet, *How Christianity Grew out of Paganism*, written nearly thirty years later, he had learnt a lesson, so he puts it that "they fully admitted the historicity of *Jesus*"—which makes a difference. He cites R. T. Herford's *Christianity in Talmud and Midrash*, but Herford's opinion on this question is merely an opinion.

Modern Jews and Christians (like Herford) start with what seems an incontrovertible fact, that Jesus really lived. What does the Talmud say? Now for Jews the Talmud is the final authority, much as, during his twelve years of tenure, Hitler became the final authority for Germans. Jesus really lived, and therefore anything in the Talmud remotely referring to somebody like him or with a similar name, no matter if the chronology is outrageously absurd, must refer to him; and if it is said that these are only confused accounts hopelessly contradicting one another, then the reply is that as the Jews were always being persecuted because of Jesus, they had to be very circumspect, and they deliberately led the "Gentile" wrong by confusing the whole issue.

But surely, however stupid the Jews thought the Gentiles were, when they were detailing the adventures of the various Jesuses in the Talmud, inferring that they were bastards, that Mary had been seduced in a way that was not nice, and so on—surely the Gentiles must have known that it was Jesus of Nazareth who was meant. Surely the Talmuds were in just as much danger by calling Jesus "so and so" as if they had called him Jesus. Moreover, why is there only one reference to "so and so" (I think) in the Mishna, and dozens in the Gemara? Is it not, as I have already pointed out, because in the early part of the Talmud there were no traditions about Jesus to talk about, while the Christian religion had later become so well established that by the year 500 A.D. it was impossible for the Jewish rabbis to ignore it in their boring and interminable discussions?

The opinion of a Jewish rabbi, as to what had happened in Jerusalem four or five centuries previously, during the Talmudic days, is worth no more than the opinion of modern Jews, or Christians like Herford, for in both cases they do not start with the question, "Did Jesus ever live?" but, "We know he lived"—how can the Talmud support our opinion? And the crushing answer is that one coming from the Christian camp far earlier than the Talmud—the year 150 A.D., with the publication of Justin's *Dialogue*.

As Mr. McCabe silently corrected his statement about Jews believing in the existence of "Christ", we can pass on to some of his other "arguments". "Today I doubt", he says in his pamphlet (p. 10), "if it [the Myth theory] has a single representative in what you may broadly call the world of scholarship". So indeed did the Christians argue about the *Age of Reason*, when Paine unleashed his formidable attack on the Bible, and where are they? Why, even such a Rationalist as Sir Leslie Stephen was so frightened at its plain language that he went out of his way to criticize adversely its style; and to clinch his opposition he re-

peated the *personal* libels of the convicted liar Cheetham against
Paine, as if they were true. The fact that he was obliged to
apologize only makes his case worse.

Mr. McCabe tells us the Myth theory "first became widely
known to Freethinkers by the writings of the late J. M. Robertson . . . (who) had as a matter of fact, borrowed the idea,
though he never acknowledged this, from an earlier Freethinker,
Robert Taylor, a man of very extensive but peculiar learning,
and Taylor may have taken it from Dupuis". If this question were
not one of historical interest I should feel inclined to let such a
personal attack go by the board. But the facts, in spite of Mr.
McCabe's "as a matter of fact", are something quite different.

Robertson himself declared that it was when he began to plan
writing *The Rise of Christianity, Sociologically Considered* as far
back as 1885, and when he believed in Jesus as a teacher, and in
his twelve disciples, that his first doubts arose. He came to the
conclusion that not only were the Twelve Apostles "demon-
strably mythical", but that "Jesus of Nazareth" turned out to be
a mixture of many Jesuses, each being in Paul's words, "Another Jesus whom we have not preached". (Introduction to
Christianity and Mythology.)

I doubt whether at that time he knew anything of Robert
Taylor but his name. The proof is that he barely refers to him
in his *Short History of Freethought*. In the longer *History of
Freethought in the Nineteenth Century,* Taylor comes in for a
long and quite favorable notice. In the *Courses of Study* (1906)
Robertson says of the *Diegesis* that it is a "work full of suggestion, but in many respects premature, and never to be followed without great caution". In the edition of 1932, when presumably Robertson had read Taylor for the first time, he says,
"The old *Diegesis* of Robert Taylor is still worth attention".
There is nothing about "great caution", the truth being, of
course, that Taylor's uncompromising stand for the non-historicity
of Jesus had caused him to be disliked by the "moderate" and
"reverent" Rationalist alike, and made them stigmatize his work
as being "untrustworthy". It was nothing of the kind, and Robertson made amends in his old age.

Of course, Taylor owed his Sun Myth theories to Dupuis, but

in the *Syntagma* and the *Diegesis*, he proves himself an acute Biblical critic; and he had come to the conclusion, in the *Syntagma*, (his first book) from the literary evidence alone that Jesus was a myth, and not altogether from Dupuis. Taylor's learning was certainly extensive, but why "peculiar"? Because he was the first Englishman to propound the mythic case?

Mr. McCabe then proceeds to demolish the other Myth protagonists quite simply. They are not "historians". Robertson is not exactly put out of court in this way, but he produced "such an impressive apparatus of comparative mythology that even his dullest and most ponderous works on the subject had a large circulation". How this proves that Jesus was an historical character is by no means clear, but there it is.

Prof. W. B. Smith is, however, definitely "not an historian but a mathematician and philosopher", and his works "made little impression". Here again I am puzzled and feel inclined to ask, so what? The real question is, had Professor Smith something to say which Historicists like Mr. McCabe could not answer? Obviously yes—otherwise he would have answered him. After all, Robert Taylor's works made "little impression", but he was right in the main.

As for Edouard Dujardin, he is "a fine literary man", but has "not the right type of mind for historical work". Prof. Arthur Drews is merely "a teacher of philosophy", and all he has done is to write "several works which were not conspicuous for their accuracy", for "he falsely says that according to the Apologist Justin, Jews of his time questioned the historicity of Jesus", and "he is responsible for the statement, often quoted in this connection, that the reference to Jesus in Tacitus was inserted in the 15th century".

The reader should note that Mr. McCabe was writing in the year 1943, when it might be presumed that some of us at least knew a little of the Jesus problem and its now extensive literature. What are we to say of a Freethinker who tells his readers that it was Drews who was "responsible" for the statement "often quoted" about the "Jesus" passage in Tacitus? There is nothing whatever about "Jesus" in Tacitus.

In the *Diegesis* written in 1829 in prison, where Robert Taylor was sent for the horrible crime of "blasphemy" will be found his many arguments against the Tacitus passage, and Taylor was not afraid, in spite of his admiration for Gibbon, to cross swords with that great historian on the question. Mr. McCabe knows nothing either of Ross's work, *Tacitus and Bracciolini*, published in 1878, and he dismisses the formidable attack on the genuineness of Tacitus written by Hochart like this: "A few French and Italian writers whose names would not interest the reader took up the idea". Considering that Hochart was writing on the question as far back as 1885, it is quite amusing to find that it was "a Prof. Drews" who is "responsible" for declaring the passage in question is a forgery.

It will also come as a surprise to find that Conybeare "whose works (*sic*) against Robertson and the mythologists are sound and scholarly, shows the passage in the 11th century manuscript of Tacitus". I have already dealt with this particular piece of nonsense, and the reader can rest assured that the only way Conybeare "showed" it was in "the 11th century" manuscript was by saying so. Anybody can say anything—what we want is proof, and of that, as Robertson "showed", we never get a trickle.

The final mythicist who is dismissed with a sneer is "a Mr. Gordon Rylands" who, alas, was but a cashier, though it is true Mr. McCabe put in the reservation "(I think)". Now whether Drews was only a teacher of philosophy or Rylands a cashier or Dujardin only a literary man or W. B. Smith a mere mathematician, is utterly beside the point, and wholly irrelevant. The real issue is their case against that of Mr. McCabe; and he makes no attempt whatever to reply to them except on points that are commonplaces of the problem, and have been answered again and again. To call Robertson, W. B. Smith, Dujardin, and Drews, as he did in the (American) "Truth Seeker" journal in 1944, "a hotch-potch of amateur historians" is no argument whatever, and is, naturally, exactly what Christian writers will bless Mr. McCabe for. It would be no argument, for example, to say of Spinoza that he was but a mere lens polisher, and was not a professor of philosophy, and therefore his system of philosophy was worthless. Nor would it be an argument to dismiss the Freethought of Foote and Holyoake by urging that both were "jail

birds", and that of Ingersoll and Bradlaugh as the Freethought of
a mere American lawyer, and a mere lawyer's clerk, while their
contemporaries, Newman, Manning, Lightfoot, and Westcott,
were all brilliant, university-trained scholars of world-wide reputation. On whose side is Mr. McCabe?

He brings forward Loisy, Guignebert, and Sir James Frazer,
as all supporters of Jesus, though Mr. McCabe makes the surprising admission that "we cannot be sure of a single biographical
detail about Jesus if we follow ordinary historical principles, so
it is not a matter of great importance whether there was such a
person or not". And this after all his body-blows at the hotch-potch
of amateur historians!

Loisy was a trained Catholic theologian who came to the conclusion that almost everything in the Gospels was unhistorical. I
am quite sure that nothing would prove more boring than an
analysis of his interminable examination of all sorts of suppositions and speculations on the Gospel texts; and his Jesus is as
vague as that of Howell Smith. Guignebert, I have already dealt
with, while even Mr. McCabe would find it difficult to explain
Frazer's very sympathetic preface to Couchoud's *Enigma of Jesus*.
Dr. Couchoud is there given very high praise indeed, though
Frazer admits that for him (Frazer) the hypothesis of a purely
mythical Christ "seems to create more difficulties than it solves".
Nevertheless, "it would be unfair to Dr. Couchoud to pronounce
a verdict on the validity of his thesis until he has adduced his full
evidence". Yet in the face of this, Mr. McCabe tells us that Frazer
"*emphatically* rejected the myth theory". The truth is, he was
most uncertain about it otherwise he would have repeated his
former pronouncement from one of his own works *Adonis, Attis,
Osiris*—a pronouncement finely criticized in Robertson's *Christianity and Mythology*.

Then Mr. McCabe finds it very difficult to meet the bare-faced
forgery in Josephus with good grace. It is "of course forged"; but
—there's always a "but" when Christian forgery has to be dealt
with by the Historicist—"who can say whether the forged passage
was not inserted instead of a reference that did not satisfy Christians"? Who, indeed? I cannot, nor can anyone else in the world.
Why did not Mr. McCabe face up to the fact that, writing when

he did, Josephus must have found Christians all around him, and yet never again mentions them? Is it conceivable that he could possibly pass by the Crucifixion, and the fact that all Christians believed in the Resurrection, without one single, solitary word or reference to them—not one tiny mention of what all Jews— if the story was true—must have found very inconvenient, in his own day?

But the great triumph of all Historicists is Paul, and while Robertson was such a fool with his stupid mythical thesis, he was quite sound on Paul—for his principal four Epistles "were not questioned by Robertson and are quite generally admitted". Let us see what Robertson himself says:

> It may be worth while for me to note that a study of the Pauline epistles, on the view that "the four" were probably genuine in the main, was a determining factor in my own resort to the mythical hypothesis. . . . So far from being a witness against the myth theory, the Pauline literature was one of the first clear grounds for that theory . . . the myth theory as it happens, is neither made nor marred by any decision as to the spuriousness of the Pauline letters. The crucial point is that, whether early or late—and the dating of them as pseudepigrapha is a difficult matter—the cardinal epistles *have been interpolated*. This became clear to me at an early stage in my studies independently of any previous criticism. That the two passages, I Cor. xi, 23-28; xv, 3-11, are interpolations, and that in the second case *the interpolation has been added to,* are as clear results of pure documentary analysis as any in the whole field of the discussion (*Historical Jesus,* p. 186).

Now this seems to me to be a far cry from saying that the four Epistles "were not questioned by Robertson". The only passages *that matter* are not merely questioned but are called "interpolations", a polite name for Christian *fraud*. And if the reader wishes to pursue the matter still further let him read the relevant pages Robertson gives to the problem in his *Christianity and Mythology*.

I have dealt with Paul in a preceding chapter and do not wish to go over the ground again; but I am fairly certain that Mr. McCabe knows the Mythicist position as well as I. That it has not impressed him is another matter, and he has a right to his opinion. But faced with the complete contradictions between the Paul of the Epistles and the Paul of the Acts Mr. McCabe calmly tells us that Acts, "which gives another account of Paul, is very unreliable . . ." Of course. Paul of the Epistles, which he thinks supports Jesus "born of a woman", though they insist throughout (as he admits) "that Jesus died on a cross and rose from the dead", is the "genuine" Paul. And to these shifts our Rationalist Historicists are forced for aid in their great stand for Jesus as a Man going about "doing good".

Mr. McCabe also finds that two of the Gospels "are generally admitted to have appeared by 80 A.D." The people who "generally admit" this are, of course, Christian apologists. The question was thoroughly and minutely discussed in *Supernatural Religion*, and in that work the thesis was maintained that the Gospels, in the form we have them, were unknown before the year 150 A.D. But its author was not a Christian and his work, needless to say, is "not generally admitted".

For Mr. McCabe "the question of the historicity of Jesus" is "so unimportant" that he thinks it a waste of time to discuss it; and he has every right to his opinion. To show Jesus in the light of Pagan Gods, all more or less similar, and all of them myths, seems to me the best way to attack Christianity. Even the most ortho- dox will not feel happy if they suspect that their Savior and Messiah, Jesus of Nazareth, is of exactly the same stuff as Osiris or Jupiter.

Dr. Conybeare, I believe, was a sort of semi-Rationalist as he certainly believed in an "historical Christ". Archibald Robertson and Howell Smith are uncompromising Rationalists who believe in an historical Jesus. Let me finally turn therefore to an orthodox Christian, whose book appeared as late as 1938—Dr. H. G. Wood's *Did Christ Really Live?*

Dr. Wood is a distinguished Quaker who had discussed the Jesus problem with John M. Robertson for many years privately. He has concentrated on this opponent as the strongest protagonist of the Myth theory, though a careful reading of his book makes me certain that he knew nothing of Dupuis, Volney, Blumenfeld, or Robert Taylor. He appears to think that if only he can show that Robertson was wrong in his theory of a Mystery Drama being behind the Passion story, and wrong in a Pagan sacrificial God being crucified, he has proved the existence of not—mark you—a mere Jesus, but a Divine Christ.

Dr. Wood regards the Gospels as "historical documents". And as far as I am able to follow him there is no reservation. They are history. Of course you can find symbolism in parts if you go out of your way to look for it, but he "would be prepared to maintain that supernatural revelation is essential to religion", and so symbolism or no symbolism (for example), "there is no accounting for the story of the Cross except that it happened so". Even "if every detail in Mark has a symbolic meaning", it "would not justify us in treating as unhistorical the details in which Christians found mystic significance". Dr. Wood is particularly careful not to land himself in a hopeless tangle of discussion on the miraculous. We do not know, for instance, if he believes that Jesus was historically carried about by an historical Devil, or that Jesus stopped an historical storm by word of command, or an historically dead Lazarus was brought to life again by the historically divine power of God Almighty on earth as an historical Christ.

Robertson's thesis on the Mystery Drama, or on a pre-Jesus God called Joshua, may be right or wrong; it is an attempt to account for the Jesus story, and a good deal of it is "speculation" based on what we know of mythology and comparative religion, and the latest researches in anthropology. But Dr. Wood must be told in plain terms that the Mythicists are not bound to accept any particular *theory* on the origin of the Gospels, or how the story of Jesus came to be written. Our case rests on the fact that there is no evidence whatever for a "Divine" Messiah (Christ) or a Noble Jesus as a Man. There is no evidence whatever for the story of his "ministry", his "Sermon on the Mount" or "on the Plain", or for anything that we are told he did. It was Dr. Wood's duty to show that there was, and to *prove* "supernatural revelation". Of course, Dr. Wood sensed this, and so he blusteringly tells us that "we [the believers] have not to advance reasons to prove that Jesus Christ is a historical character. They [the advocates of the Myth theory] have to show that he never existed and this they cannot do".

But it is for the affirmer always to prove his case. It is he who advances something, and if he says it is history it is up to him to show it. What would he have said if a believer in the *Arabian Nights* talked as he does—asked the unbeliever to prove that Aladdin or Sinbad never existed? The man who comes forward with the story of Jesus Christ being history, is exactly in the same boat as the believer in an historical Aladdin, and it is just bluster or bluff to ask *us* to show that they never existed. The evidence for a supernaturally born Christ—the one Dr. Wood believes in, remember—is no stronger than the evidence for a Wonderful Lamp. It is just as easy to believe in Aladdin's wicked uncle as to believe in the "legal" father of Jesus—Joseph—and I defy Dr. Wood or any other Christian to challenge me on that point.

In any case, Christians in general have not agreed with Dr. Wood, for they have written literally thousands of books giving us the "evidences" of Christianity, and it is these evidences which we Freethinkers have examined and found wanting. I have tried to prove this in the foregoing pages, but the "evidences" were given me first.

The Gospels are history, says Dr. Wood; therefore the Virgin Birth is history; and it is interesting to see what his fellow believers now say about that miraculous event. Bishop Gore in the *New Commentary* says, "The Virgin Birth was certainly not part of the original Apostolic message". The Rev. J. M. Thompson, in his *Miracles in the New Testament,* says, "The positive evidence for the fact of a miraculous birth must be pronounced to be exceedingly weak. The negative evidence—i.e., the evidence for the existence of views which ignore, exclude, or supplant, the Virgin Birth—is very strong". (p. 159). It is for *us* Mythicists, says Dr. Wood, to show that there never was a Virgin Birth. On the contrary, it is for him to convince Bishop Gore and the Rev. Dr. Thompson that they are wrong and that he is right.

One could go right through the Gospels and show that there is literally no validity whatever in the "evidences" of Christianity. Dean Rashdall says, in his *Contentio Veritatis,* that our belief in the "resurrection of Christ" is a "spiritual experience". "We know", he continues, "that Christ is risen, because, as St. Paul says, we are risen with Him". Is that evidence for an "historical" fact? "The tale of the physical resurrection of Jesus belongs evidently to the same circle of thought as that of the miraculous birth. This tale likewise rests on an historical substruction which falls to pieces on a careful examination." Dr. Percy Gardner, (*Exploratio Evangelica* p. 255). Thus, in the opinion of two eminent clergymen, the stories of the Virgin Birth and the Resurrection are pronounced unhistorical; and Dr. Wood, who knew this quite well, found it far more profitable to show that Robertson was wrong in presuming a pre-Christian God called Joshua, than in showing us, as he should have done, that the historical proof of these two events is unassailable.

Of course he cannot get away from the Virgin Birth. So he bluntly says (p. 152), "The stories of the miraculous birth of Jesus imply at once his historicity". He no doubt feels the same concerning the stories not only of the Resurrection of Christ but of the wholesale Resurrection of the Jewish saints at the same time. Thus, the question of the errors of Mr. Robertson are utterly beside the point and their discussion is irrelevant, as Dr. Wood has settled the whole matter by acclaiming his belief in a Divine miracle, even in the teeth of his orthodox fellow believers. Indeed, he pours scorn on the axiom, "Miracles do not happen"—an axiom, he insists, quite useless for "the purpose of historic inquiry". By accepting such an axiom, the "Christ-myth" school proves it is quite "incompetent".

We should, however, thank Dr. Wood for one or two surprising admissions. He refers to a Jew—who later became converted —Hershon, the author of *A Talmudic Miscellany*. "Robertson," he states, "was misled by Hershon who found references to Jesus in the Talmud where they do not exist" (p. 138). So at last, we have found a defender of Jesus Christ who is obliged to admit that at least some of the references to Jesus in the Talmud, confidently quoted by a Jew, (because, I suppose, he finds them there, and for no other reason) in reality "do not exist". It would be interesting to know from Dr. Wood which they are. The other admission refers to Prof. Guignebert, one of the great "historians" put forward by Mr. McCabe as not belonging to the

"hotch-potch" of amateurs, and who is a strong defender of a
genuine Jesus. "Guignebert", we are told on page 14, "who con-
tributes the volume on Jesus to the great library on '*The Evolution of Humanity*' which is appearing in France under the editor-
ship of Henri Berr, is very radical in his skepticism. He believes
in an historic person behind the Christian movement but he
doubts whether we can be sure even that his name was Jesus"!
So here we have this redoubtable defender of Jesus (whose book
on "Jesus" has been translated in English and is considered by
Howell Smith "a monument of painstaking criticism by a professional scholar, who fights shy of all extravagances") who cannot prove his historic personage was called Jesus, yet believes
he actually lived. Is there, then, anything known for certain about
this wonderful being if we can't be sure that his name was Jesus?

Dr. Wood never finds any difficulty in believing anything, and
appears to be using his imagination. He says, "Personally I do
not feel the difficulty" (p. 44). That wipes out the difficulties. In
his opinion, the matter is then settled. His argument often has
me gasping.

The "Jesus" of Dr. Wood is Jesus Christ, the Messiah of the
old but "genuine" religion of Christianity, the Son of the Living
God; and no matter what Mr. Robertson had said, no matter if
every argument he had used had been unassailable, Dr. Wood's
belief would have been exactly the same. There is not a line in
his book which gives even the semblance of an argument to
strengthen the case for an historic Jesus.

John M. Robertson has replied to most of his critics worth
replying to—and some not worth it—and I see no reason for
going over the ground again; but a word on Dr. Joseph Klausner's *Jesus of Nazareth* will not be out of place.

Like his fellow believer, Dr. Montefiore, Klausner is delighted
that the Christian world has elevated a Jew to the rank of a
Deity, and his book seems to be a song of triumph in honor of
the fact. It would therefore be impossible to persuade him
that his Great Hero never lived at all but was a mere literary
creation. Of course, Klausner knows that there are a few people
who look upon Jesus as a myth, and he duly pours his scorn
upon them. Naturally he believes in God Almighty, so we should

not be too hard on him for also believing in Jesus, though, with him, there can be no question of Christian miracles. He also believes in Judas, and apart from miracles, takes the Gospels as supplying far more than a kernel of truth. Where the Gospels do not sufficiently indicate his point of view, Klausner simply *invents*—incidents, ideas, reflections, and so on, and imagines that if he adds "this must have been" or "this could not have been" the matter is settled.

His great idea is to paint the background of the Gospels as being completely Jewish, that everything that Jesus did proved him to be a thorough Jew imbued entirely with Jewish principles, and that therefore there can be no possible doubt whatever that Jesus was a Great Jew who actually lived, exactly as we gather from the New Testament, and whose memory should be revered by all Jews so long as they recognize that he was not the Son of God. He was—almost—everything else.

Klausner puts me in mind of our Pickwickians. If an historian were to ponder on their activities 2000 years hence, how could he come to any other conclusion but that Samuel Pickwick lived?

First, there is his great biographer Charles Dickens; and an examination of Mr. Pickwick's adventures written by that author shows the most remarkable proofs of their authenticity. The background is that of London in the early years of the nineteenth century, written with such wonderful fidelity that even after the lapse of centuries its extraordinary vividness proves that it could only have been put down by a contemporary. Moreover, there is the Pickwick iconography—the portraits of Pickwick all resembling one another, and the pictures of Bath, Ipswich, and the other places visited by Mr. Pickwick, which were extant for over a century after his death. In fact, not only members of various societies like the Dickensians, the Pickwickians, and others, made annual pilgrimages to the homes and haunts of Mr. Pickwick, but so did thousands of private persons who simply reveled in seeing the actual rooms where the great man had his adventures and misadventures.

And though some of the recitals concerning him were continued in various "apocryphal" documents like "Pickwick Abroad", by another editor, (G. W. M. Reynolds), to say nothing of many other works of which the once notorious "Penny Pickwick" can still be read, one need not always take *them* as Gospel truth. The authentic memoir is that by the reliable Charles Dickens.

Then there were Pickwick cigars, and Pickwick pens, and many other similar Pickwickian items, which are still preserved in our museums. In short, anyone with all this evidence before him, who refuses to believe in a real, genuine Pickwick—and remember we claim no miracles for the Great Philanthropist—puts himself completely out of court.

I submit that it is on these lines that Klausner proceeds in giving the world his version of Jesus, and I should like to add that if Dr. Wood had been handling the case for Mr. Pickwick, he would have asked *us* to prove that Pickwick did not exist.

So much for a few defenders of Jesus as a living personality. It would have been possible to extend this chapter by another 100 pages, but I feel that what has been said covers the ground sufficiently for my purpose.

Let me now examine the alleged incomparable teachings of Jesus which are always brought forward as if they were the last word in ethics and were absolutely unique with him and nobody else.

CHAPTER XII

The Teachings
of Jesus

THERE IS A PASSAGE IN JOHN STUART MILL'S
Three Essays on Religion which has been extensively quoted by
Christians as showing what an unequivocal skeptic thinks of
"Christ". It is in the essay on Theism, which Mill had not designed exactly to go with the other two as they were not "intended to appear altogether". (*Introductory Notice.*) Mill died
before he could give it his final revision, which was a great pity
as it was his rule "never to be hurried into premature decision
on any point to which he did not think he had given sufficient
time and labor to have exhausted it to the utmost limit of his
thinking powers". The Christians who quote this passage never,
if they can help it, make this known, though I for one doubt
whether any final revision would have substantially altered Mill's
opinion. He knew very little of Biblical criticism, otherwise he
could never have penned the following:

> And whatever else may be taken away from us by rational
> criticism, Christ is still left; a unique figure, not more unlike all
> his precursors than all his followers, even those who had the

direct benefit of his personal teaching. It is of no use to say that
Christ as exhibited in the Gospels is not historical and that we
know not how much of what is admirable has been superadded
by the tradition of his followers. The tradition of followers suf-
fices us to insert any number of marvels and may have inserted
all the miracles which he is reputed to have wrought. But who
among his disciples or among their proselytes was capable of
inventing the sayings ascribed to Jesus or imagining the life and
character revealed in the Gospels. Certainly not the fishermen of
Galilee; as certainly not St. Paul, whose character and idio-
syncrasies were of a totally different sort; still less the early
Christian writers in whom nothing is more evident than that the
good which was in them was all derived, as they always
professed that it was derived, from the higher source. What
could be added and interpolated by a disciple we may see in
the mystical parts of the Gospel of St. John, matter imported
from Philo and the Alexandran Platonists and put into the mouth
of the Savior. . . . But about the life and sayings of Jesus there
is a stamp of personal originality combined with profundity of
insight, which . . . must place the prophet of Nazareth, even in
the estimation of those who have no belief in his inspiration, in
the very first rank of men of sublime genius of whom our species
can boast. (pp. 253-4)

If Mill had not been a great man—and one of the best of men—
one would have liked to tear this passage to pieces. It is bad
enough to have to meet this kind of thing from professional
Gospel blatherers who have an ax to grind (though perhaps many
of them have a family to support and cannot get out of the
religious trust). But it is obvious that Mill never set himself
seriously to study the textual problems involved in any discussion
on what Jesus said which "the fishermen of Galilee" could not
"invent". Whatever we may think of these simple fishermen it
was certainly most unlikely that any of them could write Greek
like the artist we call Luke. And if we know anything whatever
of the period in which Jesus was placed we know it to be very
unlikely also that Jesus himself spoke in Greek, in spite of a few
theologians who, faced with that fact, know that it was almost
humanly impossible for the simple fishermen of Galilee to take

down correctly every word uttered by Jesus and then translate it into New Testament Greek.

The whole passage shows a most lamentable ignorance of the progress of morality in the great countries—Egypt, Rome, Greece, and others—flourishing at the time. In his panegyric on the Talmud, Emanuel Deutch claims that almost everything, if not everything, in the teachings of Jesus can be found in the Talmud. I myself do not think that this is decisive, as undoubtedly Christians can claim that even the latest possible dates given for the Gospels puts them centuries before the compilation of the Talmud; and the counter-charge, that it is impossible to imagine the Jewish moralists going to Jesus for their moral teaching may or may not be valid. I do not know, and I do not see how anyone can know. Rules of conduct and moral apothegms must have been floating all over the then known world in some form or other, and I cannot see how it is possible to attribute any teaching of the kind to one man or to one nation.

Let the reader study McCabe's *Sources of the Morality of the Gospels* (a work I heartily commend) and he will see how wide was the field in which ethics flourished. There is a current saying, all that is new in the Gospels is not true, and all that is true is not new; Buckle puts it, "Whoever asserts that Christianity revealed to the world truths with which it was previously unacquainted, is guilty either of gross ignorance or wilful fraud". And one could leave Mill with that.

But of course there is the further question: is the teaching of Jesus so high and so unique even if borrowed from other faiths and lands? In his *Phases of Faith*, Prof. Francis Newman gives that teaching a terrible slating, as does the theist, the Rev. Charles Voysey, in his work on the same subject, *The Testimony of the Four Gospels Concerning Jesus Christ*. But one of the most bitter examinations will be found in *The Prophet of Nazareth* by Evan Powell Meredith. This work is not easy to obtain, but once read it will be very difficult indeed to look upon the teaching of Jesus in the same light as when it was taught at our mother's knee.

The real point at issue is again this, the "uniqueness" of the teaching of Jesus makes it stand out as the work of one man,

and therefore that man must have lived. But if it can be proven
that there was nothing unique in what Jesus taught, that it was
a re-hash of the current morality, and that it can be traced, as
McCabe shows, not only to Old Testament sources but to Greek
and Roman, this "proof" of his existence disappears. Mr. McCabe
points out:

> In the course of the long and exhaustive controversy about
> Christ and his message there have, of course, been many refer-
> ences to the fact that the teaching ascribed to him has ample
> parallels in earlier or contemporary thought. The conventional
> or unscholarly view of his originality is so gross and superficial
> that I have actually heard clergymen declare that his command
> to love one's neighbor as oneself—a command quoted by Christ
> from the oldest books of the Old Testament (Levit. xix, 18)—is
> one of the most signal instances of his originality! To theologians
> it is well known that parallels to almost every moral text of the
> Gospels have been quoted, and there has been of late some
> tendency to remove the stress from originality to personality.
> . . . It cannot however, be doubted that the overwhelming
> majority of Christians, and many non-Christians, are entirely un-
> aware of the extent of the research in this field. . . . The senti-
> ments attributed to Christ are already found in the Old Testa-
> ment, and it is therefore futile and superfluous to inquire at what
> time they are expressed by Jewish commentators on the Old
> Testament. They were familiar in the Jewish schools, and to all
> Pharisees, long before the time of Christ, as they were familiar in
> all the civilizations of the earth—Egyptian, Babylonian, and
> Persian, Greek and Hindu. . . . We need therefore concern
> ourselves little as to whether some rabbi or the evangelist had
> priority; neither one nor the other was original. (pages 204-9).
>
> What we have seen, however, suffices to discredit the claim
> that Jesus brought a single new element of moral idealism into
> the world. Whatever amount of distinctive phrasing or conceiv-
> ing we may find in the Gospels, the moral sentiment which is
> put in these distinctive ways was common to the whole religious
> and ethical world of the time. There is no advance whatever upon
> current morality in the Gospels. (p. 298).

I have given this long quotation from McCabe because, as he
is opposed to the Myth theory, his testimony *against* the unique-

ness of "Christ's" teaching is all the more valuable; and indeed it is a great pity that his work is not more generally known.

All this does not invalidate the fact that while some moral aphorisms in the Gospels show a high standard, at the same time it can be shown that others are particularly silly, mischievous, and untrue. "All that ever came before me are thieves and robbers" is one of those exasperating sayings which commentators are at their wits' end to explain. None the less, it is both silly and untrue. To be told that Jesus did not mean what it plainly says is the simplest way of getting out of the difficulty, and it is astonishing how often this particular expedient is resorted to when theologians have to face the fact that "our Lord" said something which it is impossible to defend. A similar instance is, "If any *man* come to Me, and hate not his father, and mother, and wife, and children, and brethren, and sisters, yea, and his own life also, he cannot be My disciple". The word "hate" is the operative one and, without exception, we are told that here it does not mean "hate" whatever it means. One commentator says, "Hate is a strong word, and of course does not imply the *feeling* of hatred, but a readiness to *act* as if one hated". (*Commentary on the New Testament*. S.P.C.K.) And Cruden, of course, says we must not take the meaning "rigorously". The teaching of Jesus is the most beautiful, the most wonderful the world has ever seen—but don't press us too hard with the "difficult" parts, as perhaps Jesus then never means what he says, or the silly sayings are spurious.

That, for example, is how Dr. Giles in his *Christian Records*, and Gregg in his *Creed of Christendom* explain away the obvious absurdities in the teachings of the unique Jesus. They are spurious, though there is no attempt whatever to prove that those parts with which they themselves agree are genuine.

It is no part of our case to discuss the teachings of Jesus except in this brief way, as a reply to the kind of nonsense similar to that which we get from J. S. Mill. And I should not have noticed his statement were it not for the fact that ever since it was published, it has formed part of the stock-in-trade of Christians who never cease quoting it as an "admission" from the enemy.

If the teaching of the Christian hero had been unique it would

have formed very strong evidence for the existence of a real
teacher, far stronger indeed than pathetic appeals to Josephus or
Tacitus. But as it is not unique, it therefore provides no proof
in support of the thesis that Jesus the man, the teacher in Judaea,
ever lived.

CHAPTER XIII

How Did the Gospels Originate?

FIRST, I MUST POINT OUT THAT THERE IS NO NEED for the Mythicist to try to solve one of the most difficult problems in religious history. For some hundreds of years the problem of the origins of Christianity has been the subject of tremendous research—and speculation. The net result of all the scholarship and patient research which has been spent on the question is— quite simply—no one knows who wrote the Gospels, or when, or where they were written and therefore the actual beginnings of the religion of Christ are lost in hopeless obscurity.

We know more than our fathers or grandfathers, but not much. And the curious thing is, that the early protagonists of the Christian faith, men like Irenaeus, Justin, Tertullian, and other Church Fathers, appear to be just as ignorant of these beginnings as we are. Even Eusebius, who is supposed to have had all, or most of, the necessary documents before him, is so vague and, in places, so absurd, that it is impossible to extract anything from his writings which would give us a sure foundation. His own attempts to get behind the veil are based on credulity and hearsay—and perhaps even on forgery.

If there is any truth whatever in Church history it can be put in the way John M. Robertson does in his *Short History of Christianity*:

> Within a hundred years from the date commonly assigned to the Crucifixion, there are Gentile traces of a Jesuist or Christist movement deriving from Jewry, and possessing a gospel or memoir as well as some of the Pauline and other epistles, both spurious and genuine; but the gospel then current seems to have contained some matter not preserved in the canonical four, and to have lacked much that those contain.

The difficulty we are faced with is that first hundred years, during which, it must be remembered, the Jewish people were almost annihilated in the war ending in the fall of Jerusalem and the later rebellion by Bar Cocheba.

That in the neighborhood of Judaea were swarms of cults of some kind must be taken for granted, for we have distinct traces of them; and therefore we should not be surprised to find that one of these became the nucleus of the religion later called Christianity. But how this came about is quite unknown, though we can speculate at will in the realm of the "may have beens" or "probablies".

It is not surprising either to find that "Gospels" began to multiply for, although "oral" tradition may have appealed to some believers, the necessity of having some written authority was perhaps soon found to be imperative. The Jews in particular were always able to appeal to such authority; and, though we do not know who were the *first* Christians, it is fairly obvious that at least some of them felt it needful to appeal to the "Scriptures" for some kind of authority; and as those Scriptures were perhaps too "Jewish", they had therefore to produce their own.

And then came a perfect shower of Gospels, Epistles, Acts, and Apocalypses, most of which are these days called Apocryphal. Although dates have been given when these were sorted out, and those contained in our New Testament labelled Canonical, the truth is that this distinction is purely arbitrary, and in point of fact, there is in all things relevant no difference between the Apocrypha and the Canon. Many of the Apocryphal Gospels were looked upon as of equal authority to the others by early Christians, and they were quoted almost as often. Indeed it is most remarkable that nearly all the old Mystery Dramas which were acted or sung in England before Wyclif, and even in his day, are based on the stories contained in the rejected Gospels. The people who wrote or produced the plays appear to have known them far better than they knew those in the Canon; or perhaps they were not allowed to use the latter.

Be that as it may, all this uncertainty as to the beginnings of Christianity and the story of Jesus remains quite unsolved. We simply know nothing positive. And so many objections can be urged against the various theories offered in support of the orthodox position that they tend to make the inquirer only more bewildered.

There is the Q document for example—the theory that behind two of the Gospels was a common source—hence the German *Quelle*, "source". Or the source for three of the Gospels; or for two or three sources. There is the problem of John and his connection with the Epistles and Revelation. There is the problem as to who was Paul and how he managed to write Epistles without Acts knowing anything about it.

Above all, was that *first* writing about Jesus? It is easy to speak about the production of Gospels, etc., but there must have been a beginning somewhere, somehow—what was it? The easiest solution is to suppose, as did Frazer, that there was a "Founder", a real man behind everything, somebody whose personality left such a vivid impression, whose sayings and teachings were so memorable, that it would have been short of a miracle if his followers had not preserved his memory in some writing which later became the nucleus of all our Gospels. That is the solution put out by the Church, directly the body of men who composed it were strong enough, or considered themselves important enough, to force such a solution of the problem on the general mass of their followers. It is believed in by almost the whole of Christendom, and as I have already pointed out by almost all Jews, and by most Rationalists.

But the minute examination of the Gospels in their various redactions and versions, of the Church Fathers and their polemics

against heretics and backsliders, and of Church history, has dis-
closed many points which the easy solution of the Church has not
solved. And even those Christians who are convinced that God
Almighty came on earth in the guise of his son Jesus Christ find
it hard to swallow all the difficulties they have to face in the
New Testament.

Take as an example such a book as *Some New Testament Problems* by the Rev. Arthur Wright, M.A. In it will certainly not be
found an easy solution of the problems involved merely because
the Church says that there was such a person as Jesus, the great
Solver of all theological problems. To apprehend Scripture truth,
Mr. Wright contends, one must understand something of the
history of the first century, of Semitic modes of thought and expression, of textual criticism and grammar, and even historical
criticism, which "is still more fundamental". And if we want to
"keep pace with the age", the old methods will not do. The old
methods are, of course, the "easy" ones—believe in Jesus Christ
and trust the Church.

And how does Mr. Wright affirm the beginnings of the Gospels? Like the majority of critics he puts Mark first, but not at
first through an *Ur-Marcus*, but an *oral* Mark which "took many
years forming". He believes that "a single lesson perhaps connected with the Passion was the first small origin of the book,
and that other lessons, one at a time, collected round the center,
the whole record expanding by degrees, sometimes in one chapter, sometimes in another, till it reached its present dimensions".
And there were three editions, the first being embedded in Luke,
the second in Matthew, and the third was written by Mark himself. Mr. Wright, of course, gives excellent reasons why his
hypothesis is a good one, and like most theologians he has a
ready answer to any objection.

For example, are the last verses in Mark genuine or not? Well,
he believes that for the true solution of this problem one must
go to Matthew where "in substance" you will find the *true* last
verses of St. Mark. And I am sure that this solution is as good as
any other.

Then take such a problem as the date of the Crucifixion, to
which he devotes four chapters. He frankly states the numerous

difficulties, and naturally hopes that he has given the right answer. It is an answer that he has come to after a long discussion
in which he deals with dozens of textual and historical puzzles,
all of which have been the subject of hundreds of books; and it
is settled by dating the Crucifixion as having taken place on Friday, March 18, A.D. 29 somewhere between 9 A.M. and 3 P.M.
In Bishop Gore's *New Commentary*, the question is not so easily
decided, for we learn that the discussion as to the date of the
Crucifixion "has unfortunately ended in no clear result". In his
Christian Records, the Rev. Dr. Giles says, "That the particulars
of this trial are of a legendary character, and will not bear close
examination, must be evident to all who are acquainted with
Roman history". Dr. Giles was a fine classical scholar, and knew
what he was talking about. But books like Mr. Wright's will continue to pour from the press.

Although he was convinced of the historicity of Jesus Dr.
Schmiedel's article on the Gospels in the *Encyclopedia Biblica*
(the first half is by Prof. E. A. Abbott) should be read by all
students, for it is a very detailed account of what we know of
the Gospels; and though written forty odd years ago, his conclusions have not been seriously challenged. One thing does
emerge from his disquisition and that is, we do *not* know how
the Gospels came into being. If anybody should have known, it
was the Church Fathers and their statements are, by our advanced critics, almost laughed out of court. Papias—we know of
him mostly through Eusebius by the way—is ridiculed. So is
Justin; and as for Irenaeus, who was the first to tell us that Luke
wrote his Gospel because of Paul, he is contemptuously dismissed:

> The whole attribution to Paul of the gospel of Lk., which,
> according to Origen, the apostle even refers to in Rom. ii, 16,
> as "my Gospel" is only an expedient which the Church fathers
> adopted to enable them to assign a quasi-apostolic origin to the
> work of one who was not himself an apostle. For this reason
> suspicion attaches also to the statement that the gospel of Mk.
> rested upon communications of Peter, especially as it is accom-
> panied with an elaborate apology for Mark's undertaking. (E. B.,
> col. 1890).

Schmiedel shows how the Church Fathers are in complete disagreement among themselves, and he elaborates the difficulties so
successfully that any reader who hopes to find out anything certain about the origin of the four Gospels and whose faith will
receive thereby additional support, will be sadly disappointed.
Schmiedel even contends that were our Gospels proved beyond
doubt to have been products of the year 50 A.D., we should still
be just as uncertain of their origin as "the chronological question
is in this instance a very subordinate one".

All this brings me to Dr. Couchoud's *Creation of Christ*, which
purports to show exactly how the Gospels originated and how
"Christ" was "brought to life" by purely literary means. I think
it is the first real attempt to show us what the beginnings of the
Gospel were like—or may have been like—apart from such
speculations as the Q document. The difference between the two
sides is that the framers or discoverers of the Q document believed in Jesus Christ and tried to show, by collating two Gospels,
that the parts common to both were very likely the primitive
document they were searching for. On the other hand, Dr.
Couchoud does not believe that anybody called Jesus Christ
ever lived at all, but that he was conceived in the first place as a
purely "heavenly being" in man's inner consciousness, and it was
only later that he was made flesh and blood—on *paper*. Thus
Christ was "created". If I may be allowed to say so, I had come
to a similar conclusion long before I read the *Creation of Christ*,
though I was, of course, quite unable to say how it was done.

If the reader has attentively gone through what I have written
so far, he will see the story of Jesus Christ did not come exactly
as the result of somebody making him up, so to speak, on the spur
of the moment. There is a long history of the *idea* behind it. "His
was a long, laborious gestation", as Dr. Couchoud puts it. But the
gestation he describes does not exactly follow the various myth
theories and symbolism which other people have found in the
Gospel stories. "The martyred God", he says, "is a new aspect,
though a surprising one, of a glorious being, the *Son of Man*, who
makes his appearance in the book of Daniel and who shall be the
judge on the day of doom". And it certainly was a long time
(Couchoud says three hundred years) before "the coming of

the Son of Man evolved uniformly a story which reaches from the book of Daniel to the Gospel according to St. Luke".

It is interesting to note how Couchoud explains that "for a true history of Christian beginnings there has been substituted a sacred history", a conclusion to which Gerald Massey had arrived over fifty years ago, though he would have called it a mythological history. And the one thing that must be borne in mind always is that Jesus Christ was no man, never was meant to be a man, not even with a capital M, but a God; he was, in short, at his earliest conception, a God.

The writings and "apocalypses" which have come down to us from "holy" men and which form the basis of so much esoteric or secret doctrine are exactly the kind of thing we should expect. Very few of these writings could have emanated from *normal* men and women. Lecky in his *Rise and Influence of Rationalism in Europe* gives a description of monks and hermits which shows why they got "heavenly" hallucinations, and led them to believe in "Saviors", "Divine Beings", "Sons of Man", and "Sons of Gods", as well as "Devils", "Angels", and "Hell".

> Abandoning every tie of home and friendship, discarding all the luxuries and most of what are deemed the necessaries of life, scourging and mascerating their bodies, living in filth and loneliness and desolation, wandering half-starved and half-naked through the deserts with the wild beasts for their only companions, the early monks almost extinguished every natural sentiment, and emancipated themselves as far as possible from the conditions of humanity. . . . They enjoyed a ghastly pleasure in multiplying forms of loathsome penance, and in trampling upon every natural desire. Their imaginations, distempered by self-inflicted sufferings peopled the solitude with congenial spirits, and transported them at will beyond the horizon of the grave. (Chap. IV).

Lecky was, of course, describing Christian monkery, but that institution was in a direct line from the monks and hermits who preceded Christianity. The Jewish prophets, whose works are in the Old Testament, must have been exactly like those described by Lecky, and the descriptions which have come down to us of John the Baptist, and James the brother of the Lord—even if

neither of them ever lived—are drawn to life. The East has
always teemed with ascetics, and no doubt they are still to be
found in their thousands, filthy, unkempt, often quite nude, living
on roots and water, lacerating themselves, and deluding the
people at large that they are therefore "holy". In essence, there
is very little difference between the lunatics who call themselves
Fakirs in India and the Catholic priest or parson who wears a
hair shirt or something worse all day, and thinks he is thereby
propitiating the Deity. Canon Liddon and Dr. Pusey both, I believe, afflicted themselves in this way in Victorian England.

Why should not some of these tortured beings, hungry, thirsty,
maddened with self-inflicted pain, give forth "apocalypses"? It
would have been surprising if they had not done so. Possibly
many hundreds were written, and those that have survived are
no doubt the best of the lot. By the word "best" is here meant
the writing which best fulfilled the purpose for which it was
written. We in this age, perhaps, have other ideas, and a good
deal of what passed as wonderful "inspired" writings in primitive
times appears to us to be uninspired balderdash. When Thomas
Paine called part of Corinthians "doubtful jargon . . . as destitute of meaning as the tolling of the bell at the funeral", it is not
surprising that his Christian contemporaries were furious—for
even Sir Leslie Stephen, an Agnostic, shared their feelings. "It
explains nothing to the understanding", added Paine; "it illus-
trates nothing to the imagination: but leaves the reader to find
any meaning if he can". And regarding such "visionary" writings
as those of Ezekiel and Daniel he thought that "they pretended
to have dreamed dreams, and seen visions, because it was unsafe
for them to speak facts or plain language". He had to confess,
however that their prophecies were "false".

But Couchoud, like Paine, hardly seems to recognize that the
"prophets" in the Bible, or out, were victims of hallucinations
brought about by privations, self-inflicted it is true, but none
the less responsible for what is called Divine Inspiration. Couchoud wants Christians to read and study the Book of Enoch, for
he claims that most of the New Testament writers knew Enoch
by heart, and it is possibly quite true. Here is a specimen of
Enoch:

He shall deliver them to the angels of torture
To punish them for having oppressed the elect.
The elect, on beholding them,
Shall laugh to see them
For the wrath of this Son of Man strikes them
And his sword is drunken with their blood.

Dr. F. C. Burkitt, in his *Jewish and Christian Apocalypses*, says that this passage has been imitated by Matt. xxv, 31-45. But surely in both cases we have specimens of religious drivel which only a half-mad hermit could pour out.

Couchoud says that "seventy years before Christ there were Christians—save for the name—in Palestine. They drew inspiration from a little book of revelations of the celestial Man"—the book of Enoch. It might have been so, and that these "Christians" were in reality the forerunners of the later Christians. And just as they followed Enoch, others made "The Assumption of Moses" their holy book, and still others may have followed someone like the ascetic who turns up in the New Testament as John the Baptist.

Here it is necessary to point out again one fact rarely taken into account by Christians. It is that the picture of Jesus they really cherish is that given in the Gospels. But the *first* account of Jesus that appeared was in Paul, whose Epistles, according to the Church were published (or circulated) before the Gospels. It is Paul's portrayal which we should study first, as indeed does Dr. Couchoud.

Paul, he says, was "a little sickly fellow, probably epileptic, possessed by electric energy and by quivering pride . . . he it was who stamped on Christianity the seal of his genius".

Paul and Barnabas, "inspired by the Spirit", undertook "a missionary expedition". I am not quite clear as to what is meant by being "inspired by the Spirit", unless it is exactly the same kind of inspiration we find in similar types of religious monks or hermits. If that is so, of course we must expect the two missionaries to have influenced some people, just as Joseph Smith, Mrs. Eddy, and Madame Blavatsky seem to have had no difficulty in "inspiring" thousands of similar-minded persons to follow them. Couchoud says:

The church (Paul's) consisted mostly of people of humble standing and of simple mind. . . . Every one of them, man and woman, learned the manner of praying aloud, uttering prophecies, healing in the Spirit, and making miracles. When a prophet stood to speak and another, seated, was inspired by the Spirit, it was the duty of the former to hold his peace. Times were when the breath of Spirit wrung from these human lyres nought but aeolian murmurs, sounds without recognizable meaning. Then it was they spoke *with tongues.* . . . Did the prophet cry "Ba' Ba' Ba'" the interpreter said "Abba'" (Father). (Gal. iv, 6). (p. 52).

As we have had similar, and even sillier, experiences in our own revival meetings, this picture of what might have happened when Paul was on a "mission" is probably quite true; but exactly what kind of a Jesus was it that the poor, deluded people of "humble standing and of simple mind" really believed was going to "work the miracle" (or whatever it was they expected)? It could not have been the Gospel Jesus because the Gospels had not then been written. If all this is true, as Couchoud contends, then nobody ought to be surprised that the Jews in Jerusalem refused to accept Paul with his new God-idea; and again, if it is true, it surely is remarkable that Josephus knew nothing whatever about it. If Paul and the Jewish priests were in such a conflict as Couchoud describes, the contemporary historian who gives hundreds of other details about the Jews, most of them unimportant, simply must have told us all about Paul and Barnabas and Peter and James, to say nothing of Titus and Stephen and Apollos (a queer name for a Jew) and even Ananias. That Paul, especially if he were an epileptic, should have had visions is nothing remarkable, nor that his "Christ Jesus" was merely a re-hash of the "Son of Man" or the other "Heavenly Being" described in Enoch, Daniel, and similar works of hallucination. But what about his followers? They were not all epileptics or hermits or half-starved visionaries—or were they? Exactly how was it possible to persuade some of them at least that there had ever been such a being as Jesus Christ or Christ Jesus? Did they really believe also that "the earthly temple had its counterpart in Heaven, and the Paschal Lamb has its celestial image in Jesus Christ"? Remember, this Jesus Christ was only an *idea* in Paul's mind.

"The stumbling-block of the Jews", continues Couchoud, "the foolishness of the Greeks, Christ Crucified was proclaimed by Paul with feverish speed." It was accepted by some of his followers, who even came to believe that they had actually seen the Lord Jesus. Couchoud claims Peter and James together with Paul as being the three "pillars" of his Church. They all disappeared about the year 65 A.D., leaving only John "as the Great Witness, the supreme warrant of the advent of the Lord". Naturally John also saw "the Lord" and put down his "visions" and prophecies in the book of the New Testament known as the Revelation of St. John the Divine. Jesus appears in it as the Lamb, and Dr. Couchoud seems to me to have discovered in this Apocalypse a beautiful religious poem, where most of us see only writing inspired by bodily suffering and therefore hallucinations amounting often to sheer gibberish. Of what use is, "I saw a woman sit upon a scarlet colored beast full of names of blasphemy, having seven heads and ten horns", except for similar visionaries like St. John the Divine? Even putting the translation in the form of poetry, as does Couchoud, does not alter its inherent nonsense.

It was Paul and John then who influenced the early Christians, Paul furiously abusing "the apostles and pillars of Jerusalem as *agents of Satan*" and John abominating "the mysticism of Paul as the *depths of Satan*". And "out of this strife developed the Christian dogmas to come".

Jesus was "the God Hero of a Divine Epic. Jesus is of heaven heavenly and he is yet to come." And more than that, "For John and for Paul, God and Jesus are one". But it was Paul's heavenly vision which was eventually to prevail.

Yet what really happened between the time when Paul disappeared, and John wrote his Apocalypse, that is, from about the year 70 to 120 A.D., "the most obscure period of Christianity", is exceptionally difficult to surmise. It should not have been so if the events Couchoud describes so dramatically had really happened, for at least part of the time is covered by Josephus minutely in his famous work, and he knows nothing whatever of the way in which Christianity had its beginnings. It is a pity that Dr. Couchoud does not explain or venture to explain why. In his *Enigma of Jesus* he makes a good deal of the fact that Josephus "says nothing of Jesus". He might have added, in his later work, nothing of so many other Christian heroes either.

Putting aside Couchoud's description of the way in which the first little Christian communities appear to have quarrelled—as they still do in these more hectic days—he comes at last to explain how the difficulty of presenting Jesus to his worshipers was overcome. It was the greatest of all problems, for it meant reconciling so many conflicting views of "our Lord". Paul, John, James, Hermas, and possibly many other writers, all put their views down, but they were all different, and the early Church or Churches had to offer something far more tangible if they wanted to keep their flocks together, especially in opposition to Judaism. And it was here that Marcion stepped in.

For Dr. Couchoud, "Marcion was one of the world's great religious geniuses and takes his place between St. Paul and St. Francis of Assisi". Most of the religious encyclopedias give a good account of what is known about him, which is very little as a matter of fact; but Dr. Couchoud has made the most of what has been gathered. Marcion was a sea captain, and it was on his voyages perhaps that he became acquainted with Paul's teachings of a "crucified" Christ, and he bitterly opposed Judaism, or Judaic Christianity, if there was such in his early days. It was he who collected ten of Paul's epistles which he "published", and he seems to have known nothing more of a New Testament when he appeared in Rome about 140 A.D. and taught there for twenty years. He certainly knew nothing of our four Gospels, though he is credited with knowing one Gospel. What, or which, was this Gospel, and what do we know about it? It is here that Dr. Couchoud differs radically from so many other critics.

Marcion believed neither in the God of the Jews nor in the Jewish Messiah, nor in any allegorical treatment of the Old Testament; it had to be taken literally, and therefore when it portrayed Jehovah as a savage God, that was because, in truth, Jehovah *was* a savage God. It was Paul to whom was revealed the true religion, Christianity, and the Divine Savior, the crucified Christ Jesus. Like Paul, Marcion opposed marriage. Tertullian and Irenaeus are our principal sources of information as to what

Marcion taught, but it must not be forgotten that they both violently opposed him as a dangerous heretic.

According to Couchoud, Marcion decided to bring Jesus, who up to then was in Heaven, and had never really come down to earth, to the people as a true terrestrial personage. In any case, Christians in his time were beginning to declare that Christ had been put to death by or under Pontius Pilate, and Marcion "accepted enthusiastically this popular pagan idea of Christ's death; its simplicity appealed to him. It was looked upon as an accomplished event, and was not hampered with a baggage of visions, interpretations, gnoses, and what not." With the help of passages in Isaiah, floating traditions and, no doubt, personal convictions, Marcion wrote his own Gospel of Jesus as living here on earth, though his immediate followers claimed its author was the Christ; that is, "that Christ had uttered all the words the Gospel contained". This Gospel and its commentary called the "Antheses" are now lost, but it has been almost pieced together from the copious quotations found in Tertullian and other polemists.

Jesus in the Gospel of Marcion was not born, but came from heaven ready-made, and though not actually a man had the *appearance* of a man. Marcion describes all sorts of happenings we know from our own Gospels, giving his reasons why they were done. Couchoud gives an excellent summary, with full authorities, and then points out, "It is clear that it has no historical element". It was the kind of work expected of a Christian leader by his humble followers; yet it "is nothing but a long parable, a vivid and sustained allegory. . . . The legend is not merely allegoric; it is didactic". And it decided "the fate of Christianity".

Dr. Couchoud is very enthusiastic about Marcion's Gospel, but coming down from the realm of enthusiasm to that of hard fact, it is by no means certain that his account of its genesis took place as he describes it. The problem of Marcion has been one which a large number of theologians have studied as minutely as possible, and they are by no means in agreement. What is certain is that the Church Fathers declared that Marcion's Gospel is simply a mutilated version of Luke. And it was not till the end of the eighteenth century, when Biblical criticism began to affirm itself, that theologians ventured on opinions which differed

among themselves as much as they differed from those held by
the Church Fathers.

A number of them claimed that Marcion formed the basis of
Luke and was its true original. Others that Marcion was "an
independent original Gospel". (See *Supernatural Religion*, which
gives an excellent summary of the controversy.) Still others
claimed that it was a Gnostic work, or that it was based on an
older work, and so on. The truth is, nobody knows, and while
the arguments, *pro* and *con*, of our clever theologians are very
ingenious, the riddle is by no means solved. Couchoud's hypothesis is a most interesting one and has the merit of attempting to
find a solution for that most difficult of all problems, the origin
of our Gospels.

But we do find something certain and that is, that Gospels
began to multiply. There was one by Basilides, who was a
Gnostic, and in his work Jesus was *not* crucified. It was Simon of
Cyrene who suffered in his place, a suggestion made also in one
of Robert Taylor's lectures. Then in Rome came that of Mark,
which tried to earn recognition because it was said to be written
by the friend of Peter; another came into being trying to correct
some tendencies in Mark, which was attributed to Matthew, the
"publican" Levi who is one of the twelve; then appeared the
Gospel of John which is supposed to have emanated from Ephesus, the brethren there despising the Marcionites. The subtly
inserted story of the "beloved disciple" of Jesus helped to make
this Gospel more and more trustworthy. Modern critics claim
that John was a Jew—it is difficult to admit this for the Gospel
certainly is anti-Semitic—who wrote poor Greek while thinking
in Aramaic.

Finally, came the Gospel of Luke, which actually was written,
contends Couchoud, by Clement of Rome, whose genius enabled
him to get the "Holy Ghost" into Christianity. He added all those
distinctive touches we know so well which give an air of reality
to the narrative, such as the taking of the census, the birth at
Bethlehem, the way in which at the age of twelve Jesus confounded the Jewish doctors in discussion, and many other things
not found in the other Gospels. The author was made to be Luke,
the friend of Paul, just as Mark was the friend of Peter, and so

in this way the "authenticity" of the Gospel was vouched for. And it was Clement who "invented" all manner of incidents and personages who now form the background of early Christianity, and who are so often called in by Christians and Rationalists alike to prove a real Jesus.

That is how, according to Dr. Couchoud, Jesus was "definitely formed", and how the Gospels came to be written. From being an idea in the minds of Daniel, and Enoch, and Paul, Jesus of Nazareth was born on earth: he was "utterly God and at the same time he is completely man". He was created by literary means and made to live much as Conan Doyle evolved Sherlock Holmes by giving life to his adventures so that people even now will walk down Baker Street and say to themselves, it was here that Sherlock Holmes used to live.

My own difficulty, however, in accepting *The Creation of Christ*, is that there seems to be far more in the origin of the Gospels than this comparatively simple explanation. Dr. Couchoud leaves out nearly all the myth influences and the way in which the story of Jesus is undoubtedly packed with bits and pieces from other religions.

As we do not know who the authors of the four Gospels were, he might well be right in postulating Marcion's as the first and Clement's as the last of the Gospels which definitely placed Jesus on the map, so to speak. But all the time there were others being written, some at least with authority, and it took many centuries before the "big four" were finally recognized as in the "canon". One could go on asking hundreds of questions by no means satisfactorily settled by Couchoud, no matter how much we may praise the ingenuity with which he pieces together his audacious speculations.

A book which always received high praise from J. M. Robertson is *The Jesus of History and the Jesus of Tradition Identified* by George Solomon, a work in which the part the books of Josephus played in the construction of the Gospels is very strongly emphasized; and I consider some of his arguments unanswerable. Jesus, he claimed, is a mixture of two men found in Josephus, the Jesus who seems to have gone about the town with "woe to Jerusalem" and been repeatedly flogged, and Judas the Galilean, who had a following of poor people, was betrayed, and died under Pontius Pilate. There was a Jesus, a robber chief, who is confused by Mr. Solomon with Judas the Galilean, but who is considered by Dr. Robert Eisler as the veritable Jesus of Nazareth in his book *The Messiah Jesus.* Indeed it should be possible to hunt out more Jesuses, and even men with different names, who might have given our Gospel writers hints in drawing the Savior of Christianity.

Solomon's book is valuable for its searching analysis of Josephus, and for the way in which some incidents in the Gospels appear to have been taken almost completely from the Jewish writer. And it is Solomon who shows how utterly impossible it was for Josephus never to have given a hint as to how Christianity grew up in Palestine had Paul and James and the others really lived, or at least, had helped in founding a new religion. If Solomon is right even in part of his theory, I cannot see how Couchoud's thesis can be maintained. Are we really to understand that Clement of Rome in his final redacting of Luke's Gospel went to Josephus for words, phrases, and incidents?

Dr. Couchoud's work is a brave attempt to account for the origin of our four Gospels, and I feel he has in all probability got nearer to the heart of the problem than many other writers; but it is still unsolved. We still remain in the realm of speculation.

This will afford no comfort to the Historicist. It still is his duty to give us evidence of the existence of Jesus, and I affirm that that is what he has completely failed to do.

CHAPTER XIV

Conclusions

IN THE FOREGOING PAGES I HAVE DELIBERATELY
avoided dealing with intricate problems in mythology and the
interminable discussions which were the delight principally of
German theologians, as to what various Christian writers meant
or did not mean by Gnostic or Greek terms in connection with
Jesus Christ. Readers who want to make a serious study of all
the questions dealing with the problem not only of Jesus Christ
but of Pagan Gods in general will find in the list of books given
in the Appendix sufficient material to last them for many years
of close application. Strauss, for example, devotes many pages to
a study of mythology, as does John M. Robertson, and the twelve
or more volumes of Frazer will, I trust, prove to any reader that
however beautiful in its simplicity may be the "genuine" teachings of Jesus, the study of comparative religion detailed with
such minuteness in those volumes tell a totally different story.

It was not necessary for me to repeat what had been done so
well by a number of writers on the Myth problem; and I have
also refrained from dealing with a number of opponents of the
Myth theory who have been well and properly dealt with by the
redoubtable author of *Pagan Christs*. I have had, of course, to

245

cover again some of the ground he and other Mythicists have so ably demolished, but I have tried in my own way to prove that the evidence for a real Jesus produced by Christians, Jews and Rationalists, is no evidence at all.

I have not attempted to show how the Gospels originated, though I must make it clear that even if we knew who their authors were, and exactly how and where they were written, this would constitute no proof whatever of the existence of such a being as they describe. Their hero is not a man (or a Man) but a God, and his miracles form an integral part of his "existence". No intelligent person outside the profession of the Church can believe in these miracles if he uses his reason, and if they are taken away, what is left of the "life" of Jesus? It has been admitted even by the orthodox that there are actually no materials for a real biography of "our Lord".

Strauss calls his own great book a *Life of Jesus*. It is, however, not a biography, but a very thorough analysis of the Apocryphal and Canonical Gospels. It was a great pity he did not carry on his investigation to its logical conclusion, which he probably would have done had he lived in these days. Renan's *Life* is just romance, very charming indeed, but by the side of Strauss—just romance. As for the numerous "Lives" by Christian writers like Farrar, it is charitable to put them on one side for they deal with God Almighty taking the shape of man and performing divine "miracles". No one who reads the *Golden Bough* with understanding can ever again believe in a God or even a God-idea.

Whatever we may think in the main of the authors of the Bible, some of them are not such fools as appears on the surface—or perhaps I ought to say that its editor or editors allowed every now and then something to slip in which would utterly confound our pious theologians. How came the writer of Galatians, whoever he was, to know that the story of Abraham and Sarah and Hagar is an "allegory"? How came Hosea to say, "I have spoken by the prophets, and I have multiplied visions, and used similitudes" (ch. xii, 10)? Did these writers know then that at least some of the events in the Bible were never real, but allegories or "visions"? How can Christians come forward with the

Old Testament in their hands, and use Isaiah as a man who prophesied the coming of Jesus when he says so unequivocally (ch. xliii, 10-11), "Ye are my witnesses, saith the Lord. . . . I am he: before me there was no God formed, neither shall there be after me. I, even I, am the Lord; and beside me there is no savior". No wonder Marcion was so bitterly opposed to Judaism in the face of that passage.

If the story of Abraham was an "allegory", and if Abraham therefore never lived, how could "Christ" be descended from him? And it is the Jesus Christ who was descended from Abraham (according to Luke) that really existed according to Christians and Rationalists. It is not some obscure personage about whom history is silent altogether, for how in the world can anyone know whether a personage about whom we know literally nothing ever existed?

I have tried to avoid discussion on disputed points of mythology which, as Howell Smith would say, may or may not be true. He himself is very uncertain about the Crucifixion: "The story of the crucifixion may, of course, be mythical; but, on the other hand, it may be true". (p. 49). This kind of reasoning leaves us in the air so to speak; and so I insist as clearly as I can that the Crucifixion as described in the Gospels never took place at all. The "obscure personage" who is so often dragged into the discussion by Rationalists may, I admit, have been crucified, but how is one to know? It is the Crucifixion in the Gospel story that I deny ever took place, and it is this side of the discussion which is so often "by-passed" by defenders of the Man Jesus, like Dr. H. G. Wood. Howell Smith considers Dr. Wood's book a "brilliant and incisive critique", but Dr. Wood prefers to discuss whether Heracles did or did not carry his pillars in the form of a cross, or some similar myth in art, rather than state an unanswerable case for the Crucifixion.

It must not be inferred from this that I deny "Pagan parallels to Gospel Myths". On the contrary, they are there on almost every page though not always *exactly* the same as in Paganism, any more than the story of Venus and the story of Astoreth are the same. When the defenders of Jesus show that, for example, the Gnostics "abhorred the idea that the heavenly father of Jesus had anything to do with the creation of the world" (*Jesus Not a Myth*, p. 53), and "Robertson suggests that Joseph's person and trade are due to a confusion of the metaphysical with the human plane", I cannot help wondering, so what? Robertson may be wrong, and still Jesus may be a myth. Robertson was desperately anxious to find Pagan parallels as an explanation of some of the stories in the Gospels, and in some instances he may have been wrong (I do *not* say he was) in seeing parallels where they do not occur. It is right that any mistake should be pointed out, but after reading the often laborious *pros* and *cons* of the question, I have sometimes felt, does it really matter? The story of Joseph as described in the Gospels is so hopelessly obscure and absurd that it surely requires no serious argument to show the old gentleman as being unadulterated fiction.

I have labored this already in the previous chapters and I recur to it again because I want to make it clear that I have deliberately avoided discussing many points simply because I have felt the real question is always: what is the evidence, from the Gospel story, or from outside the New Testament, that Jesus lived? I have found opponents much prefer to take up a point like the one whether Joshua, who is called in the Pentateuch the son of Nun ("fish"), can be a Fish himself or not. I do not know and I do not care. But I am concerned with the fact that Paul is constantly talking about a Christ Jesus crucified, and the Gospels written later than Paul, use a word which is translated "cross" but which certainly does not mean the cross upon which Jesus is always portrayed. And whether Joshua was or was not called a Fish, it is absolutely certain that Jesus was called a Fish, and I want to know why. Did his disciples and followers generally call their revered teacher a Fish for no reason whatever, merely as a sort of pet name?

And when Paul is called in as a witness by those who believe that Jesus was a man only, I ask what are we to make of Howell Smith's plea, "As a matter of fact, Paul did repeatedly claim that he was authorized by Jesus—the risen Lord—to preach the gospel" (p. 78)? Was Jesus then the "*risen* Lord" and if he was, how can we accept the "witness" of Paul for a *man* Jesus?

There are many similar points which I should like to discuss.

I hope I have dealt in a decisive way with the many queries that may come to the mind of the reader. I make no apology for rejecting miracles without reservation. And in the same way I reject, with that very learned Protestant historian Mosheim, not only the Gospels he rejects but those he accepts. His language could not be plainer: "Not long after Christ's ascension into heaven several histories of his life and doctrines, full of pious frauds and fabulous wonders, were composed by persons, whose intentions, perhaps, were not bad, but whose writings discovered the greatest superstition and ignorance. . . . Productions appeared which were imposed upon the world by fraudulent men as writings of the Holy Apostles". Does not this apply to our own New Testament? Is not the whole of the story of Jesus Christ full of fabulous wonders? And if these are removed from the life of Jesus, what remains? So little, indeed, that neither Dr. Wood on the one hand, representing Christian orthodoxy, nor Howell Smith on the other, representing Rationalism, has been able to give any life whatever to the phantom they have tried to conjure up from that dim age nearly 2000 years ago. Their Jesus is a mere shadow through whom we can see an epitome of so many of the gods of antiquity. He has been assembled and made into the hope and glory of mankind, and though he has been worshiped and adored through the centuries, he has ever remained silent—silent as the tomb, because he never had a real existence.

CHAPTER XV

Various Works and the Conclusion

SO MANY BOOKS AND PAMPHLETS HAVE BEEN DE-
voted to the Myth Problem that it would be quite a hopeless task
to deal with them in a small book like this. In many cases the
arguments appear to be the same, especially those which attempt
to show that Jesus Christ, whilst not being God—or a God—was
a mere Man (always a perfect one though) who actually lived,
going about "doing good". It is, needless to say, supremely difficult to know what the "doing good" consisted of, but the vaguer
the term the more enthusiastically it is put forward by believers,
Rationalists, Jews, and Christians alike.

However, I feel it necessary to deal with three books which
have recently come my way, particularly as one of them, by Dr.
S. J. Case, professes to be the last word, so to speak, on the
problem. "It has been said", says the publisher's "blurb" of Dr.
Case's book, *The Historicity of Jesus*, "that since its first publication no further study of the subject has been necessary". Such a
claim cannot in fairness to both sides be allowed to go unchallenged.

I shall deal first, however, with Judge C. B. Waite's *History of the Christian Religion to the Year Two Hundred,* because it is an excellent work from the Rationalistic standpoint and because it deals fully with almost all the literary evidences of Christianity. It first appeared about 1878, and its sixth edition, dated 1908, is now before me.

Robert Taylor—the "Devil's Chaplain"—in his *Syntagma* and *Diegesis,* had over 100 years ago attempted much the same task, but he was far ahead of his time. The British public received his thesis that Jesus Christ had never lived almost with horror. Even contemporary Freethinkers rejected his books as being, to say the least, "unreliable". Few were prepared to concede his case, or his explanation of Christianity based on the Solar Myth theory presented in his "Devil's Pulpit". Moreover, "justice" in the England of his day sent him to prison for "blasphemy" for three years, and poor Taylor was not always able to get all the necessary authorities and books, when writing in his prison cell. Waite's *History,* therefore, is particularly valuable, and I can strongly recommend it to all Freethinkers desirous of having in one handy book an account of what the Rev. S. Baring-Gould calls the "Lost and Hostile Gospels".

Unfortunately, Waite made a few errors, and though they do not invalidate his book or his argument they should have been corrected in his last edition. He completely confuses the "Virgin Birth" with the "Immaculate Conception"—a quite different dogma; and he re-wrote "at greater length" for his sixth edition the chapter on "Jesus Christ as a Historical Personage". He insists that "this article is important because of the determined effort of some writers to eliminate Jesus Christ from history". Almost any reader, carefully weighing what Waite has to say about the documents which he criticizes, must inevitably come to the conclusion that nearly all the "history of the Church" in the first two centuries is based on myth and fabrication; and if that be so, what evidence can be produced for the existence of Jesus Christ?

Waite, in his special chapter, produces none whatever. He simply falls back upon the well-known arguments of Christian apologists.

His first "reliable" witness (as he is called) is Paul. I have dealt lengthily with Paul and need not cover the same ground again. When Waite declares that "the Epistles of Paul stand out as a fact, utterly unexplainable and incomprehensible, except upon the hypothesis of the life and suffering of the central figure of them all", he is merely using out-dated Christian apologetic, which can easily re-coil upon himself. The "central figure of them all" in the Pentateuch is surely Jehovah, whose anthropomorphic exploits are related in detail. Does this prove that Jehovah really existed? Whoever the writer was, he believed he was dealing with a "living God" in exactly the same way as Paul—for Paul, it cannot be too strongly insisted upon, was dealing with a God and not with a man at all. It was the "suffering God" that died on the Cross, and Waite knew this as well as I. Yet he insists that "Jesus of Nazareth" was "Christ" as well; and he asks J. E. Remsburg (who rather reluctantly admitted the existence of Jesus of Nazareth but not of "Christ") whether Paul was not more likely to be right about Jesus being "Christ" than "a writer of the twentieth century".

In other words, Waite believed that Jesus of Nazareth was Jesus Christ—the God. And people who can believe this are better left alone, for they are ready to believe anything.

Naturally, Waite is in a bit of a muddle over Josephus. He hates to agree that the famous passage about Christ being more than man is a bare-faced forgery, but is obliged to do so; so he concentrates on the other passage which gives the death of James, "the brother of Jesus who was called Christ". "There is no good reason", he loftily declares, "for doubting the authenticity of this passage." On the contrary, there is every reason.

Was James a "brother" of "Christ"? That is, did God Almighty on earth have a real brother? No one knows. The Roman Catholic Church has always denied that "our Lady" was anything else but a Virgin, or had other children; and no amount of discussion has ever settled the problem on the evidence contained in the Gospels. It is quite easy to show that it is most improbable that Jesus had *real* brothers and sisters even though his "brethren" are referred to in one passage in the Gospels.

Waite sees no reason why the words "the brother of Jesus who

was called Christ" should be stricken out. Christians might forge
one passage, but they would be too pure-minded to forge another.
Or would they? Really Waite seems to be *plus royaliste que le roi.*

Did it never occur to him that if James had really been the
brother of Jesus, Josephus would have known all about Peter,
Paul, and the other Apostles as well? He would have known all
about the marvelous events related in Acts—the death of Stephen,
of Ananias and Sapphira, of the wholesale conversion of the
Jews, of the rows between the "circumcized" and the "uncircum-
cized", between Peter and Paul and Barnabas and dozens of
other things which—according to Church history—kept Jerusalem
in a state of ferment between 30 and 70 A.D. That he should have
left everything unsaid except the bare fact that James was a
brother of "Christ" is just impossible. And there are numbers of Christian writers who, to their credit, have recognized
the fact that, however painful the admission must be, the passages in Josephus regarding "Christ" are forgeries. Waite, of
course, goes to Tacitus, and he points out that the argument of
the Mythicist against the authenticity of the *Annals* "comes as near
to maintaining his position as can be expected in face of the facts
that the *Annals* were referred to by various writers in the
3d, 4th, 5th, 6th, 9th, and 12th centuries, and that several of the
books were not discovered until after the death of Bracciolini"
(the Italian writer claimed as the forger). Unfortunately, Waite
gives no authority whatever for a single statement here, and the
plain and sufficient answer is that no one with any claim to
authority could have written this nonsense. I have dealt fully with
Tacitus in other chapters in this book, to which I refer the reader.

I have nothing but praise for the rest of Waite's "History"; so
that it is a great pity that he should have tried to reply to the
Mythic position knowing practically nothing about it, and using
arguments which hardly come up to the standard of the average
Salvation Army girl.

Dr. Case's book is certainly one of the best written in favor of
a real Jesus and deserves a thorough examination. If the Mythicist is unable to meet Case squarely, he should relinquish his
championship of such an unpopular cause and join the other
side.

Exactly how much of the Gospel story Case believes is not easy
to say from his book. He defends the actual existence of Jesus
and, as far as I can see, prefers to say as little as possible about
such simple accessories as the Virgin Birth or the Resurrection, or
even the other miracles. He recognizes that *our* target is the "so-
called historical Jesus of liberal theology", and as he is presumably a supporter of this figure, he has set himself to defend it
with all the weapons at his command. A reading of his book
makes it clear to me that in the ultimate his strongest defense is
the Mythicist's (so-called) difficulty of accounting for Paul's belief in a real Jesus. His words are (p. 295):

> The very fact that Paul has no interest in proving that Jesus
> lived, but refers incidentally to such data as are mentioned re-
> garding the birth of Jesus and his association with certain people
> who were now causing the apostle to the Gentiles no little trouble,
> are features that cannot be escaped.

One might just as well say that as Moses (or whoever wrote
the Pentateuch) "had no interest in proving" that Jehovah lived,
and that Jehovah is shown quite "incidentally" talking to Adam
and Eve and Abraham and, of course, to Moses himself, this puts
the Atheist in a very great difficulty when he declares that
Jehovah never existed and "are features that cannot be escaped".

One soon discovers when reading Case his fondness for German "authorities", whom he often quotes in their original tongue.
It is not given to all of us to disentangle the meaning of erudite
theological argument in the German language, nor is it always
possible to track down Case's formidable lists of writers. Without
wishing to question the citations, it has been my fate to discover
more than once that the authority quoted—when tracked down—
often gives quite another meaning. In discussing earlier one of
the weightiest of the Jesus-the-Man champions, Prof. Guignebert, I have shown this clearly.

While admitting that "in the New Testament story of the
Apostolic age the supernatural figure of the heavenly Christ certainly stands in the foreground". Dr. Case adds, "modern critical
study, on its negative side, largely discounts the traditional history of Jesus, if it does not indeed provoke doubt about his very

existence". Very good. But where does Paul come in here? Did he believe in this "traditional" history of Jesus? Exactly what did Paul believe about Jesus which Case and the modern liberals believe, and which definitely took place? Does anybody know?

Case gives an excellent account of the many "Mythic" theories which have been put forward by various writers and this part of his work is valuable for those who are not acquainted with the books written by J. M. Robertson, Arthur Drews, W. B. Smith, Niemojewski, and a group of others. He, rightly, from his point of view, shows that "Robertson, Mead, and Drews hold to the genuineness of the principal Pauline letters" but adds in a note that W. B. Smith "seems at present to be vacillating on this question". Smith's words—he is dealing with the well-known verses in Corinthians regarding the night in which the "Lord Jesus" took bread and was betrayed—are:

> "Before they can be used in evidence of the historicity of the event in question, as witnessed by Paul, there must be given some surety that they are not interpolated, that Paul actually did write them as we now read them. No such surety has ever been given—nay, none such has ever been seriously attempted. On the contrary, all the signs are against the Paulinity and against the antiquity of the whole passage in question.

After going more into detail, Smith continues:

> Herewith the guns of this boasted battery are not only captured; they are turned destructively upon the critics that trained them. The simple primitive and long-cherished Eucharist not only does not prove the historicity of the Last Supper, but it does prove decisively the non-historicity and purely symbolic content of the incident in question . . . it is *not* an historical narrative. (*Ecce Deus*, pp. 150, 152-3).

Dr. Case is quite emphatic that Smith was "at present vacillating on this question", that is, on the authenticity of the Pauline Epistles. (*Historicity of Jesus*, p. 56, n.) The reader will now be able to see exactly how much "vacillating" there is from Smith's own words. I give them because on the Myth Problem it is more and more necessary to examine the authorities so glibly quoted by opponents.

On page 61 of his book Case points out that for the Mythicist "the New Testament Jesus is primarily a god and only secondarily a man". That is something to admit, though for most of us the New Testament Jesus is a God and never was anything else, in spite of the efforts of the Gospel writers to give him a man-like figure. Jesus walking and talking on earth gives us no more than the vague impression we get when Jupiter or Adonis walks and talks on earth.

In addition to giving the arguments from the principal Mythicists, Dr. Case tries to estimate the replies from their opponents, most of whom are Germans. Particularly severe is he on those of us who found part of our argument on the lateness of the chief Christian documents, the late dates we give for the Gospels, or our claim that the Pauline Epistles are probably products of the 2nd century. He says (p. 70) that "when one examines the argument for the spuriousness and the late dating of the letters, he finds it little more than an assertion of skepticism, which on being repeated by its advocates is too easily given the credentials of a demonstration. . . . It may be said that its exponents have presented no thorough going argument for the spuriousness of all the Pauline letters." Apart from the fact that it matters very little to the Mythic case whether or not the Epistles of Paul are "authentic", the fact remains that they have been thoroughly examined by many Freethought writers; and if their arguments are looked upon by Dr. Case as not "thorough going", that is a matter of opinion. Certainly Case himself would be quite unable to meet these arguments. Moreover, while he gives voluminous authorities on what seems to me points that hardly matter, he gives no authority whatever as being responsible for "no thorough going argument for the spuriousness of all the Pauline letters" except by just mentioning "the Dutch school represented more recently by Van Manen or the skepticism of Steck". He does not here even give us the names of their books (p. 71) or state which of their arguments he objects to, and his reply.

Dr. Case does not like the way in which the Mythicist handles the question of the dating of the Gospels. He seems to infer that if the date of their composition is not, as we claim, a late one, in fact, in the second century, the Gospels are "historical" or at least "authentic". If they can be shown to have been written at an early date—nearer the date they give for Jesus their hero—that is very good evidence that he must have been an historical person.

Here we are up against the fundamental problem as to what is "historical" or "authentic". Supposing it were indisputable that Matthew was composed say about the year 50 A.D. and that it was undoubtedly written by "Matthew the publican". Does that make the story of the Virgin Birth "historical"? Does it give credence to the story of Jesus flying about with a Devil? Are we now to believe that the Saints came out of their graves at the Crucifixion and appeared unto many after the Resurrection? The fact is, that if the Gospels were really written near the date traditionally given by the Church, it is all the more difficult to account for these ridiculous stories. One can understand believers a hundred years or so after the supposed death of their hero reverently embellishing his biography with all sorts of details their pious imagination has conjured up; but surely it is difficult to understand how, so soon after the events they describe, they can make up a lot of supernatural nonsense some of which must have been vigorously denied by the many persons who knew Jesus, had he really lived.

It was up to Case to take up the arguments given for the late dating of the Gospels in Cassels' great work *Supernatural Religion*, but he appears never to have heard of it. Rather is he concerned with a number of German "authorities", whose names and books are these days almost completely forgotten. To answer *Supernatural Religion* would have been nearly a super-human task; so, though his own work is really the last word on the subject, Case prefers to go into a detailed examination of Jensen's claim that the Gospels "are mere literary imitations of the Babylonian Gilgamesh epic". Well, we are not all agreed as to how much the Gospels owe to this epic, except that in a general way nearly all the epics and stories dealing with Gods are alike. The stories of Gods and Goddesses, their adventures and amours, had been floating about the East for many centuries. That they should in some measure copy from each other was inevitable, but to expect the Gilgamesh epic to be absolutely like the Gos-

pels, or vice versa, shows a complete misunderstanding of the
argument. Case takes a number of the actual details from the
epic and the Gospels and shows that they do not exactly pair,
and thus wants his readers to conclude that the Gospels owe
nothing to the epic, and therefore Jesus must have lived; or, if
it is preferred, that Jensen and his theories prove nothing which
show that there never was a Jesus.

Case makes the point that "practically all of Jesus' teaching is
overlooked" (p. 85) in forcing parallels between the story of
Jesus and the Babylonian epic. Here it is at once taken for
granted that Jesus really did "teach", that the "teachings" attributed to him were his own, and that therefore Jensen was
again wrong. Case, who is lavish with authorities in other instances, discreetly leaves them out here. But who says that what
are known as the "ethics" and "parables" of Jesus were actually
taught, and were original with Jesus? Why, the Christian Church,
or the Gospels, or those people who are ready to believe anything, because it is in a book.

It was up to Dr. Case to prove that "Jesus' teaching" really took
place. In the publisher's "blurb" that accompanies his later book
Jesus, a New Biography, we are told that "it uncovers the valuable residue of fact that lies beneath the shell of gospel tradition
and rescues the historical Jesus from the mass of legend, myth,
apology, and miracle that has clustered about him". Very good,
but if Dr. Case admits all this mass of "legend, myth, apology,
and miracle" some of us would like to know how much has
clustered round the "teaching", how much is "authentic", and
can be proven so to be? I think it is not unfair to reiterate that if
the Gospels can be trusted at all, then whatever is put into the
mouth of Jesus which is new, is not true; whatever is true, is not
new. But it surely is, to say the least, intriguing that Case can
slip in this little bit about the teaching of Jesus without bothering
to question it, or taking any notice that it has been most severely
questioned by Freethinkers.

Case can do no better with some other objections than to go
to Fundamentalist Christians for answers to them. For example,
the passage in Tacitus (to which I have already devoted many
pages) is put forward as being undoubtedly genuine. He objects

to the "usual way" in which we deal with it, by calling it a Christian interpolation, which he considers "unsatisfactory". But it was up to him to take up the arguments of both Ross and Hochart and show that they are invalid. Merely to say that he disagrees with them is not exactly the last word on the question.

But while Case contends for the genuineness of the Tacitean passage he cannot find much in it even when stretching his case to the utmost. "It is still a question", he says (p. 248), "whether his testimony is based on anything other than current Christian tradition." If it is, what is it worth? Really nothing at all. By the year 115 A.D. the Christian tradition was—as far as we know—fixed, and Christians were proclaiming their faith in Jesus with the same fervor as Jews did in Jehovah. That they never questioned the story of *his* "origin" but took it for granted is just what one would expect. Did anybody ever question Krishna, or Osiris, or the other Gods they were told to believe in? Does anybody in the Catholic Church even now question the story of the Virgin Birth?

Yet Dr. Case, who has hardly touched the weighty arguments of Ross and Hochart, and who imagines denying their validity is all that is necessary, calmly tells us (p. 249) that "Tacitus' reliability does not suffer by admitting that he may have had his information from current tradition; this merely robs us of the convenience of citing Tacitus as an independent witness". That is all. But it is good even to get the admission that Tacitus is not after all "an independent witness". And it is now up to the reader to decide for himself of what value such criticism is to the case for Jesus.

Of course, when Dr. Case quotes Paul, everything that writer says is quite authentic. For example, he says that Paul says, "it was characteristic of Jews to demand 'signs' in proof of the Christians' estimate of Jesus". There is not a scrap of evidence that this is true, except when Christianity was making converts and was already an established religion, say, late in the second century. Where is the evidence in support of Paul—in his day, of course? Though Case admits "legend, myth, apology, and miracle" have "clustered" round Jesus, yet he takes for granted that the "Jewish authorities" sought a "sign" as related in the Gospels "but Jesus turned away impatiently with the curt reply, 'to this generation no sign shall be given' ". There is not a scrap of evidence that the Jewish authorities sought any sign whatever, and it was up to Dr. Case to provide us with this evidence. That he believes the Gospels on this point is no proof that it ever took place, and it is typical of the way in which he deals with the problem. Unless Dr. Case can provide us with *evidence* that the Gospels are authentic accounts of the ministry of Jesus, that he knows exactly which parts are "myth, legend, apology, and miracle", and *can prove it,* I claim that going to them for what Jesus said or what the Jewish "authorities" said, is just moonshine.

All that he says on the score of the Jews asking for a "sign" (p. 150) or about "upbraiding" the Pharisees is nothing more than speculation, based on a reading of the Gospels. But as, in the form we have them, they are certainly late products of the second century, how in the world can they be in any way trusted as history? And if not history, of what use are they to prove that Jesus really lived?

We are told (p. 152) that the earliest efforts in providing a "life of Christ" were "probably" made on Jewish soil and in a Jewish atmosphere. The operative word is "probably", for no one knows, and one speculation is as good as another. But Dr. Case sees Paul coming first with his "life" and "at the other extreme" is John. Paul made the "death of Jesus an essential item in God's scheme of salvation", which no doubt is quite true; but Dr. Case might have told us why Paul's knowledge of the death of Jesus is any more to be trusted than his knowledge of God's scheme of salvation. How did Paul know what that scheme was? Did God tell him? Did he make it up, and if he did, how do we know that he did not make up the death of Jesus? Is not the plain, simple fact of the matter that Paul's idea of God and what God thinks is just "legend, myth, apology, and miracle"?

On page 155 we are told that "God's interest in Jesus was not confined to those features of his life which at first sight seemed incongruous with messianic faith. Divine approvals of a positive sort were to be found in the story of Jesus' life." Dr. Case doesn't tell us whether Paul knew anything of this or not, but it appears there were theologians contemporary with Paul "who recognized

the desirability, and found themselves equal to the task of presenting evidence from Jesus' lifetime in support of their messianic
faith."

It seems incredible that anybody but a sheer Christian Fundamentalist could write like that. How could Paul or the "theologians" know anything whatever about "God"? Did God tell
them? That they were believers in a messiah, and that they endowed a mythical being with messianic attributes is of course
possible; for in writing fiction you can let your imagination run
riot. Moreover, I do not doubt for a moment that there were
plenty of these messianic lunatics forever discussing what God
did or said, or what he was going to do for a messiah; but surely
their credulous ravings cannot be brought in as proof that there
was a real Jesus who was not a messiah, or who had nothing to
do with God, but who was just a mere Man going about "doing
good".

The truth is that all the labored pages of Dr. Case showing
what the early "theologians" and Paul thought about Jesus as a
"Messiah" is sheer fudge. If there is no Jewish God—and there
is not—then there is no "Messiah". Jewish dreams of a "savior"
who was to be the heaven-sent descendant of David are—dreams.
Endowing a purely mythical personage with them does not make
him a living being however closely the question is discussed.
First let us catch our real "Man", and we can then discuss how
he came to be regarded as a Messiah.

Every now and then Dr. Case refers to something he and
other similar-minded theologians like to call the "earliest common-
source material used in the composition of Matthew and Luke".
The fact that the four Gospels, or rather three of them, contain
similar material almost, in some cases, in the same words, has
made a number of theologians put forward some theories regarding their probable "source". One of these is that known by
the initial of the word "Quelle", the German word for "source",
and it has been increasingly adopted by the more advanced
"Higher" critics. In fact, it is now spoken of in some quarters as
if there really had been a Q document. The idea is that Mark
and some "logia" of Jesus account mostly for Matthew and Luke;
while the three document theory claims that our Synoptics are

derived from the "logia" of Papias, some account of the Perean ministry, and a Galilean source. It cannot be too strongly urged that all this is just theory, and that neither a document from the two or the three sources has ever been found. Actually, Dr. Case himself makes the admission about the "Q" document, "there is still much uncertainty". (p. 213, n.) I should think so, indeed.

The advocates for a "Man" Jesus particularly, almost always refer to what they call the "primitive" document or the "common-source material" to prove that in it we do not get the Virgin Birth, for example, or the miracles. By carefully selecting what they claim to be in this document, it is quite easy to omit many difficulties; and that is how Dr. Case, in common with many others, manages to avoid disagreeable discussions on Gospel balderdash. From page 159 of his book onwards, we get not only the sly way in which he disposes of "miracles", but also how the "early" document managed to make Jesus not one famed for "mighty works" but for "fidelity" in uttering the word of God as an "authoritative expounder of the law" and as a prophet worthy to put beside Moses. All this may be true, but just as true of a fiction as of a fact. In any case, how much of it was actually in the "primitive" document is a matter of mere speculation. All we can say with certainty is that the Gospels show Jesus as a God, as the Son of God, as equal to God, and as a worker of miracles. It is almost if not quite impossible to sort out which came first, if any at all; and to shelve all the Deity attributes and the miracles and the Devils and the Angels, and then to turn round and blandly tell us that the residue is the real Jesus, the "Man" Jesus, who went about "doing good", no doubt appeals to the "liberal Churchman" and to the "reverent Rationalist" —but not to those of us who see in the whole thing nothing but a re-hash of Pagan myths and Jewish-Christian credulity.

The result of all this inquiry into the "pragmatic phases of early Christian thinking" (p. 172) might make some people believe that there never was a Jesus—but not Dr. Case. For him it points "in a very different direction", which is not surprising considering that the object of his book was to show that Jesus really lived. Even if you point out that the Gospels teem with absurd contradictions and idiotic stories this does not "necessarily imply non-historicity for his personality". These things might well go to prove that a God like Jupiter never existed, but not if the God is Jesus. "It is too much to expect", blandly says Dr. Case again, "that we can find a full and perfect uniform portrait of the earthly Jesus in our present sources", though one would never expect such an admission even from Dr. Case, if the enormous number of lives of Jesus, packed with detail, which have been written could be piled up before him.

Dr. Case rests his thesis mainly upon Paul. He points out to begin with that the credibility or genuineness of the principal Pauline Epistles is now generally admitted. I cannot again go into this, and I find nothing in his chapter on Paul which in any way invalidates what I have written. I can only repeat my conviction that in the Epistles we have edited versions of some Gnostic documents which were full of a God in heaven called Christ Jesus (all imagination, of course), and that the late editors did their utmost to confuse the issue by bringing this God down to earth as a man. The Lord Jesus was to come again veritably in the flesh "like a thief in the night", and the faithful were to be carried back to Heaven with him, or he was to rule over them on earth (I am not quite sure as to which); and from the way Christian commentators bemoan the obscurity of a good deal of Pauline nomenclature, and from the various translations and notes the Epistles have called forth, I suspect that really even the most formidable Christian defenders of Paul are in the same boat with me. At all events Dr. Case is, as anyone can see from his own labored explanations.

That there was "a fierce personality" at the back of the Epistles may be granted, but this does not prove that they have not been edited and re-edited. And I say here as clearly as I can that the problem is not whether the Epistles are "spurious", which only means that they were written not by Paul but by some other man. The problem is, do they describe a man who really lived, and I say they describe a God—a Gnostic Being residing in Heaven and nothing but a figment of Paul's imagination.

Most commentators agree that Paul never met Jesus, but of course it is easy to show that he did if one wants to. The whole tenor of the Epistles is that Paul was speaking of, not an "ob-

jective" God but a "subjective" one, and Gerald Massey bitterly
complained how they were changed by the Christian Church to
look as if the God was an "objective" one. Even Dr. Case
acknowledges that "Paul claimed to be preaching a gospel which
looked to no human source for its authentication but which had
been received by him directly from the heavenly Christ". (p.
191). Such an admission is inevitable from anyone who has even
a superficial knowledge of the Pauline letters.

Dr. Case is asked, if Paul had any knowledge of an earthly
Jesus, why did he not use it? And his answer is, "How do we
know that he did not"? It is always the same answer. If we
point out that Josephus, actually writing a detailed contemporary
history of Pauline times, never mentions him or Peter, or indeed
any apostle or disciple or even Christianity, we are asked how
do we know he didn't somewhere else? I admit that the argument
from silence can sometimes be carried too far, but the truth is
that wherever we look for some details about a real Jesus the
answer seems to be silence or inventions.

Against everything else in the Epistles comes the statement
that "we have known Christ after the flesh", and Dr. Case would
like to claim, with some of the German theologians that he did
actually know "Christ"; but he tries in this instance to be fair,
and rather pathetically concludes that after all it may mean
only "such knowledge of Christ's earthly career as Christians in
general possess". He even admits that "the apostle freely interpreted, and at times no doubt greatly idealized, the person
of Jesus", but it would have been "a fatal shock" to the system
of Paul's "entire interpretative scheme" to deny that Jesus ever
lived. The sufficient answer to this is, that in the form we now
have them, we do not know for certain what it was that Paul
wanted to say; and I cannot again labor this point, having done
so already.

It is not surprising to find that when Dr. Case comes to the
"evidence" from the Gospels, he falls back upon all the well-worn
arguments from dates, from what Polycarp said, or from the
testimony of Irenaeus or the Diatessaron of Tatian—just as if all
this had never been dealt with or questioned and, in my opinion,
exploded by the arguments of the Mythicist. He even goes to the

"testimony" of Papias (who is called a fool by Eusebius) though it is he who quotes Papias. What Eusebius says in his *Ecclesiastical History* is very strongly "suspect" anyway, but when it is considered that he was writing in the fourth century, 300 years at least from the supposed death of Jesus, what can his testimony be worth? We agree that the story of Jesus, or rather the story of a mythical Deity in Heaven brought down to earth, was in full circulation in his day; and nobody can say at this late hour how much of his Church history is based on authentic material. As for gentlemen like Papias, or some of the other Church Fathers, one is obliged to say that it would be difficult to duplicate such a bunch of credulous fools. If Case likes to fall back on what they say, he has every right to do so; but he cannot expect any unbiased reader to admit for a moment that because they believed that Jesus was *God Almighty himself* it is "evidence" that Jesus was a *man*.

Not that Dr. Case does not show at least a critical spirit of some kind. He does not accept Papias' "explanation" of the composition of Matthew, and he admits that Harnack and Wellhausen are by no means in agreement on vital points with regard to which is the early Gospel or the "non-Markan" source. "There are still differences of opinion", he says, "about the exact dates of the several gospels"—but . . . there is always a "but", and in this case he says, "critical scholarship" agrees within "fairly well-defined limits". But here again he does not give us his reference as to who are responsible for this "critical" scholarship. All one need reply is that this "critical scholarship" has been very severely challenged by other "critical scholarship". What Prof. Brown says may be denied by Prof. Smith, and what they both say, laughed at by Prof. Robinson.

In the end, Dr. Case has to admit that on the existence of Jesus the Gospel writers are "either reliable historians or else they are mythologizers". Considering that on his own showing the Gospels are loaded with "legend, myth, apology, and miracle", it would be most interesting to learn how he knows which is which, and that by eliminating them he is quite certain the residue is a real Man Jesus going about "doing good". He does appeal to the "non-Markan tradition", though it is a purely

mythical document invented by modern theologians; and the
more he appeals to it, the more he appears to rely upon it for
the picture of Jesus as "chiefly a teacher rather than a miracle-
worker". (p. 222). I have already pointed out that it is quite
easy to invent a "tradition" in which one calmly eliminates all
the nonsense that accompanies Jesus through the present-day
Gospels.

And how does Dr. Case dispose of the miraculous? He wants to
subordinate all his argument to the thesis, and to nothing else,
that Jesus really lived; but whenever he wants to push home an
argument he does not mind referring to a miracle as if there was
not the slightest doubt that it occurred. It is in a book, and the
book is guaranteed by the Roman Catholic Church as being a
"divine" revelation. Lest it be considered that I am unfair to
Dr. Case, I quote the following:

> Especially important, as evidence for the existence of Jesus,
> is Mark's almost uniform representation that Jesus during his
> lifetime was generally misunderstood, even by his closest asso-
> ciates. The members of his own family thought him beside him-
> self, and even the Twelve showed a remarkable dullness on
> nearly every occasion when his uniqueness, might seemingly,
> easily be perceived. When he was about to feed the four thou-
> sand the disciples were as unsuspecting of the method he was
> to employ as if they had not, only a short time before, witnessed
> his miraculous feeding of the five thousand. And after the second
> incident they were still without understanding, so that Jesus
> marveled, "Do ye not yet perceive neither understand, have ye
> your heart hardened?" When he cast out demons the latter spoke
> of his messiahship in unmistakable terms and Jesus apparently
> acknowledged the accusation in the disciples' presence, yet they
> attained no conviction of his messiahship until near the close of
> his career. . . . (p. 224-25).

It is difficult to criticize this farrago of nonsense in decent
terms. Here we have Dr. Case calling in as witness that Jesus
was a *man*, the "miracle" of feeding the four thousand, as if
that really took place. He makes not the slightest attempt to
prove it. The reader need hardly be told that even if Jesus had
existed and went about "doing good", he never performed a

single *miracle* of any kind; and yet Dr. Case is prepared to shed "legend, myth, apology, and miracle" when it suits his case. When it does not, the above extract proves him to be quite as credulous as the simplest Salvation Army lassie.

The oldest motive in fiction is the belittling of the "hero". Everybody knows how often in "crime" stories the detective is baffled or beaten or nearly killed by the villain. Generally no one believes in the hero—except, of course, in the end the beauteous and glamorous and far-seeing heroine. The belittling of Jesus by his supposed Jewish opponents as well as by the disciples and apostles is just fiction—and I am quite sure that Dr. Case knows this as well as I.

As for the "messiahship" of Jesus, which I do not doubt he is prepared to defend strenuously, all one need add here is that anybody who believes in a "Messiah" is ready to believe anything. In the fiction of Jesus, his followers are shown gradually to believe in him while the "villains" the Jews, never did—nor do they now. The Jews in history have always denied that Jesus was the (or even a) Messiah, but that was only after Christianity began to emerge as a complete religion. There is simply no evidence whatever that they knew of any "Jesus of Nazareth" about the year 30 A.D.

There is still one point which must be made in the interests of truth. Historicists are moving heaven and earth to show that the Q document, or whatever they call the supposed early document or documents upon which they insist our Gospels were based, showed Jesus as no "miracle monger" or wonder worker, but as just an ordinary human being—a Man going about "doing good". But the fact remains that there were many gospels in existence before Luke took a hand at writing one, for he says so himself. That these gospels were mainly what we call Apocryphal Gospels hardly needs proof, and if this is so, then I must point out that the Jesus they deal with *is* a "miracle monger" or a "wonder worker". He is no mere Man, but a God who did marvelous things. My own contention is that, whatever were the first writings about Jesus, they must have insisted upon his being a God; for no people, however besotted they may have been, would have worshiped a mere Man, even if the Man necessitated a capital M. Only in the course of time was Jesus gradually shown to be both God and Man, and in these days desperate efforts are being made to shed the God. I hold—with John M. Robertson—that far from Mark being the earliest Gospel, because his Jesus is more of a Man than a God, that it is, in all probability, one of the latest of the Gospels, if not the latest. Just as the genuine part of Paul contained perhaps the earliest representation of Jesus the God, so such a Gnostic work like John was probably written before the Gospel of Mark. And it appears to me that in the absence of definite proof, my "speculation" is as good as Dr. Case's.

Another argument he presents as conclusive is that "the gospel representation of Jesus' historicity is practically forced upon us by his proximity to the community in which his life story first took place". There is not a scrap of evidence that this is true. If, as I have shown in dealing with the date of the Gospels in the form we have them, they were unknown before the year 150 A.D., the Jesus they describe was not in "close proximity" with his believers any more than we are in close proximity with Napoleon Bonaparte. Dr. Case adds (p. 229) "yet there is never an inkling that this claim for reality was contested or even doubted by friend or foe". Indeed! If the reader turns back to what I have said on Justin and his *Dialogue with Trypho* he will find there that a Jew, speaking about 130 years after the supposed life of Jesus had taken root—according to Case—at a time when there must have been a considerable body of Christians with many Gospels of all kinds, to say nothing of Epistles and Acts, denied that anything was known at all of this Jesus; and he appears also to have denied that there was a Crucifixion. Moreover, he knew nothing about Peter or Paul or the Apostles or the wonderful events described in Acts. And all Justin could say in reply was that Christians did not believe in empty fables! The point to note here particularly is that all this comes not from a Jew but from a Christian, and it would be absurd to take Trypho as an exception to the majority of Jews. On the contrary, it was in all probability the majority who would have then agreed with Trypho.

On the same page, Dr. Case actually refers to the Resurrection as a real occurrence which had to be defended to keep the "believer's faith" and so the "actual existence (of Jesus) was uniformly accepted as a matter of course". One can see from all this that it is also uniformly accepted by Dr. Case, including "legend, myth, apology, and miracle", by the self-same arguments which he claims persuaded the early believers. I can only repeat that if these people believed in the Resurrection, the Messiahship, the descent from David (particularly in view of the fact that this is expressly denied in the Genealogies and the Virgin Birth story) "and similar tenets of early interpretation", they would believe anything.

Naturally, Dr. Case has to admit that even the parts of the story of Jesus and the character of his teaching which he himself so thoroughly believes may have been invented. It may even "have been easily invented" (p. 231). Still, or but . . . and he goes on to show why it was not. In fact "one of the strongest arguments for Jesus' existence is the existence of the primitive community of believers". Exactly the same argument could be put forward for the reality of the God Jehovah as he, also, must have had a "primitive community of believers". He also must therefore have been a Man. Dr. Case's elaboration of his argument, together with an untranslated German quotation from Clemen supposed finally to clinch it, may have convinced him. For me, it is just a re-hash of old Christian arguments not only for Jesus the Man—going about "doing good"—but for Christ the God.

Leaving aside the Canonical Gospels, Dr. Case refers to the Apocryphal ones, even if not true in "details", as showing a belief in the existence of Jesus—as if they would be writing about him at all if they were not quite convinced of that fact. Even if the Apostolic Fathers believed in his "pre-existence and heavenly exaltation" they still believed he lived on earth. In fact if the phrase "even if" were multiplied a thousand times, I expect we should still be told all this proves the actual existence of Jesus. If the crass superstition of that parcel of fools, the Apostolic Fathers, and the idiotic "details" put in the various Apocryphal Gospels do not in themselves put these "authorities" out of court, then I'm afraid no argument ever discovered could do so. Dr. Case however hastily runs away from any elaboration here and gets on to Pliny, Suetonius, and Tacitus.

Unfortunately, we get again the same old arguments, known to all of us who have waded through Christian apologetics; and though in the case of Tacitus we are told of Ross and Hochart and their claim to the forgery of the *Annals*, yet "this extreme skepticism has failed to win any substantial approval". Except in the case of two very short phrases from Tacitus, there is not the slightest attempt to deal with the arguments against the authenticity of the passage describing Nero and the large number of Christians then in Rome and their hatred of the human race. Dr. Case prefers accepting the "genuineness of Tacitus"; it saves a lot of trouble and writing. And of course if the passage *is* a forgery, where can one go to prove the existence of Jesus in Roman history?

We come then to Philo and Josephus. The former is very regretfully admitted as saying nothing of Jesus; and the "genuineness" of the two passages about Jesus in the latter are "commonly doubted". Whether both passages are rank forgeries or have been "radically recast" has been much disputed. However, while very reluctantly throwing overboard the longer passage in Josephus, Dr. Case comes to the conclusion that in the shorter one "Josephus did mention in this incidental way 'Jesus the so-called Christ' ". Well, one opinion is as good as another. For my part I believe both are gross forgeries.

As for the "Slavonic" Josephus, that appears to be a little too much for even Dr. Case to swallow; so in it, "we cannot believe that we are here dealing with direct testimony from Josephus". For the rest, he cannot say why Josephus, who must have known all about Christianity, "possibly deliberately excluded this subject". This is another "possible" guess. On the other hand, J. Weiss, one of Case's numerous German authorities, "finds in Josephus' comparative silence a mark of his friendliness towards the Christians". That seems to be the very greatest proof that there must have been a Jesus—the complete silence of an almost contemporary. Again I can only say that if this kind of argument is the best that the last word on the subject can produce, the Mythicist has won all along the line.

Of course the number of "ifs" in this part of Dr. Case's book prove that even in the art of speculation there must be a limit. "If we had access", he says (p. 264), "to the life and thinking of contemporary rabbinical Judaism possibly we should find more frequent reference to Jesus." In this way, the testimony of the Mishna (200 A.D.) is lightly got rid of. The fact that there is only one reference in this part of the Talmud, and dozens of references to a Jesus or to various Jesuses in the later part, none of whom have the slightest likeness to the "real" Jesus, is thus gracefully dealt with. But these references, whatever they are, point out in Case's opinion, that the Jews never denied the existence of Jesus. All I need add here is that when the Talmud was compiled the most bitter controversy must have taken place between Jews and Christians, and I do not doubt for a moment that the then rabbis never questioned the existence of Jesus as they never questioned Abraham or Adam or Noah.

As it happens, Dr. Case knows this argument very well, but he insists that in spite of it, "it does not follow that this testimony [that of Tacitus and the Jewish opponents of Christianity] is wholly valueless much less that its relative scantiness and secondary character is a positive argument against Jesus' historicity". Note how the argument is here adroitly turned. It is we who ask for *evidence* that there was a real Jesus. The evidence of Tacitus, Josephus, and the Talmud (outside the New Testament) is very confidently given us. We examine this evidence and show, to use Case's own words, "its relative scantiness and secondary character"—we even show its utter uselessness. Back comes the Historicist: Well, even if it is, *you*, the Mythicist, can't use it to show that Jesus never existed. It is, says Case, "all corroborative of, and never contradictory to, Jesus' historicity". (p. 267-8). The impudent forgeries in Josephus never contradict the real existence of Jesus, they really prove it. So does the questioning of Trypho. When our opponents use this kind of tactic it seems to me that they recognize that they are waging a losing battle.

When Dupuis, and following him Robert Taylor, began this controversy about the real existence of Jesus, the Christians who did not call them mad, were obliged not only to "search the scriptures" but to bring forward the "numbers" of Pagan and

Jewish writers who corroborated "Holy Writ". All this mass of "evidence" we were confidently told permitted of no rebuttal; but the Historicist is now not quite so confident. According to Dr. Case—and please remember his book is supposed to be the last word on this problem—it now appears that "it cannot really be a matter of great importance that a Roman historian of the second century A.D., or Josephus at the end of the first century, and the Talmudists of a still later date have so little to say of the earthly Jesus. [Incidentally, Josephus has nothing whatever to say.] In the nature of the case they could not speak at first-hand. . . . The evidence for Jesus' existence is derived mainly from Christian sources . . ." (p. 268-69). Let anyone, in the face of this pathetic admission, compare the way in which all Historicists, Christian, Rationalist and Jew, invariably write reams about the "testimony" of Pliny, Suetonius, Tacitus, Josephus, and the Talmud.

But what about these "Christian sources"? I say as emphatically as I can that they show, not a "Man" Jesus but a God—and the way Dr. Case himself so airily appeals to miracles when it suits him (like the feeding of the four thousand) proves conclusively that he too looks upon Jesus as a God. He might well say that his *New Biography* of Jesus gets rid of some of the "legend, myth, apology, and miracle", but the truth is that this is impossible. Directly they are removed there is no Jesus left at all—let alone a Man Jesus.

Dr. Case in his last chapter deals with "Jesus and the latest skepticism" and I am not surprised that he refers to Conybeare's *Historical Christ*. Whether he has carefully read it is another matter, for at the outset he says that it "defends not the theological Christ but the Galilean prophet". But if that is so, why does Conybeare call his book the *Historical Christ*? Surely he should have said "Jesus", as Dr. Case himself does. I do not know if Conybeare ever was a "Freethinker", as Case assumes; my own impression is that he was "half-baked". I doubt that any Freethinker, even if he believed in Jesus as a Man (or even a man) would ever call him "Christ".

What Dr. Case has to say about the theories of John M. Robertson, Arthur Drews, Couchoud, and others calls for no

reply from me. We Mythicists are not constrained to defend
speculative theories, however attractive they may be, or even if
in our opinion they are irrefutable. I can only repeat what I
have already said, that the origins of Christianity are hopelessly
obscure, and that it can never be an easy task to account for
this religion, or indeed for many other religions. How can we
account for Judaism? That it was given by God Almighty on Mt.
Sinai to Moses?

The final position taken by Dr. Case is that Christianity cannot
be accounted for unless by a real Jesus, and that was the Jesus
found in the "early" documents, and not a theological Christ. I
deny that in his book he has produced any evidence for either
position, and I deny that he has really touched the Mythicist
claim that Jesus is just another God in the hundreds of deities
who have been worshiped, adored, and who have finally disappeared.

One of the items in the English *Thinker's Library* published by
Watts and Co., in 1946, is *Jesus: Myth or History?* by Archibald
Robertson, M.A., who has always been a stout defender of the
historicity of Jesus. This work is, however, "a lucid and balanced
statement", say the publisher's announcement, "for the general
reader, of the main arguments on the question whether Jesus was
an historical or a purely mythical character". Let us admit that
Mr. Robertson does try to give both sides as fairly as a man of
his temperament can do, and that therefore his book may prove
of great use to readers who have little time to read the massive
works of his famous namesake; for example, the six volumes John
M. Robertson devoted to the problem.

We can discount Mr. Robertson's statement that "the Mythicist
and the Historicist have each got hold of an important half-
truth"; it is only one of the pleasant ways the author has of maintaining that in his own opinion there is a case for the existence of
Jesus—which I deny. There is no more this case in the problem
of Jesus than in the problem of Osiris or Krishna.

Mr. Robertson begins with an elementary account of the Gospels and he soon strikes a controversial note. He says, "the
Synoptic Gospels are based on a common tradition, the nature
of which can be ascertained simply by marking those passages

which occur in all three". This is a delightful over-simplification, for of course it does *not* prove that they are based on a common tradition. All we are entitled to say is that these Gospels copied one another, and the only way in which we can find out a common tradition is by proving that there was a tradition. Now, according to Luke, there were many Gospels in his day. Where are they? Our Canonical Gospels, in the form we have them, are late second century productions, and nobody knows what tradition said about Jesus with certainty before their appearance.

When Mr. Robertson says that "the deity, pre-existence, and virgin birth of Jesus do not figure in the triple tradition", all he is doing is to take what Christian theologians invented, "a triple tradition", and argue from that almost anything he wants. If that does not provide enough, then the "Q" document—that is, the matter common to Matthew and Luke but not found in Mark—is put in, as if it was quite an authentic "tradition", when it is nothing but an invention or speculation of some Christian theologians (who are called by Mr. Robertson, just "critics".) The Q document, even Mr. Robertson admits, is "unlike the triple tradition". So where is this "common tradition"?

In any case, he admits also that the "Fourth Gospel gives an account of the life and teaching of Jesus utterly different from that in the Synoptic Gospels". Does this prove the "common tradition"? If a common tradition had been the case it is very difficult to see how John could never have referred to it.

As for Paul, Mr. Robertson comes to grips at once by giving us the passages in the Epistles which refer to Jesus as "born of the seed of David" (though there is nothing whatever about this in the Gospels, the genealogies giving that distinction to Joseph only), "that he had brothers" (obstinately disavowed by the Roman Catholic Church, which, at least on this point, claims to be an authority), and that "he was killed by the Jews" (which anyway is not true, for John admits that the Jews had no power then to inflict the punishment of death, and in any case it was the Romans who crucified Jesus, according to "common tradition").

Still, in accordance with his plan of giving both sides, Robertson admits "these passages however are in strong contrast to the general tone of the Epistles" (p. 7). If that is so, then our claim that the Epistles have been interpolated stands unchallenged. For Paul, who was a Gnostic, wrote of a Christ in Heaven, and never of a Jesus on earth who was but a mere Man going about "doing good". And Robertson has eventually to write, "The Jesus of the Pauline Epistles, like the Jesus of the Fourth Gospel, is a divine being". That is, of course, not altogether the Christian tradition but the Mythicist position.

The Jesus of the Apocalypse "is a wholly superhuman being", says Mr. Robertson, and this is the opinion of the writer, whoever he was, in the first "Epistle of Clement" and in "Barnabas" and in the seven Ignatian Epistles. But even Christian apologists are all prepared to agree here, though this disputation is not really our concern. I have always claimed that the Gospels and other Christian writings insist that Jesus was a God. If that is so, then certainly he never existed. What we want is *evidence* that he was a *man*.

For those who do not know it, Robertson's description of the early Christian documents and their writers is very necessary, though it is well to check him. For example, in speaking of the Shepherd of Hermas, he says, "the author never refers to Old or New Testament books, does not use the name 'Jesus' or 'Christ' at all, and rather confusingly applies the phrase 'Son of God'". . . . (p. 15.) In the translation of Hermas by Archbishop Wake the word "Christ" will be found in III Hermas, Similitude IX, 223 and 237. Hermas was at one time looked upon as an "inspired" writer and as his work is certainly superior to most of the early Christian writers this is not surprising. But it shows no knowledge of a *Man* Jesus.

Mr. Robertson's references to Justin, Papias, and Irenaeus all want checking, and in any case, I have dwelt in earlier chapters on many of their statements. Moreover, he admits that "we cannot regard the documents as authoritative". When Irenaeus claims that Jesus died an old man—quite possibly in bed, for he does not say in this passage how—it is obvious that there could have been no crucifixion under Pontius Pilate; it is not surprising that Mr. Robertson, who says as little as he can on this—it is not mentioned in his Index—is not, I am quite sure, prepared to give up this "historical" event. To do so would have meant that "Pontius Pilate would not have been immortalized" (p. 107).

On page 19, Mr. Robertson quotes Eisler's *The Messiah Jesus*, pp. 297-299, "since Thallus is said to have referred to the darkness at the crucifixion, the date in Eusebius is corrupt and should be corrected to the 207th Olympiad (A.D. 49)". There is no word of this in Eisler at the page referred to. He says, referring again to Thallus, that "the actual passage in Josephus . . . calls him 'another Samaritan'". (Josephus, *Antiquities*, xviii, 6, 4.). In 4, Thallus only is named; and in 6, there is not a word about "another Samaritan".

As for the "Christ" passage in Josephus, Robertson admits that "the forgery would not deceive a schoolboy", by which he means, of course, anybody who is intelligent enough to query it. Still, "it does not of course follow that Josephus gave no account of Jesus" (p. 21). The question is, does Josephus mention *"Jesus"*? The answer from orthodox Christians, many Rationalists, and Jews is, "Well, he does—that is, he does mention Christ if the passage is genuine, or even if it is not genuine, it has been probably changed, don't you know; and anyway how do you know he didn't?" The fact is, that the passage in Josephus mentions, not Jesus, but "Christ", and it is a rank forgery. Why it is, or whether Josephus did mention "Jesus" or "Christ" or both is a good field for futile speculation.

The other passage, the one upon which Judge Waite confidently relies, Mr. Robertson rather grudgingly admits, "is not so plainly spurious as the other". We can agree with him that it is possible to insert a rank forgery in an old work, and one that is not quite so rank. But they both are forgeries.

Pliny, one of the great "pagan witnesses", is dismissed rather shortly, because we do not know whether he regarded "Christ" as a man or a myth; but of the passage in Tacitus we are told that "no classical expert denies that the *Annals* are genuine". But surely the problem cannot rest there. We are not concerned about unnamed "classical experts" but with the arguments of men like Ross, Hochart, W. B. Smith, and others against either the authenticity of the whole of the *Annals*, or that of the particular passage which names Christ. Have these arguments been answered? I maintain that they have not, and I refer the reader to the chapters I have devoted to the question. The "witness" of Suetonius is too much for even Mr. Robertson.

When he came to the Talmud, it is a pity that he did not check his own statements at first hand. If he had read G. R. S. Mead's *Did Jesus Live 100 B.C.?* he would have made fewer errors. With the quotations he gives, I have dealt fully and the reader is again referred to them.

All Mr. Robertson's sympathies are with the Historicist in dealing with Josephus, Pliny, Tacitus, Suetonius, the Talmud, and of course, entirely with him in discussing the famous passage in Justin's *Dialogue with Trypho*. As readers already know I have shown that Trypho, a representative Jew of the second century, claimed that "Christ" if he was ever born is unknown. Robertson adroitly changes the word Christ into the "Messiah" so that it does not look like Jesus Christ but *any* "Messiah" and then claims that Trypho never meant "that Jesus is unknown" but that "the real Messiah . . . will be unknown until proclaimed by Elijah". This argument can be interminable, especially if people will never go to Justin for themselves, and see what he is driving at. I can only repeat, as emphatically as I can, that Justin's whole argument is of Jesus Christ—the Messiah predicted for the Jews by the Old Testament. It is that Messiah—Jesus Christ—who is "unknown" according to Trypho, Justin's opponent, if he ever was born; and Trypho says to Justin that it is he, Justin, who says this Messiah was crucified and rose from the dead.

Let the reader pause for a moment and ask how could a Jew talk like that if Jesus and his galaxy of Apostles and disciples with Peter, Paul, Clement, Barnabas, and others at their head had all propagated Christianity in the way we are told in Church history? Did he know nothing about them? Had he never met Jewish Christians who taunted him with the Crucifixion, as Jewish converts still do their late brothers?

From the mythicist point of view what was said by Celsus, who wrote an attack on Christianity late in the second century, all of which has been lost except the portions answered by Origen long after does not matter. He obviously looked upon the story of Jesus, which had by this time become more or less fixed, as the story of an impostor; as he made no attempt—as far as we know—to verify it in detail, it seems to me a waste of time to refer to him except by mentioning that he had got hold of what later became a sort of "Jewish Life of Christ", very "blasphemous", and utterly valueless from any point of view.

What Robertson has to say on Renan, Strauss, and other late critics is interesting, but as many of them had no doubt whatever that Jesus Christ really lived, and as some of their most telling arguments in favor of his historicity have been replied to in the course of this work, there is no need for me to deal further with them. He himself has come to see the hollowness of their assumptions, and he now emphasizes the necessity of not giving the Christian documents "the benefit of the doubt" but of asking oneself, "How much of the story do the laws of evidence compel me to accept?"

But once again Mr. Robertson—possibly to save his own belief in the historicity of Jesus—is glad to find an authority like Prof. Schmiedel, whose "foundation-pillars" for "a truly scientific life of Jesus", he accepts. Whether the word "scientific" is "writ sarcastic" Schmiedel alone knows. We therefore get Mr. Robertson gladly quoting some of these "foundation-pillars", though he must have known that both John M. Robertson and Prof. W. B. Smith made mincemeat of their pretensions.

One of Archibald Robertson's pet arguments in favor of a real Jesus is that Jesus prophesies he will come again after being put to death, and the prophecy was unfulfilled. I have dealt with it in a previous chapter, but here I should like to add that the man who wrote down the prophecy also wrote the sequel. What Mr. Robertson insists upon is, that it is impossible to imagine anybody making up a story like this of a *myth*, for the fact that Jesus never came again would make the prophecy just nonsense. But it is Mr. Robertson who says that Jesus never came again— not the writer of the "myth". It is he who says that he did rise again, and he said it with such good effect that the Resurrection has been believed in by millions of people ever since. Even at this late day people can be found to write books and get them published to defend the "fulfillment" of the prophecy.

The fact is that Robertson cuts the story in half and accepts the "prophecy" while rejecting the sequel; and he imagines he has put up a case. The man who wrote the story wrote the prophecy and quite logically gave the sequel. The two parts of the story hang together, and to pick up one part and form an argument on that while ignoring the other is quite valueless from the point of either logic or history. Needless to say, I reject both the prophecy and the sequel.

If the "Christian tradition" cannot then be depended upon, how do we come to the story of Jesus? There it is, and it has to be accounted for; and so Mr. Robertson comes at last to the Myth theory (or theories) which in 1769 began to be talked about by some disciples of Bolingbroke to Voltaire. The arguments they advanced did not convince him; and those of Volney and Dupuis later obviously do not convince Mr. Robertson. Nor is he ready to accept the ingenious hypothesis of Bruno Bauer, who also had ideas on the problem. Mr. Robertson bypasses Robert Taylor (as I could well expect) to give the credit to John M. Robertson as being "the pioneer in this enquiry", though he might have pointed out that J. M. R. came to the problem magnificently equipped through the researches of many great students of mythology and anthropology during most of the nineteenth century.

It is not my task to champion John M. Robertson's explanations or his theories of Christian origins; the reader should carefully compare what he says with Mr. Robertson's criticisms, and judge for himself. In the same way he should read Whittaker, and W. B. Smith, at first hand—Smith in particular, as he approached the problem in an original way. Prof. Drews popularized the idea of a Christ Myth with many people because he was a Theist in spite of his very radical theories. And Dr. Couchoud— in my opinion rightly—came to the conclusion that at the outset Jesus was a God and that he was brought down from Heaven and made into a man by the later writers of his "biography".

Mr. Robertson summarizes Couchoud's *Creation of Christ* and no student of the Myth theory can afford to miss the book, or at least this summary. But here again I can only say that I am not concerned with proving Couchoud is right; and even if he is

wrong in his very startling theories, this would not show that
there had ever been a Man Jesus going about "doing good".

As the reader may have gathered, I am inclined to favor the
Gnostic theory of Christian origins and for a succinct account of
this, the work of Gordon Rylands can be confidently recommended with that of Dr. Couchoud. At the same time, I do not
tie myself down to any theory because the whole question is so
very speculative. It is principally because everything connected
with the beginnings of Christianity is so vague that I hold Jesus
Christ to be a myth—analogous to Apollo or Krishna. What do
we know of *their* origins? The one thing certain in the problem
is the utter impossibility of producing any real evidence for the
existence of Jesus.

Just as one of Mr. A. Robertson's favorite arguments for Jesus
is the prophecy of coming again after being put to death so he
is constantly harking back to what Trypho said to Justin about
"Christ" or the "Messiah" not being born. "The passage", blandly
says Mr. Robertson, "has no connection whatever with the myth
theory". This is a free country, and so far we are allowed to express our own opinions on many vital matters; this being the
case, I claim that not only has "the passage" everything to do
with the myth theory, but that neither Mr. Robertson nor any of
his followers have been able to reply to its force. It is easy to
write "no connection whatever", but the phrase is no argument. I
can only repeat again that Trypho says in effect, "We know
nothing whatever of your Christ—not even if he was born; you
have made him up, or you have followed some silly yarn; and it
is *you* who say he was crucified, and rose from the dead". That
Trypho could talk as he did—including the point about "Christ"
being "born" and "crucified"—if he only meant *any* Messiah is
just unmitigated nonsense, and no amount of "no connection
whatever" can hide that fact. Mr. Robertson's bluff here quite
equals that of Dr. Conybeare. There were Jews of Trypho's day
who denied the existence of Jesus, and I say if there had been
any proof of this existence Justin would have brought up the full
force of Church "history" as recorded in Acts instead of petu-
lantly claiming that Christians do not believe "in idle fables".
Why did not Trypho know all about Paul and Peter and Barna-

bas and the damning story (for him) of so many Jewish converts? His companions roared with laughter at Justin's childish and silly arguments.

Mr. A. Robertson tries to give a summary of the arguments which Dr. F. C. Conybeare thought so devastating in his *Historical Christ*; and it is quite amusing to find that he claims Conybeare "distinguishes between the historical Jesus who, in his opinion, underlies the Synoptic Gospels (especially Mark) and the 'Christ of their own theory and imaginings' created by Paul and later theologians". This may be so, but, unfortunately, Conybeare calls his book *The Historical Christ*, and I, for one, refuse to believe that he meant "Jesus" and not "Christ". Conybeare, in fact, like so many Christian theologians, was quite ready to throw overboard a number of the silly miracles attributed to Jesus but —in my opinion—he believed that Jesus was the Heaven-sent Messiah, that is, the "Christ".

With the two Jewish writers, who like most Jews insist on the real existence of Jesus, Dr. R. Eisler and Dr. J. Klausner, I am not particularly concerned here. The former is quite certain that Jesus was not only the King of the Jews, but a robber Chieftain with 900 brigand followers; and when he was not fulfilling his royal functions, or robbing people, he would discuss the Pentateuch with Talmudic rabbis. I do not think it worth while to deal with this conglomeration of balderdash. As for Klausner, he is so proud that a Jew is worshiped by Christians as a God that not for worlds would he relinquish such innocent happiness. Jesus the Jew *must* have lived, and may he long continue to be worshiped. Mr. Robertson admits that though Klausner's *Jesus of Nazareth* is "steeped in rabbinical learning", it is "not free from inaccuracies". I quite agree.

One of the "mysteries" I have never been able to solve is the gusto with which Rationalist writers like A. Robertson and A. D. Howell Smith move heaven and earth to show that we must date the Gospels earlier than, say, the Tübingen school, or W. R. Cassels in his *Supernatural Religion*. "Howell Smith," says Mr. Robertson (pp. 91-92), "draws attention to a discovery which makes impossible the late dates assigned to the Gospels by the Tübingen school, and by mythicists from Bruno Bauer to Cou-

choud". And what is this wonderful discovery? It appears that a
papyrus containing a fragment of the Fourth Gospel has been
discovered "which in the opinion of experts cannot be later than
about A.D. 130". Here it is seen we must immediately accept the
unnamed "experts" without question. They are scholars and
could not possibly be wrong. It only shows our own incredible
ignorance if we dare to question such "experts". For my part, I
certainly do question them, just as Freethinkers in the past had
the effrontery to query the almost unbelievable bosh which
poured out from such writers as Paley, Pye Smith, Spurgeon, and
General Booth.

The real point, however, is not the dating of a "fragment". The
real point made by Cassels was that the four Canonical Gospels,
in the form we have them now, are second century productions—
they are edited and re-edited versions of earlier gospels. If one
wants to throw back these, as Mr. Robertson following Mr.
Howell Smith does, to the years 66-70 A.D., I see no reason for
not doing so. We do not know what they were about except that,
if I am allowed to "speculate", they dealt with a God called
Jesus. But what it was then claimed that this God did or said,
nobody, not even Howell Smith or A. Robertson, knows. To
claim that giving an early date, then, for the Gospels "makes an
important difference to the question of the historicity" (p. 92) of
Jesus, is just nonsense. What these writers have to prove, by
giving us the *evidence,* is that the figure depicted in the earliest
Gospels was that of a Man going about "doing good", or uttering
prophecies that he would come again when put to death or something of the sort. And neither Mr. Robertson nor Mr. Smith has
given a scrap of such evidence.

When Mr. Robertson is asked what is the difference between
Jesus and, say, Osiris, Tammuz, Mithra, and other Pagan Christs,
he has a ready answer. It appears that for the Church, Jesus is
"God *and* man, and a man, moreover who lived at a particular
moment of history, and in a particular Roman province". (p. 93).
Supposing that this is the opinion of the Church—so what? Who
in the Church says so? The Pope, the Archbishop of Canterbury,
Luther, Calvin, Irenaeus—who? The word "Church" is a collective
word and represents nobody in particular; but if any of the

gentlemen I have named are supposed to be the Church, or are of some "authority", would it be possible for Mr. Robertson to tell us what they know about a "God *and* man"? All they know is what is in the Gospels, and I am quite as good an authority on these as they are: that is, when it comes to saying that somebody described in an anonymous document relating a lot of particularly silly marvels lived or not, what does the "Church" know more than I do? The Church can claim that Jesus, living in a moment of history, is "God and man", just as the Pagans can claim that there was a terrible fight between Osiris and Set; all we want is evidence, not "claims".

I am very amused at the way in which Mr. Robertson gathers all the "important concessions" that his great namesake, John M., makes about there being perhaps one or several Jesuses behind the Gospel story. That is, when the Gospel writers claim that there was one great Jesus who was both "God and man", and John M. Robertson says that they may well have founded their myth on several itinerant monks, or preachers, or agitators, it is "an important concession", an "*embarras de richesse*", a proof that perhaps in his heart of hearts, J. M. Robertson really believed in a genuine Jesus. It is just unmitigated nonsense to talk like that. When the Gospel writers turned God into Man, they may well have put to use some stories of the dirty, credulous, hermits who infested the desert, and talked the rubbish faithfully put down by Paul in his Gnostic meanderings.

We are told that all John M. Robertson "stipulates is that we shall not pretend that the discourses of such a Jesus are accurately reproduced in the Gospels, that we shall admit a preponderant element of fiction, and that we shall on no account presume to label such a Jesus a Personality or a Figure or anything else with a big letter. Any Rationalist in these days should be able to promise so much. If that is the only issue between mythicist and historicist, the path of the peacemaker is easy". (p. 100). For this statement of what J. M. Robertson "concedes", we get no chapter and verse whatever, though *Jesus and Judas* is quoted in a previous passage as the authority for (in A. Robertson's words) "a Galilean faith healer named Jesus may have been offered as a human sacrifice by fanatical peasants at some time of social tumult." (p. 100). The reference is pp. 205-206. Here is what J. M. Robertson does say, and I ask the reader particularly to compare the quotations: "The story of an actual Galilean sacrifice, the work of a fanatical peasantry, would have to be suppressed for evangelistic purposes; even if it were known to have taken place". There is not here a word about "the Galilean faith healer named Jesus" so cleverly slipped in by Mr. A. Robertson as one of the "important concessions" of his more famous namesake.

The truth is, of course, that the "important concessions" of John M. Robertson amount to nothing more than what I have in previous pages indicated, and do not in any way show that he was ready to accept a Jesus or some Jesuses behind the Gospels in the way A. Robertson implies. Was there a real Robinson Crusoe because his story is in some measure based on that of Alexander Selkirk? To ask the question is to show its absurdity.

John M. Robertson says:

> The present writer (once described in the Hibbert Journal as being an *à priori* denier of the historicity of Jesus) actually spent a long time in trying to construct a working theorem of *three* possible historical Jesuses; one the elusive Jesus of the Talmud, first dated under Alexander Jannaeus; one a Nazarite; one not a Nazarite, and therefore 'declared to be "of Nazareth", by way of deflecting the other term. The theorem could not be carried beyond the stage of unsupported hypothesis, and had to be abandoned. . . . (*Jesus and Judas*, p. 205).

This little passage proves how much reliance can be placed on statements regarding what John M. Robertson said or did not say. I trust the reader will go to that writer's own work and never accept any statement coming from an Historicist without careful checking.

For my own part, whatever are the arguments of the fervent believers in the historicity of Jesus, however sifted from "such lumber as the Old Russian Josephus" they may be, I entirely oppose the statement which A. Robertson makes on p. 100, "that *one* starting point of the Gospel story was the existence at or about the date traditionally assigned, of a Jewish Messianic claimant bearing the common name of Joshua or Jesus, a member of the sect of Nazoraeans or Nazarenes, who was crucified as a rebel by Pilate . . ." I claim there is not a scrap of evidence to justify this assertion.

There seems no need to follow Mr. Robertson in any of his later speculations as to the "Fusion of Opposites", for example, or what he says about the Pauline Epistles. I need only say again as emphatically as I can that Paul's "Lord Jesus" or "Christ Jesus" was a pure figment of his imagination which he admits he never got from "flesh and blood". There is no more reason to give "historicity" to this particular God than to give historicity to Mormon.

Mr. A. Robertson makes a great deal of the rivalry between the Pauline and other sects, which is quite clearly shown in the Epistles and Acts; and there is no doubt whatever that this rivalry existed and that there were bitter quarrels as to who had the real "Christ" and who had the spurious one or ones. How anyone can maintain the historicity of one of these "Christs" against the others is beyond me. Why should not Paul's have been the spurious one? How do we know his was the truly original, the hero of the genuine old firm? The truth may well be that they were all inventing a new God, and found no better name than "Jesus" or "Joshua", meaning "Savior". The only rational explanation of the scores of Gospels, Acts, and Epistles in existence even at this day is that anybody who thought he could write was ready to invent his own particular "Christ" or "Jesus". And the supply of new Gospels and "Lives of Jesus" never runs out. There is always a public for them and one is just as "authentic" as the other.

Even A. Robertson has to admit—very sadly I am sure—that "human traits" can be seen added to the essentially Divine ones with which "Christ" was originally endowed (p. 105). They have been added, and the only result is "to betray the utter incongruity of the juxtaposition". Jesus is even given "a Jewish pedigree", or rather two different ones; but adds Mr. Robertson, "a later editor stultifies the pedigree by ascribing to him a virgin birth after the pattern of pagan demigods". Now, there is not a scrap of evidence that this is true—it is just one of Mr. Robertson's "speculations". We simply do not know under what conditions the Virgin

Birth story came into the Gospels, and we certainly know nothing whatever about a "later editor" stultifying anything whatever. The reader should note how easily these statements are made and how they are put forward with that air of authority which is intended to mislead the keen reader, but which, when analyzed, are found to be pure assumption, a merry game at which Christians have always been such tremendous victors, and which is now, alas, so often the wonder-weapon of the reverent Rationalist.

Whatever Mr. Robertson believes on the subject, and he certainly believes that there was a Jesus, I think we can now leave him in the happy position of not perhaps being quite so certain as he once was.

There is one little pamphlet to which I should like to call the reader's attention before taking my final leave. It is Gerald Massey's *The Historical Jesus and Mythical Christ*. Massey's great work was in the realm of Egyptian mythology. He wrote a number of massive works which for reasons, not difficult to conjecture, never received the attention they deserved. Massey stoutly maintained that Jesus Christ was a Myth, and short shrift was always given to any writer who maintained such an unpopular position. But in this small pamphlet he managed to pack a tremendous amount of information, and no one reading it could ever afterwards have any doubt that the Christian mythology is merely the old Egyptian under different names, and of course with some reservations.

For Massey, "Jesus" is Jehoshua Ben Pandira of the Talmud, who lived about the year 100 B.C. He was an historical character, he claims, and was hanged on a tree on the eve of Passover. Massey made inquiries of many Jewish rabbis, and he declares they always denied any identity between the Jehoshua of the Talmud and Jesus of Nazareth. It does not seem to me, however, that their opinion on the subject has any value.

What is worth noting, however, is that Christians—and even Rationalists like Mr. A. Robertson—insist that Jehoshua Ben Pandira and Jesus of Nazareth are the same. Mr. Robertson says (p. 101, n.): "The Jews had an obvious motive for dating Jesus a hundred years earlier. They thus countered the Christian argument that the catastrophe of A.D. 70 was a punishment for their rejection of Jesus". No reference again is given to Jewish or Christian writers as "authority" for this statement. If I may be allowed to say so, the "catastrophe" is always urged by those Christians and Jews who are proselytizing for Christianity, and is a very *modern* argument. In other words, this "note" is just a pure speculation on Mr. Robertson's part.

Massey claims that the "false" Christ so utterly repudiated by Paul, was Jehoshua "of whom James was a follower". When we come to the real Christ, the true Christ of Paul, Massey insists that he can "only be explained by means of the Mythos and those conditions of primitive sociology which are mirrored in mythology and preserved in theology". And he proceeds to show how some of the mythological scenes reproduced in Egypt "have been copied or reproduced as historical in the Canonical Gospels, where they stand like four corner stones to the Historic Structure, and prove that the foundations are mythical".

Massey stands almost entirely for the astronomical "Christ". He gives some extraordinary facts, which can be explained only his way. And he insists: "It is not I that deny the divinity of Jesus the Christ; I assert it. He never was, and never could be, any other than a divinity; that is, a character non-human and entirely mythical, who had been the pagan divinity of various myths that had been pagan during thousands of years before our Era".

The man who can write like this was bound to be ignored even by Rationalists like A. Robertson and A. D. Howell Smith. But the reader should, if possible, procure a copy of this fine pamphlet and he will see how the Egyptian Mythos has been cleverly changed into Christianity, and how purely mythical Egyptian scenes are believed in literally by millions of Christians and even acute critics like Dr. S. J. Case. Here is a final citation:

> I could keep on all day, and all night, or give a dozen lectures, without exhausting my evidence that the Canonical Gospels are only a later literalized réchauffé of the Egyptian writings; the representations in the Mysteries, and the oral teachings of the Gnostics which passed out of Egypt into Greece and Rome—for there is plenty more proof where this comes from. . . . The Christian legends were first related of Horus the Messiah, the

Solar Hero, the greatest hero that ever lived in the mind of man—
not in the flesh—the only hero to whom the miracles were natural,
because he was not human. From beginning to end the history is
not human but divine, and the divine is the mythical. . . .

That, of course, is the Mythicist position. The people who
plead for a real Jesus simply do not understand Myth and Miracle
except in a very superficial way. The real problem is now not so
much as to whether there is a God or a Son of God or a Virgin
Mother. The real problem is why do people still believe in these
primitive and childish fancies? And not until they understand
how they came to hold such superstitious ideas will they realize
that all Gods, whatever they are called, spring only from the
unenlightened mind of man.

Bibliography

THE BIBLE. The Variorum Teacher's Edition published by Eyre and Spottiswoode is probably the best for all students. It is brilliantly edited.

THE ENCYCLOPEDIA BIBLICA. Indispensable. Its special articles, e.g. The Gospels, Paul, Texts and Versions, and many others are of the highest value. Best edition is the one volume edition, 1914.

OUR BIBLE AND THE ANCIENT MANUSCRIPTS. by Sir F. G. Kenyon. Excellent account of the history of the text and translations.

L'ORIGINE DE TOUS LES CULTES. (1795) by C. F. Dupuis. The unabridged edition is difficult to obtain. Dupuis' own abridgment is in the "Classiques Garnier". The chapter dealing with Christianity has often been translated, e.g., in the Thomas Scott series. Packed with research and learning in favor of the Astro-myth theory.

THE SYNTAGMA. THE DIEGESIS. THE DEVIL'S PULPIT. (1828-31) All by (the Rev.) Robert Taylor. The first two works are a searching examination of the literary evidences of Christianity. The third is an attempt to explain many of the Bible stories in terms of the Sun and Astro-myths. All still of great value.

THE EXISTENCE OF CHRIST DISPROVED. (1841). by "a German Jew", probably J. C. Blumenfeld. Excellent, but dated.

SUPERNATURAL RELIGION. by W. R. Cassels. Pop. edition, 1905, Watts & Co. The finest work on the dates and authorship of the Gospels ever written. Three quarters of the reply by Canon J. B. Lightfoot (perhaps the ablest scholar of his day in the Church) in *Essays on Supernatural Religion* is irrelevant; and he deliberately avoided any discussion on Miracles and the Resurrection. Cassels' *Reply to Dr. Lightfoot's Essays* is a crushing rejoinder.

ANCIENT FAITHS IN ANCIENT NAMES. 2 volumes. (1868-9) by Thomas Inman, M.D. Very scarce. A summary by the author with an essay by John Newton on "Baal Worship" can be had from the Truth Seeker Co., New York, entitled *Ancient Pagan and Modern Christian Symbolism.* Treats symbolism fully from the phallic point of view and is packed with much other learning.

ANTHROPOLOGY. PRIMITIVE CULTURE. (1871-81) Both by Sir E. B. Tylor. Fundamental works which led to the modern study of comparative religions.

THE GOLDEN BOUGH. 12 or more volumes. Condensed and abridged by the author in one volume, 1922, Watts & Co. Perhaps the fullest and most important study ever made in comparative religion. Though Frazer in this work avers his belief in an historical Jesus, this belief runs counter to the whole of his thesis. No serious student of the Jesus problem can afford to miss this great work.

ANCIENT EGYPT. by Gerald Massey. (1907). Very scarce. A veritable encyclopedia on Egyptian belief and parallels to Christianity. Massey also published a number of lectures, e.g., *The Historical Jesus and the Mythical Christ, Paul as a Gnostic Opponent,* and many others supporting the Myth theory. All of great value.

TACITUS AND BRACCIOLINI. by W. J. Ross. (1878). A masterly analysis of the problem of the *Annals* of Tacitus, without, it should be added, any reference to the disputed passage regarding "Christ". Indispensable.

THE GOSPEL HISTORY AND DOCTRINAL TEACHING. Anon. By the author of *The Religions of Mankind, their Origin and History.* (1873).

THE FOUR GOSPELS AS HISTORICAL RECORDS. Anon. (1895). An enlarged version of Thomas Scott's *English Life of Jesus,* possibly by the Rev. Sir G. W. Cox. Both this and the preceding work are full of the most searching analysis of the "history" contained in the Gospels and there are few books on the orthodox side in any way comparable to them. Their conclusions are devastating.

BIBLE MYTHS. by T. W. Doane. (1884). A very valuable compilation. Nearly 200 standard authorities are called upon to show the parallels between Paganism and Christianity. Reprinted, 1949, by the Truth Seeker Co.

PAGAN CHRISTS. CHRISTIANITY AND MYTHOLOGY. SHORT
HISTORY OF CHRISTIANITY. THE JESUS PROBLEM. THE
HISTORICAL JESUS. JESUS AND JUDAS. by John M. Robertson. (Revised editions up to 1927). These six volumes give a
magnificent statement of the case for the non-historicity of
Jesus, together with Robertson's often annihilating replies to
opponents. No student of the question can afford to miss these
great and original contributions to the most perplexing problem
in religion.

THE EVOLUTION OF CHRISTIANITY. DID JESUS EVER
LIVE? by L. Gordon Rylands. (1927-35). A fresh presentment of the
case. Deals fully with Gnostic influences.

THE CHRIST MYTH. WITNESSES TO THE HISTORICITY OF
JESUS. by Prof. Arthur Drews (1910-12). The evidence for a pre-
Christian Jesus fully discussed in the first work. In the second
the Christian evidences for the historical existence of Jesus fully
analyzed and "found wanting". Both works created a *furor* in
Germany and produced innumerable "replies".

ECCE DEUS. by Prof. W. B. Smith. (1912). An exceptionally fine
analysis of the Gospels from the point of view of symbolism
which, it is urged, is the only explanation of many of the incidents connected with Jesus. In addition there is a drastic analysis
of Christian evidences. A unique work.

SOURCES OF THE MORALITY OF THE GOSPELS. by Joseph
McCabe. (1914). The standard work on this subject. Fully
documented and invaluable.

THE PROPHET OF NAZARETH. by Evan Powell Meredith. (1864).
Perhaps the most drastic criticism of the life and teaching of
Jesus ever written. Its thoroughness perhaps accounts for its
scarcity and lack of recognition. Highly recommended.

THE ORIGINS OF CHRISTIANITY. by Thomas Whittaker. (1933).
A valuable exposition of Van Manen's theories on the authorship
of Paul and other matters appertaining to the Myth theory.

ANCIENT HISTORY OF THE GOD JESUS. by Edouard Dujardin.
Abridged English version by A. Brodie Sanders, M.A. (1938).
Cleverly sustains the theory of a Pre-Christian Jesus, the God of
a prehistoric Mystery Religion. Notable addition with new views
on the Myth theory.

DID JESUS LIVE 100 B.C.? by G. R. S. Mead. (1903). Indispensable
for the study of the Talmud as a proof of the existence of Jesus.
One of the best books on the question.

THE ENIGMA OF JESUS. (1924). THE CREATION OF CHRIST.
(1939). by Dr. P. L. Couchoud. A brilliant discussion of the
Jesus Problem. In the later work, formulates the view that Marcion, by writing a "biography" of Jesus as a man, brings him down
from heaven where he had been placed by Daniel, Enoch, and
Paul. Revolutionary and plausible.

THE RISE OF CHRISTENDOM. by Edwin Johnson, M.A. (1890).
Although its thesis cannot be maintained, it is a work well worth
study. Johnson claims that Islam was the first of the three great
religions beginning about the year 800 A.D., followed by Judaism
a century or so later and then by Christianity. Provocative and
full of suggestion.

THE CHRIST. THE BIBLE. John E. Remsburg. Two lucid exposi-
tions of the Bible and the Jesus story. Published by the Truth
Seeker Co.

In addition to the above, a study of the many books dealing with the
more or less orthodox position is recommended. Strauss' *Leben Jesu*
(1835), translated by George Eliot (1846), though not a "life", is
perhaps the greatest of those works which drastically criticize the
Gospels yet uphold a "man" Jesus. Another fine work is *The Quest
of the Historical Jesus* by Dr. Albert Schweitzer (1910). From the
Rationalist side comes Howell Smith's *Jesus Not a Myth* with which
I have dealt in the text; and from the orthodox, comes Dr. H. G.
Wood's *Did Christ Really Live?* (1938). These two books will
enable the reader to decide for himself the kind of "Jesus" and
"Christ" that emerges when the Myth theory is criticized. *Jesus the
Nazarene* by Maurice Goguel (1926) and the two works by Prof.
Charles Guignebert, *Le Probleme de Jesus* (1914)—not yet translated
—and *Jesus* are also well worth study. For special books on the Bible
and on other religions like Mithraism, Hinduism, etc., the indispensable
handbook is John M. Robertson's *Courses of Study* (Watts & Co.,
1932).

Index

Of Heaven and Earth: Essays Presented at the First Sitchin Studies Day, edited by Zecharia Sitchin. ISBN 1-885395-17-5 • 164 pages • 5 1/2 x 8 1/2 • trade paper • illustrated • $14.95

God Games: What Do You Do Forever?, by Neil Freer. ISBN 1-885395-39-6 • 312 pages • 6 x 9 • trade paper • $19.95

Space Travelers and the Genesis of the Human Form: Evidence of Intelligent Contact in the Solar System, by Joan d'Arc. ISBN 1-58509-127-8 • 208 pages • 6 x 9 • trade paper • illustrated • $18.95

Humanity's Extraterrestrial Origins: ET Influences on Humankind's Biological and Cultural Evolution, by Dr. Arthur David Horn with Lynette Mallory-Horn. ISBN 3-931652-31-9 • 373 pages • 6 x 9 • trade paper • $17.00

Past Shock: The Origin of Religion and Its Impact on the Human Soul, by Jack Barranger. ISBN 1-885395-08-6 • 126 pages • 6 x 9 • trade paper • illustrated • $12.95

Flying Serpents and Dragons: The Story of Mankind's Reptilian Past, by R.A. Boulay. ISBN 1-885395-38-8 • 276 pages • 6 x 9 • trade paper • illustrated • $19.95

Triumph of the Human Spirit: The Greatest Achievements of the Human Soul and How Its Power Can Change Your Life, by Paul Tice. ISBN 1-885395-57-4 • 295 pages • 6 x 9 • trade paper • illustrated • $19.95

Mysteries Explored: The Search for Human Origins, UFOs, and Religious Beginnings, by Jack Barranger and Paul Tice. ISBN 1-58509-101-4 • 104 pages • 6 x 9 • trade paper • $12.95

Mushrooms and Mankind: The Impact of Mushrooms on Human Consciousness and Religion, by James Arthur. ISBN 1-58509-151-0 • 180 pages • 6 x 9 • trade paper • $16.95

Vril or Vital Magnetism, with an Introduction by Paul Tice. ISBN 1-58509-030-1 • 124 pages • 5 1/2 x 8 1/2 • trade paper • $12.95

The Odic Force: Letters on Od and Magnetism, by Karl von Reichenbach. ISBN 1-58509-001-8 • 192 pages • 6 x 9 • trade paper • $15.95

The New Revelation: The Coming of a New Spiritual Paradigm, by Arthur Conan Doyle. ISBN 1-58509-220-7 • 124 pages • 6 x 9 • trade paper • $12.95

The Astral World: Its Scenes, Dwellers, and Phenomena, by Swami Panchadasi. ISBN 1-58509-071-9 • 104 pages • 6 x 9 • trade paper • $11.95

Reason and Belief: The Impact of Scientific Discovery on Religious and Spiritual Faith, by Sir Oliver Lodge. ISBN 1-58509-226-6 • 180 pages • 6 x 9 • trade paper • $17.95

William Blake: A Biography, by Basil De Selincourt. ISBN 1-58509-225-8 • 384 pages • 6 x 9 • trade paper • $28.95

The Divine Pymander: And Other Writings of Hermes Trismegistus, translated by John D. Chambers. ISBN 1-58509-046-8 • 196 pages • 6 x 9 • trade paper • $16.95

Theosophy and The Secret Doctrine, by Harriet L. Henderson. Includes *H.P. Blavatsky: An Outline of Her Life,* by Herbert Whyte, ISBN 1-58509-075-1 • 132 pages • 6 x 9 • trade paper • $13.95

The Light of Egypt, Volume One: The Science of the Soul and the Stars, by Thomas H. Burgoyne. ISBN 1-58509-051-4 • 320 pages • 6 x 9 • trade paper • illustrated • $24.95

The Light of Egypt, Volume Two: The Science of the Soul and the Stars, by Thomas H. Burgoyne. ISBN 1-58509-052-2 • 224 pages • 6 x 9 • trade paper • illustrated • $17.95

The Jumping Frog and 18 Other Stories: 19 Unforgettable Mark Twain Stories, by Mark Twain. ISBN 1-58509-200-2 • 128 pages • 6 x 9 • trade paper • $12.95

The Devil's Dictionary: A Guidebook for Cynics, by Ambrose Bierce. ISBN 1-58509-016-6 • 144 pages • 6 x 9 • trade paper • $12.95

The Smoky God: Or The Voyage to the Inner World, by Willis George Emerson. ISBN 1-58509-067-0 • 184 pages • 6 x 9 • trade paper • illustrated • $15.95

A Short History of the World, by H.G. Wells. ISBN 1-58509-211-8 • 320 pages • 6 x 9 • trade paper • $24.95

The Voyages and Discoveries of the Companions of Columbus, by Washington Irving. ISBN 1-58509-500-1 • 352 pages • 6 x 9 • hard cover • $39.95

History of Baalbek, by Michel Alouf. ISBN 1-58509-063-8 • 196 pages • 5 x 8 • trade paper • illustrated • $15.95

Ancient Egyptian Masonry: The Building Craft, by Sommers Clarke and R. Engelback. ISBN 1-58509-059-X • 350 pages • 6 x 9 • trade paper • illustrated • $26.95

That Old Time Religion: The Story of Religious Foundations, by Jordan Maxwell and Paul Tice. ISBN 1-58509-100-6 • 220 pages • 6 x 9 • trade paper • $19.95

Jumpin' Jehovah: Exposing the Atrocities of the Old Testament God, by Paul Tice. ISBN 1-58509-102-2 • 104 pages • 6 x 9 • trade paper • $12.95

The Book of Enoch: A Work of Visionary Revelation and Prophecy, Revealing Divine Secrets and Fantastic Information about Creation, Salvation, Heaven and Hell, translated by R. H. Charles. ISBN 1-58509-019-0 • 152 pages • 5 1/2 x 8 1/2 • trade paper • $13.95

The Book of Enoch: Translated from the Editor's Ethiopic Text and Edited with an Enlarged Introduction, Notes and Indexes, Together with a Reprint of the Greek Fragments, edited by R. H. Charles. ISBN 1-58509-080-8 • 448 pages • 6 x 9 • trade paper • $34.95

The Book of the Secrets of Enoch, translated from the Slavonic by W. R. Morfill. Edited, with Introduction and Notes by R. H. Charles. ISBN 1-58509-020-4 • 148 pages • 5 1/2 x 8 1/2 • trade paper • $13.95

Enuma Elish: The Seven Tablets of Creation, Volume One, by L. W. King. ISBN 1-58509-041-7 • 236 pages • 6 x 9 • trade paper • illustrated • $18.95

Enuma Elish: The Seven Tablets of Creation, Volume Two, by L. W. King. ISBN 1-58509-042-5 • 260 pages • 6 x 9 • trade paper • illustrated • $19.95

Enuma Elish, Volumes One and Two: The Seven Tablets of Creation, by L. W. King. Two volumes from above bound as one. ISBN 1-58509-043-3 • 496 pages • 6 x 9 • trade paper • illustrated • $38.90

The Archko Volume: Documents that Claim Proof to the Life, Death, and Resurrection of Christ, by Drs. McIntosh and Twyman. ISBN 1-58509-082-4 • 248 pages • 6 x 9 • trade paper • $20.95

The Lost Language of Symbolism: An Inquiry into the Origin of Certain Letters, Words, Names, Fairy-Tales, Folklore, and Mythologies, by Harold Bayley. ISBN 1-58509-070-0 • 384 pages • 6 x 9 • trade paper • $27.95

The Book of Jasher: A Suppressed Book that was Removed from the Bible, Referred to in Joshua and Second Samuel, translated by Albinus Alcuin (800 AD). ISBN 1-58509-081-6 • 304 pages • 6 x 9 • trade paper • $24.95

The Bible's Most Embarrassing Moments, with an Introduction by Paul Tice. ISBN 1-58509-025-5 • 172 pages • 5 x 8 • trade paper • $14.95

History of the Cross: The Pagan Origin and Idolatrous Adoption and Worship of the Image, by Henry Dana Ward. ISBN 1-58509-056-5 • 104 pages • 6 x 9 • trade paper • illustrated • $11.95

Was Jesus Influenced by Buddhism? A Comparative Study of the Lives and Thoughts of Gautama and Jesus, by Dwight Goddard. ISBN 1-58509-027-1 • 252 pages • 6 x 9 • trade paper • $19.95

History of the Christian Religion to the Year Two Hundred, by Charles B. Waite. ISBN 1-885395-15-9 • 556 pages. • 6 x 9 • hard cover • $25.00

Symbols, Sex, and the Stars, by Ernest Busenbark. ISBN 1-885395-19-1 • 396 pages • 5 1/2 x 8 1/2 • trade paper • $22.95

History of the First Council of Nice: A World's Christian Convention, A.D. 325, by Dean Dudley. ISBN 1-58509-023-9 • 132 pages • 5 1/2 x 8 1/2 • trade paper • $12.95

The World's Sixteen Crucified Saviors, by Kersey Graves. ISBN 1-58509-018-2 • 436 pages • 5 1/2 x 8 1/2 • trade paper • $29.95

Babylonian Influence on the Bible and Popular Beliefs: A Comparative Study of Genesis I.2, by A. Smythe Palmer. ISBN 1-58509-000-X • 124 pages • 6 x 9 • trade paper • $12.95

Biography of Satan: Exposing the Origins of the Devil, by Kersey Graves. ISBN 1-885395-11-6 • 168 pages • 5 1/2 x 8 1/2 • trade paper • $13.95

The Malleus Maleficarum: The Notorious Handbook Once Used to Condemn and Punish "Witches", by Heinrich Kramer and James Sprenger. ISBN 1-58509-098-0 • 332 pages • 6 x 9 • trade paper • $25.95

Crux Ansata: An Indictment of the Roman Catholic Church, by H. G. Wells. ISBN 1-58509-210-X • 160 pages • 6 x 9 • trade paper • $14.95

Emanuel Swedenborg: The Spiritual Columbus, by U.S.E. (William Spear). ISBN 1-58509-096-4 • 208 pages • 6 x 9 • trade paper • $17.95

Dragons and Dragon Lore, by Ernest Ingersoll. ISBN 1-58509-021-2 • 228 pages • 6 x 9 • trade paper • illustrated • $17.95

The Vision of God, by Nicholas of Cusa. ISBN 1-58509-004-2 • 160 pages • 5 x 8 • trade paper • $13.95

The Historical Jesus and the Mythical Christ: Separating Fact From Fiction, by Gerald Massey. ISBN 1-58509-073-5 • 244 pages • 6 x 9 • trade paper • $18.95

Gog and Magog: The Giants in Guildhall; Their Real and Legendary History, with an Account of Other Giants at Home and Abroad, by F.W. Fairholt. ISBN 1-58509-084-0 • 172 pages • 6 x 9 • trade paper • $16.95

The Origin and Evolution of Religion, by Albert Churchward. ISBN 1-58509-078-6 • 504 pages • 6 x 9 • trade paper • $39.95

The Origin of Biblical Traditions, by Albert T. Clay. ISBN 1-58509-065-4 • 220 pages • 5 1/2 x 8 1/2 • trade paper • $17.95

Aryan Sun Myths, by Sarah Elizabeth Titcomb, Introduction by Charles Morris. ISBN 1-58509-069-7 • 192 pages • 6 x 9 • trade paper • $15.95

The Social Record of Christianity, by Joseph McCabe. Includes *The Lies and Fallacies of the Encyclopedia Britannica,* ISBN 1-58509-215-0 • 204 pages • 6 x 9 • trade paper • $17.95

The History of the Christian Religion and Church During the First Three Centuries, by Dr. Augustus Neander. ISBN 1-58509-077-8 • 112 pages • 6 x 9 • trade paper • $12.95

Ancient Symbol Worship: Influence of the Phallic Idea in the Religions of Antiquity, by Hodder M. Westropp and C. Staniland Wake. ISBN 1-58509-048-4 • 120 pages • 6 x 9 • trade paper • illustrated • $12.95

The Gnosis: Or Ancient Wisdom in the Christian Scriptures, by William Kingsland. ISBN 1-58509-047-6 • 232 pages • 6 x 9 • trade paper • $18.95

The Evolution of the Idea of God: An Inquiry into the Origin of Religions, by Grant Allen. ISBN 1-58509-074-3 • 160 pages • 6 x 9 • trade paper • $14.95

Sun Lore of All Ages: A Survey of Solar Mythology, Folklore, Customs, Worship, Festivals, and Superstition, by William Tyler Olcott. ISBN 1-58509-044-1 • 316 pages • 6 x 9 • trade paper • $24.95

Nature Worship: An Account of Phallic Faiths and Practices Ancient and Modern, by the Author of Phallicism with an Introduction by Tedd St. Rain. ISBN 1-58509-049-2 • 112 pages • 6 x 9 • trade paper • illustrated • $12.95

Life and Religion, by Max Muller. ISBN 1-885395-10-8 • 237 pages • 5 1/2 x 8 1/2 • trade paper • $14.95

Jesus: God, Man, or Myth? An Examination of the Evidence, by Herbert Cutner. ISBN 1-58509-072-7 • 304 pages • 6 x 9 • trade paper • $23.95

Pagan and Christian Creeds: Their Origin and Meaning, by Edward Carpenter. ISBN 1-58509-024-7 • 316 pages • 5 1/2 x 8 1/2 • trade paper • $24.95

The Christ Myth: A Study, by Elizabeth Evans. ISBN 1-58509-037-9 • 136 pages • 6 x 9 • trade paper • $13.95

Popery: Foe of the Church and the Republic, by Joseph F. Van Dyke. ISBN 1-58509-058-1 • 336 pages • 6 x 9 • trade paper • illustrated • $25.95

Career of Religious Ideas, by Hudson Tuttle. ISBN 1-58509-066-2 • 172 pages • 5 x 8 • trade paper • $15.95

Buddhist Suttas: Major Scriptural Writings from Early Buddhism, by T.W. Rhys Davids. ISBN 1-58509-079-4 • 376 pages • 6 x 9 • trade paper • $27.95

Early Buddhism, by T. W. Rhys Davids. Includes ***Buddhist Ethics: The Way to Salvation?,*** by Paul Tice. ISBN 1-58509-076-X • 112 pages • 6 x 9 • trade paper • $12.95

The Fountain-Head of Religion: A Comparative Study of the Principal Religions of the World and a Manifestation of their Common Origin from the Vedas, by Ganga Prasad. ISBN 1-58509-054-9 • 276 pages • 6 x 9 • trade paper • $22.95

India: What Can It Teach Us?, by Max Muller. ISBN 1-58509-064-6 • 284 pages • 5 1/2 x 8 1/2 • trade paper • $22.95

Matrix of Power: How the World has Been Controlled by Powerful People Without Your Knowledge, by Jordan Maxwell. ISBN 1-58509-120-0 • 104 pages • 6 x 9 • trade paper • $12.95

Cyberculture Counterconspiracy: A Steamshovel Web Reader, Volume One, edited by Kenn Thomas. ISBN 1-58509-125-1 • 180 pages • 6 x 9 • trade paper • illustrated • $16.95

Cyberculture Counterconspiracy: A Steamshovel Web Reader, Volume Two, edited by Kenn Thomas. ISBN 1-58509-126-X • 132 pages • 6 x 9 • trade paper • illustrated • $13.95

Oklahoma City Bombing: The Suppressed Truth, by Jon Rappoport. ISBN 1-885395-22-1 • 112 pages • 5 1/2 x 8 1/2 • trade paper • $12.95

The Protocols of the Learned Elders of Zion, by Victor Marsden. ISBN 1-58509-015-8 • 312 pages • 6 x 9 • trade paper • $24.95

Secret Societies and Subversive Movements, by Nesta H. Webster. ISBN 1-58509-092-1 • 432 pages • 6 x 9 • trade paper • $29.95

The Secret Doctrine of the Rosicrucians, by Magus Incognito. ISBN 1-58509-091-3 • 256 pages • 6 x 9 • trade paper • $20.95

The Origin and Evolution of Freemasonry: Connected with the Origin and Evolution of the Human Race, by Albert Churchward. ISBN 1-58509-029-8 • 240 pages • 6 x 9 • trade paper • $18.95

The Lost Key: An Explanation and Application of Masonic Symbols, by Prentiss Tucker. ISBN 1-58509-050-6 • 192 pages • 6 x 9 • trade paper • illustrated • $15.95

The Character, Claims, and Practical Workings of Freemasonry, by Rev. C.G. Finney. ISBN 1-58509-094-8 • 288 pages • 6 x 9 • trade paper • $22.95

The Secret World Government or "The Hidden Hand": The Unrevealed in History, by Maj.-Gen., Count Cherep-Spiridovich. ISBN 1-58509-093-X • 270 pages • 6 x 9 • trade paper • $21.95

The Magus, Book One: A Complete System of Occult Philosophy, by Francis Barrett. ISBN 1-58509-031-X • 200 pages • 6 x 9 • trade paper • illustrated • $16.95

The Magus, Book Two: A Complete System of Occult Philosophy, by Francis Barrett. ISBN 1-58509-032-8 • 220 pages • 6 x 9 • trade paper • illustrated • $17.95

The Magus, Book One and Two: A Complete System of Occult Philosophy, by Francis Barrett. ISBN 1-58509-033-6 • 420 pages • 6 x 9 • trade paper • illustrated • $34.90

The Key of Solomon The King, by S. Liddell MacGregor Mathers. ISBN 1-58509-022-0 • 152 pages • 6 x 9 • trade paper • illustrated • $12.95

Magic and Mystery in Tibet, by Alexandra David-Neel. ISBN 1-58509-097-2 • 352 pages • 6 x 9 • trade paper • $26.95

The Comte de St. Germain, by I. Cooper Oakley. ISBN 1-58509-068-9 • 280 pages • 6 x 9 • trade paper • illustrated • $22.95

Alchemy Rediscovered and Restored, by A. Cockren. ISBN 1-58509-028-X • 156 pages • 5 1/2 x 8 1/2 • trade paper • $13.95

The 6th and 7th Books of Moses, with an Introduction by Paul Tice. ISBN 1-58509-045-X • 188 pages • 6 x 9 • trade paper • illustrated • $16.95